# Cloud Native Go

## Building Web Applications
## and Microservices for the Cloud
## with Go and React

Kevin Hoffman
Dan Nemeth

 Addison-Wesley

Boston • Columbus • Indianapolis • New York • San Francisco • Amsterdam • Cape Town
Dubai • London • Madrid • Milan • Munich • Paris • Montreal • Toronto • Delhi
Mexico City • São Paulo • Sidney • Hong Kong • Seoul • Singapore • Taipei • Tokyo

For information about buying this title in bulk quantities, or for special sales opportunities (which may include electronic versions; custom cover designs; and content particular to your business, training goals, marketing focus, or branding interests), please contact our corporate sales department at corpsales@pearsoned.com or (800) 382-3419.

For government sales inquiries, please contact governmentsales@pearsoned.com.

For questions about sales outside the U.S., please contact intlcs@pearson.com.

Visit us on the Web: informit.com/aw

Library of Congress Control Number: 2016956519

ISBN-13: 978-0-672-33779-6

ISBN-10: 0-672-33779-7

1   16

**Editor-in-Chief**
Mark Taub

**Executive Editor**
Greg Doench

**Development Editor**
Mark Renfrow

**Managing Editor**
Sandra Schroeder

**Senior Project Editor**
Lori Lyons

**Project Manager**
Dhayanidhi

**Copy Editor**
Larry Sulky

**Indexer**
Cheryl Lenser

**Proofreader**
Bavithra

**Editorial Assistant**
Olivia Basegio

**Cover Designer**
Chuti Prasertsith

**Compositor**
codeMantra

❖

*This book is dedicated to the A-Team. Four men, sent to Pivotal for crimes they didn't commit, who now roam the countryside in search of developers in need of guidance: innocent people who need help moving their software to the cloud. If you need cloud apps, they will find you.*

*Without these brave men, the act of writing software would have become so boring and unbearable that this book would never have been written. In fact, the authors may have given up their lives of service to the cloud, only to while away their remaining days as baristas in a smelly hipster coffee shop.*

### The A-Team is:

*Dan "Hannibal" Nemeth*

*Chris "Murdock" Umbel*

*Tom "Face" Collings*

*Kevin "B.A." Hoffman*

❖

# Contents at a Glance

# Contents

# Preface

When Dan and I set out to write this book, we didn't want it to be a reference book or "yet another syntax book." Instead, we wanted to put to good use our experience building cloud native solutions for Pivotal customers and nearly a lifetime of combined experience building software for companies of just about every size, shape, and industry.

This book starts off with a philosophical chapter, *The Way of the Cloud*, because we firmly believe that the secret to building good software has more to do with the mindset and discipline of the developers than it does the tooling or language.

From there, we follow The Way of the Cloud in everything we do as we gradually, in a test-driven and highly automated fashion, take you through a series of chapters designed to increase your skills building cloud native services in Go. We cover the fundamentals of building services; middleware; the use of tools like git, Docker, and Wercker; and cloud native fundamentals like environment-based configuration, service discovery, and reactive and push-based applications. We cover patterns like Event Sourcing and CQRS, and combine everything in the book into a final sample that you can use as inspiration for your own projects.

Another of our strongly-held beliefs is that the act of building a piece of software should be as fun (or more!) as using that software. If it's not fun, you're doing it wrong. We wanted the joy we get from building services in Go to infect our readers, and hopefully you will have as much fun reading this book as we did writing it.

# About the Authors

**Kevin Hoffman** helps enterprises bring their legacy applications onto the cloud through modernization and building cloud native services in many different languages. He started programming when he was 10 years old, teaching himself BASIC on a rebuilt Commodore VIC-20. Since then, he has been addicted to the art of building software, and has spent as much time as he can learning languages, frameworks, and patterns. He has built everything from software that remotely controls photography drones to biometric security, ultra-low-latency financial applications, mobile applications, and everything between. He fell in love with the Go language while building custom components for use with Pivotal Cloud Foundry.

Kevin is the author of a popular series of fantasy books (*The Sigilord Chronicles*, http://amzn. to/2fc8iES) and is eagerly awaiting the day when he will finally be able to combine his love for building software with his love for building fictional worlds.

**Dan Nemeth** currently works at Pivotal as an Advisory Solutions Architect, supporting Pivotal Cloud Foundry. He has been writing software since the days of the Commodore 64. He began coding professionally in 1995 for a local ISP writing CGI scripts in ANSI C. Since then, he has spent the majority of his career as an independent consultant building solutions for industries ranging from finance to pharmaceutical, and using various languages/frameworks that were vogue at the time. Dan has recently embraced Go as a homecoming, of sorts, and is enthusiastically using it for all of his projects.

Should you find Dan away from his computer, he will likely be on the waters near Annapolis either sailing or fly fishing.

# Acknowledgments

This book would not have been possible without the nearly infinite patience of my family, especially my wife. Despite me having said on numerous occasions in the past that I would never again write a technical book, here I was, writing another tech book. They put up with long nights, me wearing ruts into the floor pacing, and the loss of quality time in order to get this book finished. I am more proud of this book than I am of any other I've worked on in the past, and that is directly related to the invaluable support of family, friends, and a brilliant co-author.

—*Kevin Hoffman*

# The Way of the Cloud

*"If you do not change your direction, you may end up where you are heading."*

Lao Tzu

As we mentioned in the preface, our goal in this book is to teach you to build cloud native applications. However, the phrase *cloud native,* as part of the gestalt, carries with it a lot of implied baggage that we would like to leave behind, such as an explicit focus on applications rather than humans and philosophy, and a reliance on the original "12 factors"[1] to define and characterize applications.

While application-focused guidelines are certainly valuable, we feel that a cloud native culture starts with the people building and designing the applications, and if those people have embraced the right philosophy, then that will be obvious in the beauty of the applications they produce. The passion of any artist is always visible in the works they produce, and web applications and microservices are no different in this regard.

Building applications for the cloud is more than just learning a new set of libraries or a different programming language. It involves mastering new disciplines, building and fostering new habits, and looking at the world differently.

The Chinese character 道 (dao) has many interpretations, but when used in terms of philosophy, it means *the way* or *the path*. It refers to the path, or the way in which one does a thing, such as leading a life or building software. To describe our own personal philosophy of embracing cloud native development and architecture, we call this path 雲道 (yúndào), which means *the way of the cloud*.

In this chapter, we will introduce you to *the way of the cloud*. The way has many virtues that we feel are exemplars, and everything we have built for this book, from the prose to the code

---

1  12 Factors, Heroku's now dated guidelines for building cloud applications: http://12factor.net.

and supporting sites, exudes the passion we have for *the way*. Hopefully, by the time you have finished this book, you will be as passionate about *the way* as we are.

We will be discussing:

- The virtues of *the way of the cloud*
- Justifications for choosing the Go language for cloud native microservices development

# The Virtues of the Way of the Cloud

Contrary to popular belief, there are days when what we do isn't all rainbows and unicorns. At some point, something happens and our passion becomes a chore. We trudge to work and we go through the motions of adding code, praying it works, and deploying. We lose sight of the fact that what we build is *art*, and we fail to give our craft the love and devotion it deserves.

In one degree or another, this has probably happened to us all at some point in our careers. Hopefully an inspiring boss, a new technology or language, or a new job turned things around and rescued us from this pit.

For us, this rescue came in the form of *the way of the cloud*. It changed our perspective on software development and how we see the world. We can see the art in what we build now, and software has become *fun* again, and there is no way we can go back to building applications any other way.

Throughout our years of building software for enterprises, startups, hobbies, and everything in between, we have developed a set of virtues that we feel give us the best chance at creating scalable, reliable, and predictable software that embraces the cloud and everything it has to offer.

While there's nothing that says these virtues can only apply to cloud software, this book is about *cloud native* software development and so throughout the book, every code sample we produce and every topic we discuss will exude the virtues below. In fact, we followed these virtues in producing this book—everything from the prose to the code to the companion site.

## Favor Simplicity

### The Way of the Cloud

Favor simplicity in everything that you do.

Question everything that appears to defy simplicity. What you're building is already complex enough; there is absolutely no need to inject further complexity or ceremony into your work.

Question every tool. Ask yourself if the tool is making your life easier, or compensating or apologizing for complexity elsewhere in the system. If the answer is the latter, *ditch the tool, and the reason for using it.*

Question all of your code. If it's too complex to read, change the language or framework that's causing that complexity. If there is so much magic happening behind the scenes in the code you *can't see* that it's difficult to figure out what happens when or where, *change the code.*

Here is the litmus test for simplicity:

- Is your IDE optional?

- Can you build and deploy from the command line?

- Can a new team member quickly figure out what's going on just by reading the code?

Tools and IDEs must make our lives better by automating routine tasks, and simplifying manual tasks by reducing frustration or time. Tools must *never* be mandatory. If you have to use a specific IDE because your code will not generate or compile without it, then you are absolutely not following *the way of the cloud*, and not favoring simplicity.

Anything that you can do from the command line can be automated by a script or a continuous delivery tool. Therefore, if you can build, test, and deploy your application from a command line, then you can automate all of those tasks.

This may seem like a harsh stance, and you have every right to disagree with us. However, at least until you finish reading this book, try and apply this virtue to all of your development efforts. You will not be disappointed.

The only people who claim that you cannot have cloud native and simplicity at the same time are those apologizing for complexity they either created or aren't willing to give up.

## Test First, Test Everything

### The Way of the Cloud
Employ Test-Driven Development. Test everything, everywhere.

Testing is your first and best defense against the evils of *hope-based computing.*

Pretty much everyone can agree that testing is a good idea, but few teams ever agree on how much testing should be necessary. Before we answer that, consider this: why do we test our software?

Of course we want bug-free software, and we want our customers to be happy, and we'd like to make hojillions of dollars while we're at it. But, the core of testing is none of those things. At the most basic level, testing gives us *confidence.*

Have you ever been in a room when someone is about to exercise some feature of your application in front of some very important or influential people? Do you remember the feeling of panic wash over you right before the crucial test?

### Fear

Fear is the direct result of lack of testing.

It is that fear of what might happen, that *uncertainty* of how your application performs that can plague an entire system, causing untold stress, system failures, and the worst: customer-discovered bugs in production.

What we need to do is replace our fear with confidence. Confidence is a cumulative effect in our system that starts with confidence in the smallest testable unit. From there, confidence builds as our codebase expands and we maintain the integrity of our tests.

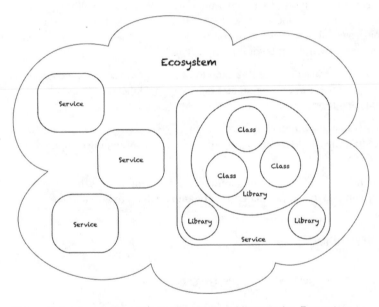

Figure 1.1   Areas of Testing Confidence in a Microservice Ecosystem

Figure 1.1 shows this in detail. When we have full confidence in a class because it has been fully tested with unit tests, then we can have confidence in a library because we have confidence in all of the classes in that library. The converse is the important lesson here: if you do not have confidence in the building blocks of your application, then you have *far less* confidence in your application as a whole. Confidence decreases exponentially as you travel outward from class to library to service without testing.

We can only have confidence in our service if we have confidence in all of the libraries that make up this codebase. Finally, we can only have confidence in our ecosystem of services if every service within the ecosystem has been fully tested, both internally and at the seams via integration testing among multiple services.

You may often run into situations on teams where leadership doesn't feel that the time spent on extensive testing is worth it. It's pretty easy to manipulate a spreadsheet to back up the assertion that adequate testing costs too much money. Therefore, to counter that thinking, consider the following analogy:

When you build your applications locally, you've got all the tools you could imagine at your disposal. You can connect to a debugger, you can set and hit breakpoints. In some cases you can even pause an app, manipulate data in memory, and then resume it. This gives you a *false sense of confidence*, and can even make you think integration and unit testing is unnecessary, given how much time you've spent in the debugger.

Consider then a situation where what you're building isn't just a piece of software being deployed on a computer sitting a few feet from you. Imagine that what you're building is actually a spacecraft, being launched into deep space. Once launched, you can't touch it, you can't grab a screwdriver and make last-minute adjustments, and if something fails catastrophically a few million miles from home, that's the end of the line.

When you deploy to the cloud, you are relinquishing a lot of hands-on control. It might not be as complicated as launching a satellite, but you give up instantiation control, you can't set breakpoints, and you generally don't have runtime introspection.

The next time someone waves a spreadsheet at you claiming that testing costs too much money, simply reply and ask them the cost of complete and total failure of the product at every level, because that is the real cost of skimping on tests.

This brings us back to confidence. If you have confidence in the fact that your application will function as it should, you can use that confidence as a bedrock for other huge benefits, like continuous delivery (discussed next).

The bottom line is you should adopt Test-Driven Development[2], and you must build confidence in the services you produce by testing everything inside and out of every service you build.

## Release Early, Release Often

### The Way of the Cloud

Every checkin is a potential production release, deployed via CD pipeline.

In the previous section, we talked about the fear of people using your application because you lack the confidence that it will behave as it should. There is another kind of fear that we need to confront head-on: the fear of releasing.

---

2  For more information on Test-Driven Development, check out: Beck, Kent. (2003) *Test-Driven Development: By Example*. Addison-Wesley Professional.

There are organizations where it is the norm for a release to be a stop-the-world event. It is planned months in advance, emergency personnel are on standby, ambulances and firefighters are in position, and nearly every person who ever checked in a line of code, or oversaw the checkins, is on the phone at midnight in order to carry out this release. The Guinness Book of World Records is on the phone so they can be there to record the event just in case, for the first time in history, nothing goes wrong.

Companies that operate this way try to mitigate the problem by throwing more resources, more people, and more infrastructure and controls at a release. Sometimes they will even delay releases, and release *less often*. This is the exact opposite of what you should do.

The only way to get over the fear of releasing is to *release more frequently*.

The cascade of benefits starts when every developer on your team firmly believes that every single commit to the source control system could end up in production within a matter of days. This leads to a level of rigor and discipline that most people don't normally apply to their code. Additionally, if you know your code is going to be released rapidly, you are far more likely to test your code, because the last thing you want is a production release with low confidence, right?

## Automate Everything

### The Way of the Cloud

Everything that can be automated, should be automated.

Now that we have confidence that our code is being tested, being written in a way that facilitates testing, and that we're releasing so regularly that we no longer fear the looming specter of release, we can start making our lives better and increasing productivity.

*Anything you do more than once per day is a candidate for automation.*

The first and probably most important thing to automate is your release process itself. Within minutes of a checkin, some automated system should be running tests on your code, validating that the code meets your standards, and deploying an immutable build artifact to some environment where it can be used for manual and integration testing.

Things that you do manually are error-prone. As the easily distracted humans that we are, we can forget steps, we can do steps in the wrong order, and we can do extra steps we don't need. Once we've certified an automated process, it gives us even more confidence.

We should be able to reach a point where, after a push to source control, if no sirens go off, no Darth Vader heads light up, and no angry e-mails get sent out, then we have confidence that our changes did not cause unit or integration tests to fail. There's still more testing that needs to be done prior to production, but we have enough confidence that our checkin is a release candidate ready to go through the pre-production certification process.

With that, we leave you with one final guideline on automation:

*Any frequently repeated part of your process that cannot be replaced with a button or a script is too complicated, too brittle, or both.*

Only when you have embraced automation, and you are able to go from commit to cloud automatically, can you really start to reap the benefits of cloud native development and scale out from building a single microservice to building microservice ecosystems.

## Build Service Ecosystems

### The Way of the Cloud

Everything is a service, including your application.

Before discussing ecosystems, we want to air our gripes with the term *microservices*[3]. As with any buzzword, it has become overused and watered down. We firmly believe that all services should be microservices, so the prefix *micro* is completely unnecessary.

For years, we were in love with building monoliths. Even when the whole "n-tier" or "3-tier" application fad was hip and trendy, those n-tier applications were still monoliths. They were just slightly more organized monoliths.

In a monolithic application, every concern and functional requirement of a system is met inside one giant *thing*. This inhibits the simplicity, ease of automation, and ease of release that are fundamental to the way of the cloud.

In a monolith, any time anything changes, you must perform a release of the entire application. This encourages the five-alarm "all hands" release party that we want to avoid. Applications like this are hard to maintain, slow to start, slow to stop, and often have dependencies so tightly coupled that they are difficult to deploy in the cloud.

A **microservice** is really just a service that adheres to a slightly looser definition of the **Single Responsibility Principle (SRP)** that arose from patterns for object-oriented design. It is a *service that does one thing*.

An application is just a microservice that exposes one or more endpoints that render a GUI (e.g. HTML).

Entire books have been written (with more likely to come!) on the concepts of microservices and how to decide what should be a service, what shouldn't be, and where to cut at the seams of your existing monoliths in order to refactor them into smaller services.

---

3  For more information on microservices, check out: Newman, Sam. (2015) *Building Microservices*. O'Reilly Media.

The purpose of this virtue of the way of the cloud is to imagine that you aren't building giant monoliths; you are instead building services that co-exist within an ecosystem. This reinforces habits like building strongly versioned contracts into your RESTful endpoints, testing service interaction as part of your release process, and planning for flexibility to allow for unforeseen, future consumers of your services.

# Why Use Go?

Now that you've suffered through us having wind-bagged our way through *the way of the cloud*, you might be wondering: why Go? What makes Go the ideal language to use for building cloud native services and applications?

There are three main reasons why we've chosen Go as our preferred language for building cloud native applications: simplicity, open source, and ease of automation.

## Simplicity

There is a compelling beauty in the simplicity of Go. On the surface, it could even pass for a simplified variant of ANSI C, but it is powerful enough to handle today's most demanding software requirements.

This simplicity isn't just on the surface—everything about Go eschews unnecessary complexity, ceremony, and cruft. It doesn't compile to intermediary bytecode like Java or .NET, it produces native binaries. As such, this simplicity doesn't come at a price, it actually improves performance.

Once you get over the initial fear of not being able to be productive in a language that doesn't have classes, pure functional programming[4], or a billion other bells and whistles, you may end up like us and love the purity of a language that shuns magic and artifice, and gives you raw, pure power to be productive and finally enjoy programming again.

## Open Source

Go isn't just an open source language, it is a language embraced and supported by a community of people who thrive on open source and all that it provides. As you'll see throughout the book, sharing open source modules via GitHub and other repositories is a first-class concept within the language and its core tooling.

---

4  Go does allow higher-order functions and functions-as-data, but lacks some features FP purists would consider mandatory. This debate is far too heated for discussion in this book.

## Easy Automation and IDE Freedom

As we mentioned earlier in this chapter, if you can control an aspect of your build cycle with a script, then you can automate it. Everything that you do with Go, from compilation to executing tests or performing static analysis, can be done from a simple command line.

Another extended benefit to using Go is that it enables your freedom to choose whatever text editor you like. For more details on getting set up with an IDE and customizing your Go development environment, make sure to check out our recommendations at cloudnativego.com.

Go to the book's companion website, github.com/cloudnativego/, for access to code files used in this book and additional material.

# Summary

In this chapter we touched on some philosophy, some theory, and laid down some definitions and guidelines. We firmly believe that the mindset of the development is the critical factor that will lead to the success or downfall of any cloud native project.

This is why we introduced *the way of the cloud* early in the book, and as you will see as you make your way through the remainder of it, this philosophy colors every decision we make, every line of code we write, and every test we automate.

We also talked about the serendipitous nature of how well Go lends itself to building simple, elegant, highly efficient, super-fast microservices. Go isn't our favorite language because it has the fanciest libraries or the most ways to write obfuscated code. Rather, Go is our favorite language because of the *absence* of those things and the incredibly low impedance mismatch between our intent and our code.

# 2

# Getting Started

*"The secret of getting ahead is getting started."*

Mark Twain

As we will demonstrate throughout this book, having the right environment (local or for your automated builds) is crucial to the success of any development project. If a workstation has the right tools and is set up properly, developing on that workstation can feel like a breath of fresh air. Conversely, a poorly set up environment can suffocate any developer trying to use it.

We're not going to write any of our own code in this chapter. Instead, we're going to focus on the *bare minimum* set of tools needed so that when we do get to write code in the next chapter, it will be easy and relaxing.

In this chapter, we are going to:

- Install Git, and ensure we have a GitHub account.

- Install and configure the Go command-line tools.

- Test everything to make sure our environment works.

## The Right Tools for the Job

My grandfather always used to tell me to "always make sure you have the best tools." This is a little different than the age-old sage advice *always use the right tool for the job*. I think my grandfather was trying to impart a couple of pieces of wisdom in one fairly dense sentence.

First, if you're going to cut corners, *don't cut corners on tooling*. Anything that makes your life easier, reduces friction, and reduces stress is at least worth evaluating. Second, and probably most importantly, I think he was trying to impart the idea that you should be using the tool *best suited* to the job. Hammers make terrible screwdrivers, screwdrivers make terrible wrenches, and huge bloated IDEs often make for excessive code and configuration files or they contribute to the excessive rage of the developers using them.

We will always cheerlead for the minimalist approach, but that doesn't mean we're against tooling altogether, we're just against *tooling for tooling's own sake*. Throughout this book we're going to use a number of command-line tools and websites, but we're not going to force you to use an IDE. We strongly believe that any language or framework that forces you to use a specific IDE comes pre-equipped with code smell and debt.

As such, we're going to talk about the Git command-line tools, the Go command-line tools, and how to verify your environment. How consenting adults type code in the privacy of their own homes is their own business.

# Setting Up Git

It might seem strange that the first thing we ask you to do in this book is install Git. Go is an open source language. The language and its tooling are intrinsically connected to github and the open source community. What this means is you really can't have a functioning Go developer workstation without also having source control clients like git, mercurial, and bazaar installed.

If you're using a Linux workstation or a VM, then you can basically sit back and let `apt-get` do all the work for you, and install `git`, `mercurial`, and `bazaar` one package at a time. If you're using Windows then we suggest you upgrade to the Windows 10 anniversary edition and install *Bash for Windows* (seriously, it's real, and no Windows Go developer should be without it).

If you are on a Mac, then you're going to want **Homebrew**.

## Installing Homebrew

Homebrew is your friend. As a developer working on a Mac, this is quite possibly one of the most useful tools at your disposal. Homebrew is a tool that allows you to install other tools, many of which are required for Go. To install Homebrew on your Mac (any linebreaks in the below command are for formatting only and shouldn't be typed):

```
ruby -e "$(curl -fsSL
  https://raw.githubusercontent.com/Homebrew/install/master/install)"
```

If you do not have Ruby installed, then you have likely not installed the Xcode command-line utilities. Those you can install with the following command in a shell:

```
xcode-select --install
```

To verify that your Homebrew installation completed successfully, issue the following command:

```
brew doctor
```

This command will examine your Homebrew installation. It might point out some directories that you need to take ownership of, and it might also display a message indicating that your copy of Homebrew is outdated. At this point, if Homebrew is outdated, follow the directions indicated to update.

Next, install Homebrew **Cask**, which labels itself as "the missing Apps manager for the Mac":

```
brew install caskroom/cask/brew-cask
```

At this point, your Homebrew installation should be working and now you are ready to use Homebrew to install the other pre-requisites for Go.

## Installing the Git Client

Before doing anything, type the following in a shell:

```
$ git --version
```

If you see a relatively new version (ours was 2.8.2 at the time), you should be ready to go. Note that you might have Apple's Git (it will say so in the version) if you have done any tinkering with Xcode for Mac or iOS development. If you get an error and Git isn't available, then use Homebrew to install it:

```
$ brew install git
```

If you have Apple's Git installed, but it is an older version than the one you find in Homebrew, then you can simply install Homebrew's Git over top of Apple's.

## Installing Mercurial and Bazaar

As we mentioned earlier, Go is intrinsically linked with the open source community, and, in turn, with open source version control repositories. GitHub is not the only source of third party Go packages you might be interested in using. You'll also need to install two other repository tools, `mercurial` and `bazaar`, if you want to ensure that your Go environment works properly.

To install these, just get them from Homebrew:

```
$ brew install mercurial
$ brew install bazaar
```

Now, just to double check that you have all of the revision control clients you need installed, issue the following commands to Homebrew to check the status of the installations:

```
$ brew info git
$ brew info mercurial
$ brew info bazaar
```

## Creating a GitHub Account

As you'll see later when we discuss setting up your Go workspace, the vast majority of third-party packages in Go are stored in GitHub. If you ever want to share your own packages, you'll likely do that through GitHub. In short, if you're doing anything beyond the simplest of activities in Go, you'll want to be able to interact with GitHub.

If you do not have a GitHub account yet, then bookmark this page and go get a free account right now. Do not continue to the next page or do anything else until you have created this account. To us, GitHub is like oxygen, and we cannot survive without it. You can see both of our GitHub accounts at https://github.com/autodidaddict (Kevin) and https://github.com/dnem (Dan).

# Setting Up Go

We strongly recommend that you peruse Go's official "getting started" page here: https://golang.org/doc/install. There are a number of different ways to install Go, depending on your operating system and preferences.

On the Mac, you can download an installer package but, to be consistent with the other tools we've installed and to allow for the simplest path to keeping those tools up to date, we recommend you install Go via Homebrew. When you do, you should see output that looks similar to the following:

```
$ brew install go
==> Downloading
https://homebrew.bintray.com/bottles/go-1.6.2.el_capitan.bottle.tar.gz
################################################################## 100.0%
==> Pouring go-1.6.2.el_capitan.bottle.tar.gz
==> Caveats
As of go 1.2, a valid GOPATH is required to use the `go get` command:
  https://golang.org/doc/code.html#GOPATH

You may wish to add the GOROOT-based install location to your PATH:
  export PATH=$PATH:/usr/local/opt/go/libexec/bin
==> Summary
   /usr/local/Cellar/go/1.6.2: 5,778 files, 325.3M
```

## Configuring your Go Workspace

With Go installed, you need to set up a Go workspace. You can pick any directory you like, but this directory needs to be one to which you have unfettered access. All of the code you write will happen in this directory, and all of the packages you download will be downloaded into paths below this directory.

Once you've chosen this directory, modify your profile so that every time you open a terminal, the $GOPATH environment variable points to this directory.

Next, modify your profile to ensure that your $PATH environment variable also contains $GOPATH/bin. This will allow you to execute Go applications that you have installed.

For example, let's say you have decided that your Go workspace will be in a directory called `Go` directly below your home directory. If your user account was called `goguru`, then you would set your `$GOPATH` environment variable to `/Users/goguru/Go`, and add `/Users/goguru/Go/bin` to your path.

All packages, including the ones that you create yourself as applications or as shared packages, are stored in sub-directories below `$GOPATH/src`. For example, if you were creating a chess game, and your GitHub account name was `autodidaddict`, the root directory of the code for that game would be at `$GOPATH/src/github.com/autodidaddict/go-chess`.

The organization of your Go workspace is not arbitrary. It is essential to being able to properly locate and vendor (or download and cache locally) dependencies for everything you build. As Go newbies, the number one cause of problems for us was failure to adhere to the basic rules of Go workspace structure.

If you find yourself seeing bizarre compilation failures when working with the samples in this book or with other Go code, make sure you double-check the location of that code within your Go workspace.

## Testing Your Environment

Like everything else we do, we need to test before we write code. In this case, there are a couple of smoke tests we can run to ensure that our Go workspace and all of our command-line utilities are working properly.

The first thing we can do is to exercise the `go get` command, which fetches an external dependency from a repository (usually GitHub) and copies it into our current Go workspace in the appropriate directory.

To see this in action, you can `go get` a simple "hello world" app we've made available on GitHub for this book:

```
$ go get github.com/cloudnativego/hello
```

In keeping with Go's idioms, *no news is good news*. It should look like nothing happened, but we can now go into the source directory for this package in our local Go workspace and see the same files that reside on GitHub:

```
$ cd $GOPATH
$ cd src/github.com/cloudnativego/hello
$ ls
Godeps          Procfile        README.md        buildlocal       main.go
  manifest.yml              wercker.yml
```

So far so good. Now, we can test to see if the Go compiler will actually build the contents of this directory:

```
$ go build .
```

Again, we should see nothing if all went according to plan. If we look at this directory again, however, we'll notice that there is now a `hello` executable. We can run this like we do any other native application:

```
$ ./hello
[negroni] listening on :8080
```

You don't need to worry about what Negroni is yet, but it looks enough like a web server that we can probably issue this command:

```
$ curl http://localhost:8080
Hello from Go!
```

If we see "Hello from Go!" then we know that our Go workspace is working and that we've installed all of the requisite command-line tools and clients we need to support Go development.

Now it's time to write some Go code!

## Summary

Nobody likes a chapter that doesn't have any code in it, but sometimes these things are necessary. In this chapter we took a look at the command-line tools and configuration necessary to set up your workstation in preparation for the code you'll be writing throughout the rest of the book.

If you didn't successfully get through the "Testing Your Environment" section, we encourage you to go back and try and get that squared away. Nothing in the rest of the book will work properly if your Go workspace isn't set up right.

If you're all set, then it's time to start diving into the simple elegance of the Go language!

# 3

# Go Primer

*"I like a lot of the design decisions they made in the [Go] language. Basically, I like all of them."*

Martin Odersky, creator of Scala

This chapter provides a primer on a select subset of Go language topics. We will be covering the aspects of Go that we will use most frequently throughout this book, including:

- A "hello world" sample.
- Introduction to functions.
- Manipulating and storing data with structs.
- Using methods on structs.
- Working with packages.
- Creating your own packages.

If you need a complete reference and thorough delve into the language and all of its many intricacies, then we highly recommend Mark Summerfield's *Programming in Go: Creating Applications for the 21st Century* from Addison-Wesley or *The Go Programming Language* by Alan A. A. Donovan and Brian W. Kernighan[1].

One thing that you will discover as you go through this chapter, the rest of this book, and other books focused more on the Go language details, is that Go is *not* an object-oriented programming language. The sooner you come to grips with this reality, the better your learning experience will be. We view the lack of real object-oriented primitives in the Go language as a refreshing change that is a shining example of favoring simplicity.

---

[1] Yes, *that* Brian Kernighan, of Kernighan and Ritchie fame. In the history of the C programming language, he's kind of a big deal.

The other thing you will notice, which we briefly mentioned in Chapter 1, *The Way of the Cloud*, is that Go is all about sensibility and simplicity. It wasn't designed to satisfy some checklist of required features for fancy languages, nor was it designed to be the one language to rule them all, and in the darkness bind them.

Go is a practical language that can be used to solve real-world problems. For better or worse, most people seem to view Go as a niche language best suited to building small, command-line interface applications. We intend to use this book to prove that Go is capable of far more than that, especially when it comes to cloud native applications and microservices.

Don't worry if it doesn't seem like this chapter covers the entire language. We will be introducing you to new concepts as we go, but this chapter provides the building blocks upon which the remainder of the book is built.

## Building Hello Cloud

We have mixed feelings about "hello world" samples. On the one hand, many people despise them and feel they offer little to no value. On the other hand, you have to start somewhere, and printing "hello, world" seems to be a mainstay for the first code sample of any book.

In our case, we're going to print "hello, cloud" to the console, as shown in Listing 3.1.

Listing 3.1   **hello-cloud.go**

```
package main

import "fmt"

func main() {
        fmt.Println("Hello, cloud!")
        fmt.Println("你好, 云!")
}
```

This listing is fairly straightforward, and represents one of the most basic Go applications that you can write. The first line declares the package name (we'll talk about packages later), which, in our case, is main.

After this we import a package called fmt. This package provides the basic formatting functions and exposes a very C-like experience for reading, writing, and formatting strings. In this code listing, the fmt package is imported so that we have access to the Println function.

Next we define a function (also discussed later in the chapter) called main. All Go applications need a main function as the entry point. The next call to Println prints the phrase *Hello, cloud!* to the standard output device. The second print function illustrates a subtle aspect of Go, wherein strings are arrays of bytes, yet all Go strings can contain Unicode (even multi-byte) characters. A discussion on Unicode code points (Go calls them **runes**) is beyond the scope of this chapter[2].

To run the application, just issue the following command at a shell or command prompt:

```
go run hello-cloud.go
```

For this command to work, you don't *have* to be in a directory in your Go path (defined in Chapter 2, *Getting Started*), but you should get in the habit of being in your Go path for everything you do, even the simplest of samples. This habit will serve you well when it comes time to use third-party packages.

In this case, since this sample is publicly available, you might be executing it from

```
$GOPATH/src/github.com/cloudnativego/go-primer.
```

You can also run this sample in the Go Playground, an extremely useful web site that will let you quickly experiment with bits of Go code without messing up your current project. It also makes for a quick and handy substitute if you're on the go (see what we did there?) and don't have access to a full development environment. The Go Playground can be found at http://play.golang.org.

## Using Basic Functions

Functions in Go can take zero or more arguments, and they can return zero or more values. With a few extremely useful exceptions, Go function syntax looks very much like classic C function syntax. For those of you used to adding methods to classes, this may feel a bit awkward. There are no classes in Go, just functions, and visibility of those functions is determined by package scope, and whether or not the function is exported.

A really simple function to perform a virtual die roll might look something like this:

```
func dieRoll(size int) int {
        rand.Seed(time.Now().UnixNano())
        return rand.Intn(size) + 1
}
```

This function, named dieRoll, takes a single parameter called size, which is an integer parameter. First we seed the randomizer (which requires the use of the rand package) with the current time. If we had seeded it with a constant value, we would have returned the exact same die roll every time. Next, we use the return keyword to return a value from the function, a random number from 1 to the size of the die.

---

2  A great blog post on the subject of runes, strings, and their ilk can be found at https://blog.golang .org/strings.

## Randomization in the Playground

It's worth pointing out that the Go Playground uses a fixed clock time, which means your randomization will use a fixed seed and you'll always end up rolling the exact same die. It might be a fun experiment to run this same code locally and in the playground to observe this phenomenon.

If we were to invoke this function as follows, it would be equivalent to rolling our favorite Dungeons and Dragons die, the D20:

```
dieRoll(20)
```

Unlike functions from most languages, Go allows us to return multiple values. This does not mean that Go has added object-oriented overhead with concepts like tuples or pattern matching, as the following function illustrates:

```
func rollTwo(size1, size2 int) (int, int) {
        return dieRoll(size1), dieRoll(size2)
}
```

This function actually calls our original `dieRoll` function twice. As you can see from the method signature, it returns two anonymous values (i.e. we did not assign variable names to them), both of which are integers. Go also gives us the ability to name our return values. If we do this, then before the first line of our function executes, Go will have initialized the named return values to their defaults.

Take a look at the full sample in Listing 3.2, which defines several functions and illustrates the various ways we can use multiple return values.

Listing 3.2  **basic-functions.go**

```
package main

import (
        "fmt"
        "math/rand"
        "strconv"
        "time"
)

func dieRoll(size int) int {
        rand.Seed(time.Now().UnixNano())
        return rand.Intn(size) + 1
}

func rollTwo(size1, size2 int) (int, int) {
        return dieRoll(size1), dieRoll(size2)
}
```

```go
func returnsNamed(input1 string, input2 int) (theResult string, err error) {
        theResult = "modified " + input1 + ", " + strconv.Itoa(input2)
        return theResult, err
}

func main() {
        fmt.Printf("Rolled a die of size %d, result: %d\n", 6, dieRoll(6))

        res1, res2 := rollTwo(6, 10)
        fmt.Printf("Rolled a pair of dice (%d,%d), results: %d, %d\n",
                6, 10, res1, res2)

        named, err := returnsNamed("globule", 42)
        fmt.Printf("Named params returned: '%s', %v\n", named, err)
}
```

One important thing to take away from this code sample is the syntax for invoking a method and capturing multiple return values. One of the most frequently used idiomatic Go patterns is the definition of a function that returns a value and an error that will be `nil` if nothing went wrong. You will see this pattern used throughout the book and likely most Go samples or open source projects you encounter.

Also note that the names of the return values are *only* defined within the scope of the function definition. They do *not* have to match the names of the variables you use in another scope to capture the results.

Executing this application will display output that looks something like this:

```
$ go run basic-functions.go
Rolled a die of size 6, result: 5
Rolled a pair of dice (6,10), results: 1, 6
Named params returned: 'modified globule, 42', <nil>
```

Never confuse simple with primitive. In Chapter 1 we alluded to the fact that Go isn't necessarily a pure functional programming language. That doesn't mean we can't do some pretty powerful things with functions.

Let's say we wanted to have two different die roll functions, one real one and one fake one. We then want to have an array of these die roll functions and we invoke them without the calling code knowing whether it is invoking the real or the fake. In a classic OOP setting, we might create an interface called `IDieRoller`, then create two concrete classes that implement a `rollDie` method.

This is not how Go does things and it is our firm belief that all that extra work is unnecessary. In Go, we can just create a type definition such that any function that matches our signature can be treated as that type, which can then be passed around as parameters to functions or stored as data on structs or in arrays.

First, let's define the `dieRollFunc` type:

```go
type dieRollFunc func(int) int
```

As long as this type definition is in scope, any function that takes an integer and returns an integer can be treated as though it were a die roll function. Now let's write a function that returns a slice of functions:

```
func fakeDieRoll(size int) int {
        return 42
}

func getDieRolls() []dieRollFunc {
        return []dieRollFunc{
                dieRoll,
                fakeDieRoll,
        }
}
```

An extremely important distinction to make is that these are not pointers to parameter-bound functions (though, much to many people's surprise, Go is perfectly capable of **currying**[3]). These are just the raw functions that must be passed an integer when invoked.

The following code uses a new Go keyword, range, to loop over the contents of our slice, providing both an index and a function that we can invoke:

```
var rolls = getDieRolls()
for index, rollFunc := range rolls {
        fmt.Printf("Die Roll Attempt #%d, result: %d\n", index, rollFunc(10))
}
```

Now if we re-run our application with the examples of treating functions as data, we should see output that looks something like this:

```
Die Roll Attempt #0, result: 3
Die Roll Attempt #1, result: 42
```

This will always print **42** for the second parameter while the first uses our previously defined randomly generated die roll function.

Functions in Go are as important as classes and methods in other programming languages, and you shouldn't let the simple syntax fool you into thinking that simplicity implies a lack of power or utility.

## Working with Structs

**Structs** in Go are just typed collections of fields. We have a tremendous amount of flexibility with structs. We can nest them, we can create anonymous structs, and, as we'll see in the next section, we can create methods that operate on structs.

---

3  There is plenty of information online about this; just search for "functional programming golang".

To get started, let's create a simple struct that holds a person's name and age:

```
type person struct {
        name string
        age  int
}
```

We start with the `type` keyword, indicating that we are declaring a type (we saw this earlier when working with functions), followed by the name of the struct (in this case it is `person`) and finally the keyword `struct`. What follows is the collection of fields belonging to this type.

To create a struct, we have a number of different conventions we can use. All of the following lines of code can create a person struct:

```
var p = person{}
var p2 = person{ "bob", 21 }
var p3 = person{ name: "bob", age: 21, }
var p4 = &person{}
var p5 = &person{ "bob", 21 }
var p6 = &person{ name: "bob", age: 21, }
```

The first line shows us how we create an empty struct. The second line uses the order in which the fields are defined to let us supply initial values sequentially. The third line lets us set values for the fields in any order we like because were supplying the name of each field.

The next three lines accomplish the same thing, but instead of creating a struct, they create a *pointer to* a struct. Don't worry about working with pointers—it's nowhere near as complex as it is in C or C++.

We can access the individual fields within a struct variable using traditional dot (".") syntax that most of us are already familiar with.

Let's expand our simple struct with new features, where we'll create a multi-level struct for storing information about potential enemies in a multiplayer game server, as shown in Listing 3.3.

Listing 3.3   **go-structs.go**

```
package main

import (
        "fmt"
)

type power struct {
        attack  int
        defense int
}
```

```go
type location struct {
        x float32
        y float32
        z float32
}

type nonPlayerCharacter struct {
        name  string
        speed int
        hp    int
        power power
        loc   location
}

func main() {
        fmt.Println("Structs...")

        demon := nonPlayerCharacter{
                name:  "Alfred",
                speed: 21,
                hp:    1000,
                power: power{attack: 75, defense: 50},
                loc:   location{x: 1075.123, y: 521.123, z: 211.231},
        }

        fmt.Println(demon)

        anotherDemon := nonPlayerCharacter{
                name:  "Beelzebub",
                speed: 30,
                hp:    5000,
                power: power{attack: 10, defense: 10},
                loc:   location{x: 32.03, y: 72.45, z: 65.231},
        }

        fmt.Println(anotherDemon)
}
```

The first struct we see is power, which contains a grouping of offensive and defensive ratings. Next, we see the location struct, which contains a set of three-dimensional coordinates.

Finally, we have the nonPlayerCharacter struct, which houses a name, speed, hit points, location, and power of the non-player character. Ideally this information would be used by algorithms running in a game server, like determining combat resolution, calculating distances or collisions between characters, and other common game operations.

We use the struct creation syntax to create a new NPC (non-player character), demon, and a second NPC, anotherDemon. When we print these out we see output similar to the following:

```
Structs...
Alfred (1075.123047,521.122986,211.231003)
Beelzebub (32.029999,72.449997,65.231003)
```

It's worth pointing out here that the displayed values have slight resolution and rounding errors compared to the original inputs. This is normal, and issues like this are common when using floating point data types.

# Introducing Go Interfaces

Among all of our favorite features of Go, **interfaces** is definitely in the top five. In the previous section, we showed you how you can create logically grouped bundles of data called structs. In this next section, we'll show you how you can extend structs with functionality and how that applies to interfaces.

# Adding Methods to Structs

We can use structs (or virtually any type, really) as anchors for methods. This means we can have functions designed to operate specifically on structs. This feature is what gives Go the illusion of object-oriented functionality to the casual observer. This is an unfortunate misperception, because *Go is not object-oriented.*

To get started, let's create a couple of interesting structs to play with.

```
type attacker struct {
        attackpower int
        dmgbonus    int
}

type sword struct {
        attacker
        twohanded bool
}

type gun struct {
        attacker
        bulletsremaining int
}
```

In the preceding code, we've set up two types: gun and sword. Both of these types share a sub-structure called attacker. We don't have to repeat the name twice if the name matches the data type. *Do not confuse this syntax with structure inheritance...or any other kind of inheritance.* Make sure you tell all your friends that Go is not object-oriented.

Now let's use Go's method syntax to add a `Wield` method to both the `sword` struct and the `gun` struct.

```
func (s sword) Wield() bool {
        fmt.Println("You've wielded a sword!")
        return true
}

func (g gun) Wield() bool {
        fmt.Println("You've wielded a gun!")
        return true
}
```

We can now create guns and swords and wield them individually, like so:

```
sword1 := sword{attacker: attacker{attackpower: 1, dmgbonus: 5}, twohanded: true}
gun1 := gun{attacker: attacker{attackpower: 10, dmgbonus: 20}, bulletsremaining: 11}
fmt.Printf("Weapons: sword: %v, gun: %v\n", sword1, gun1)
sword1.Wield()
sword2.Wield()
```

This is excellent, and we're now able to create methods that operate on specific types, which in our case has been structs. For future reference, and you'll see it in samples later in the book, we don't just have to anchor methods to structs.

## Exploiting Dynamic Typing in Go with Interfaces

Now we're at a point where we can talk about interfaces and the power they bring to the Go language.

Let's say we want to create a function that automatically wields any weapon, whether it's a gun or a sword. In a traditional object-oriented language, we might create an interface called *IWeapon* or something similar, and then we would *explicitly* declare that certain classes implement that interface.

Go has no such explicit requirements. We can declare an interface that indicates something is a weapon with the following simple code:

```
type weapon interface {
        Wield() bool
}
```

What separates Go from so many other languages is that we do not have to declare that a struct or other type "is a weapon". It is automatically known to be a weapon simply by virtue of whether or not Go can find methods of the indicated signature in scope.

A lot of programmers like to call this "duck typing", which is a nod to the following quote from the "duck test", which you can read more about on Wikipedia:

If it looks like a duck, swims like a duck, and quacks like a duck, then it probably is a duck.

The Duck Test

Go doesn't really care about whether your type swims or looks or even quacks. All it has to do is *behave* like a duck. As such, we would like to propose that going forward, such type matching should be called "will it blend?" typing rather than "duck" typing (feel free to use the hashtag #wibtyping to make yourself trendy). If it blends, it blends, regardless of the device's shape, size, origin, or originally intended purpose.

With this interface in hand, we can then create a function that will perform a wield on anything wieldable:

```
func wielder(w weapon) bool {
        fmt.Println("Wielding...")
        return w.Wield()
}
```

Now we can pass our sword and our gun variables to the wielder function:

```
wielder(sword1)
wielder(gun1)
```

This results in the following output:

```
Weapons: sword: {{1 5} true}, gun: {{10 20} 11}
Wielding...
You've wielded a sword!
Wielding...
You've wielded a gun!
```

So far so good. However, what happens if we're having a really bad day and we feel a sudden urge to wield a chair? How would that work?

```
chair1 := chair{legcount: 3, leather: true}
wielder(chair1)
```

If we try and compile this code after just creating the chair struct, we'll get an error that looks like the following compilation output:

```
cannot use chair1 (type chair) as type weapon in argument to wielder: chair does not
implement weapon (missing Wield method)
```

However, if we give the chair struct a `Wield` method, then the "will it blend?" (or, in our case, "does it wield?") test will pass and we now get output that looks like this:

```
Weapons: sword: {{1 5} true}, gun: {{10 20} 11}
Wielding...
You've wielded a sword!
Wielding...
You've wielded a gun!
Wielding...
You've wielded a chair!! You having a bad day?
```

One of the most important take-aways from this section is that you don't have to explicitly declare what your type does. If it satisfies an interface—*any* interface—then your type can be used wherever that interface is used. This is especially powerful when the type author and interface author are not the same and can be used for extremely powerful extension mechanisms.

Going back to some of the first structs we created in this chapter, we can enhance them with methods. Go includes the built-in interface `Stringer` in the `fmt` package. Anything that conforms to the `Stringer` interface can be represented as a string. In our case, let's represent our three-dimensional in-game location as a string:

```
func (loc location) String() string {
        return fmt.Sprintf("(%f,%f,%f)", loc.x, loc.y, loc.z)
}
```

Remember, we're not explicitly telling Go that the struct "implements Stringer". We've implicitly satisfied that contract by exposing a `String` method. We can also add more utility methods, like computing the distance between locations (and thus allowing the computation of distance between two NPCs):

```
func (loc location) euclideanDistance(target location) float64 {
        return math.Sqrt(
                (loc.x-target.x)*(loc.x-target.x) +
                        (loc.y-target.y)*(loc.y-target.y) +
                        (loc.z-target.z)*(loc.z-target.z))
}

func (npc nonPlayerCharacter) distanceTo(target nonPlayerCharacter) float64 {
        return npc.loc.euclideanDistance(target.loc)
}
```

This gives us the ability to access these utility methods for debugging and calculation purposes in the game:

```
fmt.Printf("Npc %v is %f units away from Npc %v\n", demon, demon.
distanceTo(anotherDemon), anotherDemon)
```

If we wanted to, we could create an interface called something like `Distancer`, which would then allow functions to operate on a whole suite of types that are capable of computing their distance to other points.

## Working with Third-Party Packages

The Go language encourages developers to create small, reusable software components through the use of packages. Throughout this chapter we have been using packages, though we haven't made too big of a deal out of it until now.

For example, we used the `fmt` package to print to the console and format strings. We used the `math` package to get the square root function we needed to compute Euclidean distance. We used the `math/rand` package to get random number generation. You get the idea.

So far we have been using packages that are in the core Go libraries. As a result, all of the packages we've needed up to this point have already been in our Go workspace (the folder tree under $GOPATH).

This is just the tip of the iceberg. There is a wealth of packages available publicly, written by talented and passionate developers, just sitting there waiting for us to use. There are libraries for everything from building web applications to working with in-memory graphs to printing ASCII art banners.

For this sample, we're going to work with a package called `tablewriter`. This package resides on GitHub and allows us to print fancy, cleanly formatted tables as output to the console. This might seem superficial, but you'd be surprised how many times we've needed crisp columnar displays in console and log output.

Before we can use this package, we need to get it. For Go, this means we execute the `go get` command at a command prompt, as shown below:

```
go get github.com/olekukonko/tablewriter
```

This will fetch the package in question and put it in our Go workspace. If this command works, we should see no output, but we can go look at the directory $GOPATH/src/github.com/olekukonko/tablewriter and we will see a bunch of *.go files, some Markdown (discussed later) files, and a subdirectory. In short, this is the contents of the GitHub repository.

Most package developers provide a README in their GitHub repository that explains how to use the package they've developed. Before proceeding with our code sample, go check out the README for `tablewriter` at https://github.com/olekukonko/tablewriter.

Now that we have a decent idea of how we can use this third-party library, and we've used `go get` to fetch it, let's create a Go application that uses the table writer to output a list of NPCs that have appeared in earlier samples in this chapter. This package consumer is shown in Listing 3.4:

Listing 3.4   **go-package-consumer.go**

```go
package main

import (
        "os"

        "github.com/olekukonko/tablewriter"
)

func main() {
        data := [][]string{
                []string{"Alfred", "15", "10/20", "(10.32, 56.21, 30.25)"},
                []string{"Beelzebub", "30", "30/50", "(1,1,1)"},
                []string{"Hortense", "21", "80/80", "(1,1,1)"},
                []string{"Pokey", "8", "30/40", "(1,1,1)"},
        }
```

```
    table := tablewriter.NewWriter(os.Stdout)
    table.SetHeader([]string{"NPC", "Speed", "Power", "Location"})
    table.AppendBulk(data)
    table.Render()
}
```

Most of this is copied directly from the author's sample, though we have changed the column headers and data to describe characters roaming our fictional game server and their locations.

Running the application gives us the following output:

```
$ go run go-package-consumer.go
+-----------+-------+-------+----------------------+
|    NPC    | SPEED | POWER |       LOCATION       |
+-----------+-------+-------+----------------------+
| Alfred    |    15 | 10/20 | (10.32, 56.21, 30.25)|
| Beelzebub |    30 | 30/50 | (1,1,1)              |
| Hortense  |    21 | 80/80 | (1,1,1)              |
| Pokey     |     8 | 30/40 | (1,1,1)              |
+-----------+-------+-------+----------------------+
```

If this fails to compile, or you get import failures related to tablewriter, make sure that you've properly downloaded the package and that you are building the code for this sample in your Go workspace.

We're huge fans of not re-inventing the wheel, and having access to an overwhelming supply of third-party libraries means we will be well-stocked with all kinds of Go wheels for the foreseeable future.

## Creating Your Own Packages

Now that we've seen how to work with structs, how to create simple functions, how to create methods that apply to structs, and how to use packages built by other people, we're ready to create our own package.

Go's ecosystem of publicly available, open-source packages may be enough to solve every problem that we have and we may never need to create a single package. However, if we do end up solving a new problem or creating a nice set of code that we would love to share, we should share it. Go is all about open source, as are we, and every time we create a reusable package we make sure it's available on GitHub in case someone else might want to use it.

Creating a package in Go is actually pretty straightforward. Up to this point, all of our code has resided in the main package. This tells Go that it will find a main method, and that the code is executable as an application. A non-main package indicates a package intended to be imported and used by other Go code.

## Exporting Functions and Data

If you've been paying close attention to the code samples we've built so far, you might have noticed that all of our structs, fields, and functions started with a lower-case letter and all of the methods we've been using from other packages have started with capital letters. This isn't just an arbitrary naming convention like you see in other languages. This naming convention has actual, compiled consequences.

Packages are a unit of scoping in Go. We don't have OOP member access keywords like `public` or `private`, but we can still control the visibility of our code. Any type that we create (including functions) in Go that begins with a lower-case letter is considered *package-private*, or *not exported*. Any type that we create that begins with a capital letter is exported, and visible to anyone using our package.

As a package developer, you can think of it this way: everything with a capital letter is your public API, while everything with a lower-case letter is for internal use only.

## Creating a Package

It would be a shame not to share with the world all of the amazing work we've done with non-player characters, so let's create a package that will expose our groundbreaking code to the general public.

First, we'll create an `npcs` directory below the `go-primer` directory we've been working in. This means we'll be working in `$GOPATH/src/github.com/cloudnativego/go-primer/npcs`. It's possible for you to do this in another directory, but things will go horribly wrong if you're not in a valid Go workspace.

By convention, many package developers prefer to create a `types.go` file that contains the types to be used or exported by the package. Some developers like to split exported and private types into two different files, but that's usually only if you have an overwhelming number of types. As with all the patterns we show in this book, you're free to adopt or reject them, but we like to remain consistent throughout the samples.

Listing 3.5 contains our `types.go` file:

Listing 3.5  **npcs/types.go**

```
package npcs

// Power describes the attack and defense power of an NPC
type Power struct {
        Attack  int
        Defense int
}
```

```
// Location describes where in the virtual world an NPC exists
type Location struct {
        X float64
        Y float64
        Z float64
}

// NonPlayerCharacter represents metadata for an in-game creature
type NonPlayerCharacter struct {
        Name   string
        Speed int
        HP     int
        Power Power
        Loc    Location
}
```

There are a couple of things that may look different from the last time we worked with NPC structs. This time around, all the structs begin with capital letters, as do all of their fields. You can mix and match exported and private fields in a single struct if you like. Additionally, we now have comments above each of our exported types. This isn't just a nice thing, this is a rule enforced by most Go static analyzers, and required if we end up using a documentation generation tool.

The methods that we will expose to package consumers are going to go in a separate file called npcs.go, shown in Listing 3.6:

Listing 3.6  **npcs/npcs.go**

```
package npcs

import (
        "fmt"
        "math"
)

func (loc Location) String() string {
        return fmt.Sprintf("(%f,%f,%f)", loc.X, loc.Y, loc.Z)
}

// EuclideanDistance returns the distance between two in-game locations
func (loc Location) EuclideanDistance(target Location) float64 {
        return math.Sqrt(
                (loc.X-target.X)*(loc.X-target.X) +
                        (loc.Y-target.Y)*(loc.Y-target.Y) +
                        (loc.Z-target.Z)*(loc.Z-target.Z))
}
```

```
// DistanceTo returns the distance between two in-game characters
func (npc NonPlayerCharacter) DistanceTo(target NonPlayerCharacter) float64 {
        return npc.Loc.EuclideanDistance(target.Loc)
}


func (npc NonPlayerCharacter) String() string {
        return fmt.Sprintf("%s %s", npc.Name, npc.Loc)
}
```

We're exporting all of these functions so they need to have capital letters, and they are operating on structs and fields that have been exported.

With this sub-package created, we're now ready to use it in a client application, as shown in Listing 3.7:

Listing 3.7    **custom-package-consumer.go**

```
package main

import (
        "fmt"

        "github.com/cloudnativego/go-primer/npcs"
)

func main() {
        mob := npcs.NonPlayerCharacter{Name: "Alfred"}
        fmt.Println(mob)

        hortense := npcs.NonPlayerCharacter{Name: "Hortense",
            Loc: npcs.Location{X: 10.0, Y: 10.0, Z: 10.0}}
        fmt.Println(hortense)

        fmt.Printf("Alfred is %f units from Hortense.\n",
            mob.DistanceTo(hortense))
}
```

Now that we have made the world a better place with our magnificent NPC package, we can run our sample package consumer, and bask in its glory:

```
$ go run custom-package-consumer.go
Alfred (0.000000,0.000000,0.000000)
Hortense (10.000000,10.000000,10.000000)
Alfred is 17.320508 units from Hortense.
```

## Summary

This chapter provided a brief primer on the basics of the Go programming language. It is by no means a complete language reference or even a language tutorial. The scope of this book is narrowly focused on microservices and cloud native patterns and practices, but we wanted to make sure you had exposure to the fundamentals of the language before getting into the details of building microservices.

If you found this chapter to be a little overwhelming, then you might want to pause this book and skim through a few chapters of the books we referenced at the beginning of the chapter. Readers who already have some experience with Go hopefully found this chapter to be a handy refresher.

# 4

# Delivering Continuously

*"Programming is not a zero-sum game. Teaching something to a fellow programmer doesn't take it away from you."*

John Carmack

The art of building software is a craft that takes many years to perfect. In the early years of our careers, we often equate lines of code with the quality or the cool factor of an application: the more lines of code we write, the better the developers we are.

Once we get over that misconception, we tend to go the other way. We believe that the fewer lines of code we write, the better our code is, and the better the developers we are.

At some point in our professional development we start to realize that there is no direct correlation between lines of code and application quality. Whether we are searching for high or low water marks, *lines of code* is almost always a distraction from reality.

We learn valuable lessons by watching things go horribly, terribly wrong. After we've been on the phone at midnight with a menagerie of other IT types, all bracing for the impact of the inevitable doom that is "the release", our perspective on things changes.

Ultimately we come to the conclusion that what we seek is *confidence*. We want to know, before our application is deployed, that our application will do what it should, when it should, and do so in a predictable fashion. We gain this confidence not by avoiding the dreaded release, but by releasing *all the time*.

In this chapter we'll talk about continuous integration and continuous delivery, including the following topics:

- Introduction to Docker and Dockerhub, powerful tools for cloud-based CI and immutable artifacts.

- Introduction to Wercker, a CI tool useful for indie developers, startups, and even full enterprises.

- Automatically building your projects after every Git commit.

- Automatically deploying build artifacts as part of a CI pipeline.

# Introducing Docker

Docker is a container tool that utilizes Linux kernel features such as **cgroups** and **namespaces** to provide isolation of network, file, and memory resources without resorting to a full virtual machine. Lately, Docker has been gaining tremendous momentum and is seeing rising adoption numbers in many industries.

## Why use Docker?

Docker gives us the ability to create an immutable release that will run anywhere, regardless of what is or is not installed on the target environment (Docker, however, does have to be installed). For example, if I deployed a Docker image containing a service to Docker Hub (http://hub.docker.com), anyone with the base Docker install on their machine could run that service. They wouldn't have to worry about installing dependencies, compilers, or any other supporting infrastructure. Their development machine would not get polluted trying to set up configuration and dependencies for that service. Everything can be contained inside the Docker image.

For more information on Docker, including details on how to create your own Docker files and images and advanced administration, check out the book *Docker Up and Running* from O'Reilly Media by Karl Matthias and Sean P. Kane.

As you'll see later in this chapter, we're going to be able to publish Docker images to Docker Hub directly from our continuous integration tool—all done online, in the cloud, with almost no infrastructure installed on your workstation.

## Installing Docker

When installing Docker on a Mac, the preferred method is to install Docker *Toolbox*. If you see older documentation referring to something called *Boot2Docker*, this is deprecated and you should *not* be installing Docker this way.

For details on how to install Docker on your Mac, check out https://docs.docker.com/engine/installation/mac/. At the time of this writing, we had Docker version 1.8.1 installed. Make sure you check the documentation to ensure you're looking at the newest installation instructions before performing the install.

If you happen to have a Mac newer than 2010 that has 4GB of RAM and does *not* already have VirtualBox installed on it, and you're running Yosemite or better, then you can actually install a Mac-native application for Docker without the need for VirtualBox virtualization. Check Docker's website for those instructions.

We have written our samples assuming the use of Docker Toolbox, so if you're using the new Mac-native application your experience might be slightly different (and hopefully smoother!).

### Installation via Homebrew

You can also manually install Docker and all pre-requisites via Homebrew. It's slightly more involved, but makes it easier to stay updated and is consistent with how we've installed everything else. You'll need to install Docker, Docker Machine, and VirtualBox all through Homebrew if you don't intend to use Docker Toolbox.

If you've managed to install Docker Machine properly, then the first thing you're going to want to do is start it. Since Docker relies on features specific to the Linux kernel, what you're actually doing is starting up a virtual machine (facilitated by VirtualBox) that emulates those Linux kernel features in order to start a Docker server (called the *daemon*).

To start Docker Machine, enter the following command at your terminal.

```
$ docker-machine start default
Starting VM...
Started machines may have new IP addresses. You may need to re-run the `docker-machine env' command.
```

If you've named your machine something other than default, then replace `default` with the name of your machine. If you opt for all the defaults during Docker Toolbox installation, then it will install a Docker Machine named `default`.

It may take a few minutes to start the Docker machine depending on the power of your computer. There are a number of environment variables that need to be set (in *every* terminal window you intend to use with Docker) in order to properly communicate with the Docker server for doing things like running applications, listing images in your registry, etc. To see what those values need to be, type the following in your shell:

```
$ docker-machine env default
export DOCKER_TLS_VERIFY="1"
export DOCKER_HOST="tcp://192.168.99.100:2376"
export DOCKER_CERT_PATH="/Users/khoffman/.docker/machine/machines/default"
export DOCKER_MACHINE_NAME="default"
# Run this command to configure your shell:
# eval "$(docker-machine env default)"
```

This gives you the shell commands necessary to configure your terminal with the right Docker environment. To make these commands happen and modify your environment, you can use the following command once your Docker machine is running:

```
$ eval "$(docker-machine env default)"
```

Docker Toolbox comes with a shortcut to a pre-configured Docker shell that allows you to skip this step, but we find that shell awkward and cumbersome, so we just run the `eval` command to "Dockerify" an existing terminal window.

Now you should be able to run all Docker commands in the terminal to examine your installation. One that you'll find you may run quite often is `docker images`. This command lists the Docker images you have stored in your local repository.

## Running Docker Images

Now for the fun part! If you choose, you can manually download and install Docker images to make them available on your machine, or you can actually run them directly from Docker Hub (or a private registry, if you've configured one within your enterprise).

As an example, if you run the following command, it will launch our "hello world" web server sample directly from Docker Hub.

```
$ docker run -p 8080:8080 cloudnativego/book-hello
[negroni] listening on :8080
[negroni] Started GET /
[negroni] Completed 200 OK in 71.688µs
```

The output shows what it looks like after that image has been cached locally. If you're doing this for the first time, you will see a bunch of progress reports indicating that you're downloading the layers of the Docker image.

This command maps port 8080 *inside* the Docker image to port 8080 *outside* the Docker image. As mentioned, Docker provides network isolation, so unless you explicitly allow traffic from outside a container to be routed inside the container, the isolation will essentially be a firewall.

Since we've mapped the inside and outside ports, we can now hit port 8080 on the IP address of our Docker machine (note that this is *not* localhost).

> **Note**
>
> If a machine is running, you can ask Docker for the IP address of that Docker machine using the command `docker-machine ip default`. If you want the IP address of a machine other than `default`, just use the name of that machine.

```
$ curl http://192.168.99.100:8080
Hello from Go!
```

This command shows that we can download a fully functioning piece of software from Docker Hub, cache the image locally, *and* execute the Docker image's run command. Even if we didn't install a single tool for Go or configure our Go workspace, we could still use this Docker image to launch our sample service.

Once we start to wrap our heads around all of the power and utility that Docker provides, we start seeing tremendous possibilities, like deploying our build artifacts as Docker Hub images.

> **Tip**
>
> If you're doing a lot of development with a lot of different Docker images, there's a chance you could exceed your virtual host's disk capacity storing all that stuff. Those images are just caches, so there should be no permanent consequences from doing an occasional cleanup. If you run into this, you might find the following two shell commands useful:
>
> Delete all Docker containers—`docker rm $(docker ps -a -q)`
>
> Delete all Docker images—`docker rmi $(docker images -q)`

# Continuous Integration with Wercker

Depending on your background, you may already have experience with Continuous Integration servers. Some of the more popular ones are servers like Jenkins, TeamCity, Concourse, and, for the Microsoft world, Team Foundation Server (TFS). For this chapter, and the rest of the book, we will be using a CI tool called **Wercker**.

These tools all attempt to provide a software package that helps developers embrace CI best practices. In this section of the chapter, we will provide a brief overview of CI, and then walk through setting up Wercker to automatically build an application.

## Continuous Integration Best Practices

While sifting through Wikipedia, one occasionally finds pearls of wisdom amid the endless sea of trivia facts. The section on continuous integration (CI) best practices is particularly well done and informative. The following is a review of that content including some commentary on how each of these guidelines applies to what we're doing int this book:

- **Maintain a code repository**—As we discussed in Chapter 2, getting yourself familiar with GitHub is essential for working through this book.

- **Automate the build**—Setting up build automation is the goal of this chapter.

- **Make the build self-testing**—Test-Driven Development isn't just something we do once in a while, it is part of *the way of the cloud*, as you'll see in Chapter 5. All code we write is tested, and CI servers must execute those tests.

- **Commit to the baseline every day**—Another virtue of *the way of the cloud* is *release early, release often*. This is reflected in CI best practices by constantly committing to the baseline. The longer you wait before committing to the baseline (the branch that produces production releases), the less confidence you have and the more you *fear* the release process.

- **Build every commit**—Every time you check in code, your CI tool should execute a build, which involves running unit tests, evaluating test coverage, and often running static analysis tools.

- **Keep the build fast**—If your build is too slow or cumbersome to automate, this is a smell that something else may be wrong. Your builds should be fast, so you can see them pass or fail quickly. Slow, bulky, prolonged builds eventually become enough of a nuisance that people start turning them off, or disabling test runs.

- **Test in a production clone**—We'll show you a number of ways you can accomplish this throughout the book, including deploying your services to a local cloud.

- **Make it easy to get deliverables**—As we mentioned in the previous section, our deliverables will all be exposed in Docker Hub, making it brain-dead simple to fetch our build artifacts. Wercker doesn't force you to use Docker Hub, however, as you can pull build artifacts from the website or the command-line tools.

- **Everyone can see the results of the latest build**—If no one knows the build is failing, there is absolutely no reason to have automated builds. If a build goes red, it should immediately become top priority to make it go green again. Wercker makes it easy to see the results of builds, but also has a client application that will notify you instantly when builds fail. It's important that your tool make build status visible, but it's up to you and your team to build the discipline to treat failed builds with the severity they demand.

- **Automate deployment**—We'll see in this chapter how we can use Wercker to deploy Docker images automatically at the end of a successful build. If deploying is a manual process, it becomes an error-prone process. Manual deployments are slow and cumbersome, and teams tend to avoid them, leading to longer delays between deploys and a loss of confidence.

## Why use Wercker?

With all of the CI tools already available on the market, why would we recommend using one like Wercker? We evaluate all tools against the virtues of the *way of the cloud*, and Wercker came out on top for our needs for this book.

First and foremost, the infrastructure for Wecker doesn't reside on our workstations. We have to install a command-line client, but that's it. The builds happen in the cloud. Secondly, we can get started using Wercker without handing over a credit card. This is a huge showstopper when it comes to our desire to favor simplicity. Having to commit to payment terms dramatically raises the stress level of a developer, often needlessly.

Finally, Wercker itself is *simple*. It's incredibly easy to set up, does not require advanced training, a doctorate in continuous integration, or a ritual sacrifice in hopes that builds will work.

> **Tip**
>
> If you spend more time debugging your build tool than your product, you're using the wrong tool.

With Wercker, there are three basic steps to get going, and then you're ready for CI:

1. Create an application in Wercker using the website.

2. Add a `wercker.yml` file to your application's codebase.

3. Choose how to package and where to deploy successful builds.

## Creating a Wercker Application

Head over to wercker.com right now and create an account. You can choose to log in to
Wercker using your GitHub account, which streamlines everything and makes for one less set
of credentials you need to worry about. It also makes it easier for Wercker to talk to GitHub
when setting up builds.

Once you've got an account, then it's a simple matter of clicking the *Applications* menu
at the top and choosing the *create* option. If prompted for whether you want to create an
organization or application, choose *application*. Organizations allow multiple Wercker users
to collaborate, all without having to supply a credit card. Figure 4.1 shows a wizard-style page
for setting up a new application. As Wercker is always changing and upgrading their UX and
features, this screenshot could be out of date by the time you read this.

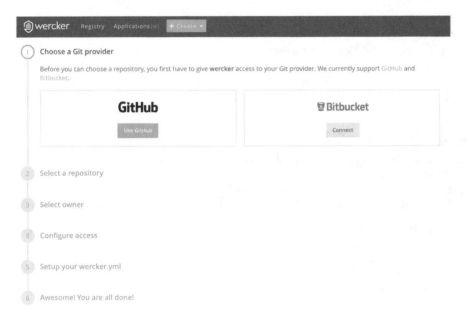

Figure 4.1    Creating an Application in Wercker

Source: wercker.com

You don't have to specifically follow along, as there will be an exercise later in the chapter on
creating a Wercker build. After choosing between GitHub or Bitbucket, you are then prompted
to choose a repository. This is a source code repository to which Wercker will link the new
application. Figure 4.2 shows a list of application builds in Wercker.

When commits happen in this repository, Wercker will kick off a build according to your
preferences and configuration.

Applications

🔍 Search on name or owner

FILTER ON:   All   Mine   cng

| NAME | OWNER | UPDATED |
|------|-------|---------|
| B  blog 🔒 | cng | 2 months ago |
| H  hello | cng | 2 months ago |
| V  vcap 🔒 | cng | 2 months ago |
| G  gogo-service 🔒 | cng | |

Figure 4.2   List of Applications in Wercker

Source: wercker.com

During step 5 of the application creation process, Wercker can attempt to generate a `wercker` `.yml` file (discussed next) on your behalf. We have found that, at least for Go applications, this rarely ever results in the configuration we want, so we always create our own Wercker configuration files.

## Installing the Wercker CLI

You'll want to be able to invoke Wercker builds locally so you can have a reliable prediction of how the cloud-based build is going to go. Both the local build and the cloud build rely on the use of Docker. Essentially, your code is bundled into a docker image of your choosing (defined in your `wercker.yml`) and then you choose what gets executed and how.

To run Wercker builds locally, you'll need the Wercker CLI. For information on how to install and test the CLI, check out http://devcenter.wercker.com/learn/basics/the-wercker-cli.html. Wercker updates their documentation more frequently than this book will be updated, so please mark your spot in this book while you go and install the Wercker CLI according to their documentation. At the time of this writing, Wercker's documentation still refers to using Boot2Docker as a means to installing Docker. Ignore this, and use the directions we supplied earlier on getting up and running with Docker. Just skip to the section of their documentation entitled "Getting the CLI".

If you've installed the CLI properly, you should be able to ask the CLI for the version, as shown below:

```
$ wercker version
Version: 1.0.295
Compiled at: 2015-10-23 06:19:25 -0400 EDT
Git commit: db49e30f0968ff400269a5b92f8b36004e3501f1
No new version available
```

If you are running an older version of the CLI, you might see something like this, prompting you to automatically update:

```
$ wercker version
Version: 1.0.174
Compiled at: 2015-06-24 10:02:21 -0400 EDT
Git commit: ac873bc1c5a8780889fd1454940a0037aec03e2b
A new version is available: 1.0.295 (Compiled at: 2015-10-23T10:19:25Z, Git commit:
db49e30f0968ff400269a5b92f8b36004e3501f1)
Download it from: https://s3.amazonaws.com/downloads.wercker.com/cli/stable/
darwin_amd64/wercker
Would you like update? [yN]
```

If you have trouble performing an automatic update (which happened to us several times), then it's just as easy to re-run the `curl` command in Wercker's documentation to download the latest CLI.

## Creating a Wercker Configuration File

A Wercker configuration file is a YAML file that contains three main sections, corresponding to the three main pipelines available:

- **Dev**—This defines the list of steps for the development pipeline. As with all of the pipelines, you can specify a **box** to use for the build, or you can globally specify a box to use for all pipelines. A box is either one of Wercker's built-in pre-made Docker images or can refer to any Docker image hosted by Docker Hub.

- **Build**—This defines a list of steps and scripts to be performed during the Wercker build. Not that unlike many other servers like Jenkins and TeamCity, the build steps are in a configuration file residing in the codebase, not in opaque configuration hidden by the server.

- **Deploy**—This is where you define how and where your build is deployed.

> **YAML**
>
> According to http://www.yaml.org/, YAML stands for "YAML Ain't Markup Language". It is a human-readable, machine-parseable text format. Many will disagree with us, but we feel that YAML is to JSON what JSON was to XML. We don't recommend using YAML as the payload format for RESTful services, but it is ideally suited to configuration and metadata storage.

While this book was being written, Wercker came out with the concept of **workflows** that extend the capabilities of pipelines with branches, conditional builds, multiple deployment targets, and other advanced features. For simplicity's sake in this book, we'll focus on pipelines.

When editing YAML configuration files, you should be wary. While we traditionally favor standard text editors over IDEs, you *will* want to use something that can parse and format YAML properly while editing it. It is very sensitive to whitespace and tabs and if your spacing is off, things will break. Most editors, including Emacs and Atom, have plugins for dealing with YAML.

If you're interested in learning more, check out http://www.yaml.org/start.html as a starting point. To read the YAML in Listing 4.1, you just need to know the main key points of YAML:

- YAML is pronounced "yeah-mul".

- Structure is indicated via indentation of one or more spaces.

- Items within a sequence are preceded by a dash.

- Key-value pairs (e.g. map items) are denoted by a colon following a key *with no intervening whitespace*.

Finally, one last thing before going through the configuration file. If you aren't sure about your YAML and you want to verify the syntax, check out http://www.yamllint.com/, an online YAML validator. This tool has saved much bacon and pulled many feet from the fire.

Listing 4.1 contains the `wercker.yml` file from our opinionated *hello world* sample.

Listing 4.1   **wercker.yml**

```
box: golang

dev:
  steps:
    - setup-go-workspace:
        package-dir: github.com/cloudnativego/hello

    - script:
        name: env
        code: env

    - script:
        name: go get
        code: |
          cd $WERCKER_SOURCE_DIR
          go version
          go get -u github.com/Masterminds/glide
          export PATH=$WERCKER_SOURCE_DIR/bin:$PATH
          glide install

    - internal/watch:
        code: go run main.go
        reload: true

build:
  steps:
    - setup-go-workspace:
        package-dir: github.com/cloudnativego/hello

    - script:
        name: env
        code: env

    - script:
        name: go get
        code: |
```

```
        cd $WERCKER_SOURCE_DIR
        go version
        go get -u github.com/Masterminds/glide
        export PATH=$WERCKER_SOURCE_DIR/bin:$PATH
        glide install

  # Build the project
  - script:
      name: go build
      code: |
        go build

  # Test the project
  - script:
      name: go test
      code: |
        go test -v $(glide novendor)

  - script:
      name: copy files to wercker output
      code: |
        cp -R ./ ${WERCKER_OUTPUT_DIR}


deploy:
 steps:
   - internal/docker-push:
       username: $DOCKER_USERNAME
       password: $DOCKER_PASSWORD
       cmd: /pipeline/source/hello
       port: "8080"
       tag: latest
       repository: cloudnativego/book-hello
       registry: https://registry.hub.docker.com

   - cng/cf-deploy:
       api: $API
       user: $USER
       password: $PASSWORD
       org: $ORG
       space: $SPACE
       appname: wercker-step-hello
       docker_image: cloudnativego/book-hello
```

There are three pipelines in this file: dev, build, and deploy. In the dev pipeline, we're essentially using Wercker and Docker to create a clean slate Docker image and then run our application directly.

In Listing 4.1, the value of the box key is golang. This means that we're using a baseline Docker image that comes with Go already installed on it. This is essential because the baseline Docker image for a Wercker build needs to have the build tools required for your application.

This is sometimes a difficult concept to grasp. When you build with Wercker, you aren't using your local workstation's resources (even if the build is technically *local!*). Instead, you are using the resources available to a Docker image. As a result, if you want to compile Go applications with Wercker, you need to start with a Go-enabled Docker image. This makes total sense if you want builds to produce identical artifacts whether they run locally or in Wercker's cloud.

The first script that we run in this build is called go get. Whatever name you put in for the script will actually show up in the build output, as shown on the Wercker website in Figure 4.3.

This step lets us go get anything we might need that isn't part of the base image. In our case, we're using a tool called *Glide* to help us manage and vendor our Go dependencies. Glide sits on top of the new vendored dependency management available in Go 1.5 and later, and gives us the ability to update dependencies and lock them in on specific versions, something that is difficult or impossible to do with stock Go tools.

|  | | |
|---|---|---|
| ✓ Build **passed** on ꝑ master | | |
| Message | | |
| #cd37c26  Fix typo in wercker.yml - *Kevin Hoffman* | | |
| Steps | | C |
| ✓ get code | 3 sec | ≈ |
| ✓ setup environment | 2 sec | ≈ |
| ✓ wercker-init | 0 sec | ≈ |
| ✓ setup-go-workspace | 1 sec | ≈ |
| ✓ go get | 10 sec | ≈ |
| ✓ go build | 3 sec | ≈ |
| ✓ env | 1 sec | ≈ |
| ✓ go test | 4 sec | ≈ |
| ✓ integration tests | 5 sec | ≈ |
| ✓ copy files to wercker output | 1 sec | ≈ |
| ✓ store | 3 sec | ≈ |

Figure 4.3   Build Steps Execution Status

Source: wercker.com

The next script, `go build`, actually performs the build. Because we've installed Glide and we're using Go 1.6 (or later), we can just use the simple `go build` command to compile.

This will execute the command within a temporary Go workspace as defined by the contents of a `vendor/` directory beneath the application that was created when Glide was initialized and was checked into source control. This directory, and the Glide tool, allow us to vendor our dependencies and store them with our application. This adds a bit of bloat to our GitHub repository, but is worth every byte when it comes to predictable builds.

Without a dependency management tool like Glide we might set ourselves up for situations where we accidentally re-vendor dependencies during build or deploy steps. This completely violates our goal of pushing immutable artifacts.

### Using Glide

All the documentation you need on Glide can be found at http://github.com/Masterminds/glide. You essentially have three commands that will be used from the command line in your daily development routine:

- **`glide init`**—Creates a `glide.yml` and `glide.lock` file based on project dependencies.
- **`glide up`**—Gets the latest versions of dependent packages and updates the glide .lock file
- **`glide install`**—Installs all of the packages identified in the `glide.lock` file.

After we build, we execute all the tests within the project. Note that we use `go test -v $(glide novendor)` to execute our tests. This just returns a value that tells Go what files to examine, based on Glide's configuration.

Assuming our tests pass, we use the `$WERCKER_OUTPUT_DIR` environment variable to copy our application binary into a location that will show up in the final Docker image produced by the build.

The deploy section of the `wercker.yml` file refers to deploying the resulting build artifact, which we'll discuss shortly.

Starting with Chapter 5 of this book, all of the code samples in our GitHub organization come with `wercker.yml` files. Everything we built for this book was done cloud-first and with continuous integration in mind. You can use these Wercker configuration files as starter templates for your own projects. Also note that some samples might use workflows while others use the classic pipelines.

## Running a Wercker Build

The easiest way to run a Wercker build is to simply commit code. Once Wercker is configured, your build should start only a few seconds after you push. Obviously we still want to use the regular Go command line (e.g. `go build`, `go test`, etc.) to build and test our application locally. The next logical step after that is to see how the application builds using the Wercker pipeline (and therefore, within an isolated, portable Docker image). This is *invaluable* for eliminating the "works on my machine" problems that arise regularly during development projects.

We usually have a script with our applications that looks like this to invoke the `wercker` build command:

```
rm -rf _builds _steps _projects
wercker build --git-domain github.com --git-owner cloudnativego --git-repository
gogo-service
rm -rf _builds _steps _projects
```

Running this script (assuming there's a Wercker build associated with a repository at `github .com/cloudnativego/gogo-service`, as indicated in the preceding command line) will look a little something like this:

```
$ ./buildlocal
--> Executing pipeline
--> Running step: setup environment
Pulling from library/golang: latest
Already exists: 6d1ae97ee388
Already exists: 8b9a99209d5c
Already exists: 2e05a52ffd47
Already exists: 80887d145531
Already exists: ec064956c4f0
Already exists: c8a688c71293
Already exists: 03f519453f95
Already exists: b449de9eb16c
Already exists: 7ab9945f3cbe
Already exists: 7cb2cf0c147e
Already exists: b56020e12f7a
Already exists: 1c3154f0cc14
Already exists: d556268f76ae
Already exists: 0eca3aede538
Digest: sha256:1cbd73c3a58097c777d85ad289aed4d0af45325288899ddae5a082d5e7a49c46
Status: Image is up to date for golang:latest
--> Running step: wercker-init
--> Running step: setup-go-workspace
Using /go as root dir
package-dir option not set, will use default: /go/src/github.com/cloudnativego/
gogo-service
$WERCKER_SOURCE_DIR now points to: /go/src/github.com/cloudnativego/gogo-service
Go workspace setup finished
--> Running step: go get
go version go1.5.2 linux/amd64
--> Running step: go build
--> Running step: go test
ok      github.com/cloudnativego/gogo-service      0.005s
--> Running step: copy files to wercker output
--> Steps passed: 17.92s
--> Pipeline finished: 19.03s
```

Everything up to "Status: Image is up to date" is the command-line tool ensuring that we have the latest layers for the Docker image we're using as a baseline (`library/golang: latest`, as indicated in the output).

> **Caution**
>
> Make sure you either keep an eye on the versions of your baseline images, or you fix them to specific release versions. We have seen issues with weird compilation errors when the version of Go changes in the *latest* image. If the version of Go in the *latest* image is different than what you're using to build outside of Wercker, you could have inconsistent, or failing, builds.

The rest of the output shows the steps indicated in the `wercker.yml` file like `go get`, `go build`, and `go test`. We use the `-v` parameter when executing `go test` so we get an itemized list of each test executed and the results.

## Deploying to DockerHub

Once we can successfully build our application locally with the Wercker CLI and remotely trigger a build either by Git commit or by pushing a button on the website, we're ready to set up deployments.

By default, the build artifacts from each individual build are only available within Wercker. You can download the artifact from the website or you can pull it with the Wercker command line.

As an added bonus, we can also deploy our artifacts to a number of locations. Wercker has several built-in deployment steps and there are plug-ins available for many other deployment targets (as you'll see later in the book, we've written a Wercker step for deploying DockerHub images to Cloud Foundry).

First, we can set up a deployment target in the Wercker website, as shown in Figure 4.4.

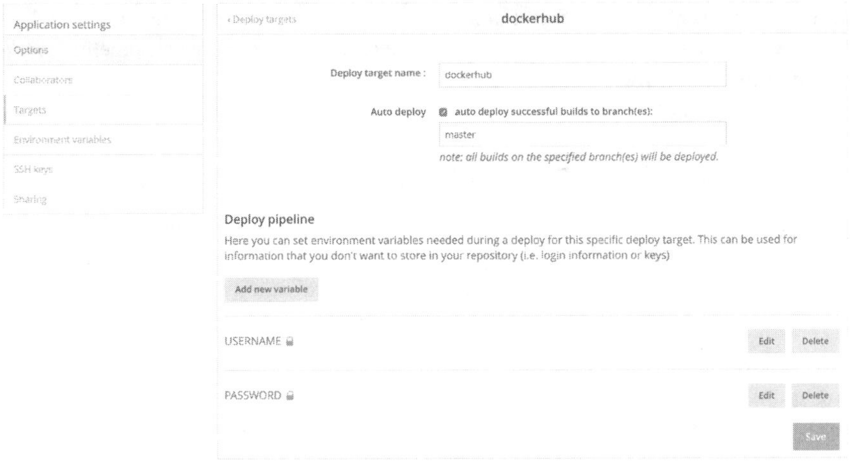

Figure 4.4    Configuring Deployment Targets in Wercker

Source: wercker.com

Figure 4.4 shows a deployment target called `dockerhub`. This target is configured to automatically deploy from the **master** branch. This means that the `deploy` step in our Wercker configuration file will be referenced at the end of every build after every commit:

```
deploy:
 steps:
  - internal/docker-push:
        username: $USERNAME
        password: $PASSWORD
        cmd: /pipeline/source/gogo-service
        port: "8080"
        tag: latest
        repository: cloudnativego/gogo-service
        registry: https://registry.hub.docker.com
```

The properties required for the `internal/docker-push` step are documented in Wercker's documentation. One of the main points to see here is that we've provided some additional metadata for the Docker image, such as the run command, the default port mapping, and a tag. Additionally, we've indicated the Docker Hub repository into which this image will be deployed (`cloudnativego/gogo-service`).

The other important aspect of this configuration is that the user name and password required to obtain write access to a Docker Hub repository are not embedded within the `wercker.yml` file, but are instead substituted with secure environment variables we defined in the deployment target configuration on Wercker's website (see Figure 4.4).

In addition to automatic deployment upon successful build, we can also manually push a build artifact to Docker Hub either by pushing a button on the website or by using the Wercker CLI.

At this point in the chapter, you should feel pretty comfortable with both Docker and Wercker and how those two technologies are going to fit into the continuous integration pipelines we're going to be using throughout the book.

## Reader Exercise: Create a Full Development Pipeline

Since we do not have access to your GitHub account or to your Wercker account (you did create a Wercker account earlier in this chapter, didn't you?) we can't walk you though a full development pipeline sample without handing out our own credentials and compromising our accounts. Despite the hilarity that might ensue from this, we decided against it.

However, this is an ideal opportunity for you to pause before we get any further into actual Go programming and try and put the last few chapters to practical purpose. As an exercise to you to cement your knowledge of building development pipelines, we would like you to create your own end-to-end continuous integration and delivery pipeline.

It sounds complicated, but there really isn't that much to it. In fact, we'll give you some steps to follow:

1. Create a new Go application (remember, package is named `main`) in `$GOPATH/src/github.com/`*`youraccount`*`/pipeline`.

2. This application can have a single `main.go` file that just emits "hello world" (or whatever you would like) to the console.

3. Make sure the application runs (`go run`) and builds (`go build`) locally.

4. Commit your work to GitHub. If this works, you should be able to go to a second computer (or a different workspace on your computer, if you're feeling adventurous) and `go get` the application you just created straight from GitHub.

5. Go over to Wercker and create a new application called `mypipeline` (or something more creative). Choose the `github` integration and point it to your public GitHub repository.

6. Finish configuring the Wercker application and skip the `wercker.yml` step. Instead, create your own using the template we provided earlier during our discussion of Wercker. In your `wercker.yml` you can use Go commands directly, and won't need to run with `godep`.

7. Make sure you can build your application locally using the Wercker CLI.

8. Add a deployment target for your application that will push to Docker Hub. You can follow the same directions we used earlier.

9. Make a subtle change to your application and commit that to GitHub. Now go to Wercker and watch your build succeed.

10. Watch your application then get deployed to Docker Hub. It should then show up in the location you chose in your `wercker.yml` file, e.g. `dockerhub.com/`*`(youraccount)`*`/pipeline:latest`.

11. Use the `docker run` command we showed you earlier to execute your application from the Docker Hub image. If all has gone well, you should now see your console output.

12. Play around with committing changes to GitHub and watching the changes appear in the Docker Hub image you run just a few minutes later.

This might seem like a long way to go just to emit some text to the console, but we need to keep your eye on the big picture: you've just set up a continuous delivery pipeline that automatically puts new release artifacts out on Docker Hub just minutes after every GitHub commit.

You're starting your development project from a stable, testable, continuously deployed foundation. From here on in, if you adhere to TDD principles and *the way of the cloud*, you will be able to iteratively add any feature with the confidence that it can be deployed to production after checking into source control.

Having this type of infrastructure at your disposal will pay dividends far and above the twenty minutes or so it takes to get the initial pipeline set up.

### Advanced Challenge: Integrate Third-Party Library

As an advanced challenge, modify the code you wrote already for the reader challenge to utilize some third-party package (the table-writer package from Chapter 3 is an ideal candidate).

To get this to work, refer back to the portion of the chapter where we used the Glide tool to vendor in dependencies. If you check in the vendor directory and you're using Glide as per our samples, your local and remote Wercker builds should all work properly.

## Summary

In this chapter we didn't include a single line of sample Go code. Embracing the concepts of continuous integration and continuous delivery are essential to *the way of the cloud* and we feel that both of these practices are *mandatory* in order to have the level of confidence in your applications and services that is necessary in today's world of rapid change, agile methodologies, and cloud-based infrastructure.

We talked about using Wercker as our tool of choice for continuous integration, which relies upon Docker for the creation and execution of immutable build artifacts. While you are certainly free to choose your own CI server, we explicitly chose Wercker for its ease of use, simplicity, and wallet-friendliness. In other words, even if your enterprise chooses to go another way, it'll cost you absolutely nothing to create build pipelines in Wercker as you make your way through this book.

We hope that you have gone through the reader exercise, as setting up build pipelines should be something you do so much out of habit that it should be muscle memory. We're also going to be building at least one Wercker build per chapter throughout the rest of the book, so familiarity with this tool is key.

Having completed the reader exercise, and ideally the advanced version of it, you should now have the core Go skills and infrastructure tools you need to roll up your sleeves and dive into the rest of the book, which will lead you down a path of progressively more intricate and powerful cloud native application development in Go.

# 5

# Building
# Microservices in Go

*"The golden rule: can you make a change to a service and deploy it by itself*
*without changing anything else?"*

Sam Newman, *Building Microservices*

Every service you build should be a microservice, and, as we've discussed earlier in the book, we generally disagree with using the prefix *micro* at all. In this chapter we're going to be building a service, but this chapter is as much about the process as it is about the end result.

We'll start by following the practice of **API First**, designing our service's RESTful contract before we write a single line of code. Then, when it does come time to write code, we're going to start by writing *tests* first. By writing small tests that go from failure to passing, we will gradually build out our service.

The sample service we're going to build in this chapter is a server implementation of the game of Go. This service will be designed to enable clients of any kind to participate in matches of Go, from iPhones to browsers to other services.

Most importantly, this service needs a name. A service written in Go that resolves matches of the game of Go can be called nothing less than **GoGo**.

In this chapter, we're going to cover:

- API First development disciplines and practices.
- Creating the scaffolding for a microservice.
- Adding tests to a scaffolded service and iterating through adding code to make tests pass.
- Deploying and running a microservice in the cloud.

# Designing Services API First

In this next section we're going to design our microservice. One of the classic problems of software development is that what you design is rarely ever what you end up developing. There is always a gap between documentation, requirements, and implementation.

Thankfully, as you'll see, there are some tools available to use for microservice development that actually allow a situation where *the design is the documentation,* which can then be integrated into the development process.

## Designing the Matches API

The first thing that we're going to need if we're creating a service that hosts matches is a resource collection for matches. With this collection, we should be able to create a new match as well as list all of the matches currently being managed by the server shown in Table 5.1.

Table 5.1   **The Matches API**

| Resource | Method | Description |
| --- | --- | --- |
| /matches | GET | Queries a list of all available matches. |
| /matches | POST | Creates and starts a new match. |
| /matches/{id} | GET | Queries the details for an individual match. |

If we were building a game of Go that we were hoping to sell for real money, rather than as a sample, we would also implement methods to allow a UI to query things like **chains** and **liberties**, concepts essential to determining legal moves in Go.

### Designing the Moves API

Once the service is set up to handle matches, we need to expose an API to let players make moves. This adds the following HTTP methods to the moves sub-resource as shown in Table 5.2.

Table 5.2   **The Moves API**

| Resource | Method | Description |
| --- | --- | --- |
| /matches/{id}/moves | GET | Returns a time-ordered list of all moves taken during the match. |
| /matches/{id}/moves | POST | Make a move. A move without a position is a pass. |

# Creating an API Blueprint

In our desire to simplify everything we do, some time ago we started to eschew complex or cumbersome forms of documentation. Do we really need to share monstrous document files that carry with them decades of backwards compatibility requirements?

For us, **Markdown**[1] is the preferred form of creating documentation and doing countless other things. It is a simple, plain text format that requires no IDE or bloated editing tool, and it can be converted and processed into countless formats from PDF to web sites. As with so many things, the debate over which format people use for documentation has been known to spark massive, blood-soaked inter-office battles.

As a matter of habit, we typically create Markdown documents that we bundle along with our services. This allows other developers to quickly get a list of all of our service's REST resources, the URI patterns, and request/response payloads. As simple as our Go code is, we still wanted a way to document the service contract without making someone go sifting through our router code.

As it turns out, there is a dialect of Markdown used specifically for documenting RESTful APIs: **API Blueprint**. You can get started reading up on this format at the API Blueprint website https://apiblueprint.org/.

If you check out the GitHub repository for this chapter (https://github.com/cloudnativego/gogo-service), you'll see a file called `apiary.apib`. This file consists of Markdown that represents the documentation and specification of the RESTful contract supported by the GoGo service.

Listing 5.1 below shows a sample of the Markdown content. You can see how it describes REST resources, HTTP methods, and JSON payloads.

Listing 5.1 **Sample Blueprint Markdown**

```
### Start a New Match [POST]

You can create a new match with this action. It takes information about the players
  and will set up a new game. The game will start at round 1, and it will be
  **black**'s turn to play. Per standard Go rules, **black** plays first.

+ Request (application/json)

        {
            "gridsize" : 19,
            "players" : [
            {
                "color" : "white",
                "name" : "bob"
            },
            {
                "color" : "black",
                "name" : "alfred"
            }
            ]
        }
```

---

1  Links to references on Markdown syntax can be found here: https://en.wikipedia.org/wiki/Markdown.

```
+ Response 201 (application/json)

    + Headers

            Location: /matches/5a003b78-409e-4452-b456-a6f0dcee05bd

    + Body

            {
                "id" : "5a003b78-409e-4452-b456-a6f0dcee05bd",
                "started_at": "2015-08-05T08:40:51.620Z",
                "gridsize" : 19,
                "turn" : 0,
                "players" : [
                    {
                        "color" : "white",
                        "name" : "bob",
                        "score" : 10
                    },
                    {
                        "color" : "black",
                        "name" : "alfred",
                        "score" : 22
                    }
                ]

            }
```

## Testing and Publishing Documentation with Apiary

In Chapter 1, *The Way of the Cloud*, we cautioned against relying too heavily on tools. Tools should make your life easier, but they should never be mandatory. The API Blueprint Markdown that contains the documentation and specification for our service is just a simple text file, however, there is a tool that can do a *lot* to make our lives both easier and more productive.

Apiary is a website that lets you interactively design your RESTful API. You can think of it as a WYSIWYG editor for API Blueprint Markdown syntax, but that's just the beginning. Apiary will also set up mock server endpoints for you that return sample JSON payloads. This saves you the trouble of having to build your own mock server, and lets you remain in API First mode until after you've gone through the motions of exercising various rough drafts of your API.

In addition to exposing mock server endpoints, you can also see client code in a multitude of languages that exercises your API, further assisting you and your team in validating your API—all before you have to write a single line of server code.

The API Blueprint document for the GoGo service is available in our GitHub repository as well as on Apiary for viewing at http://docs.gogame.apiary.io/. Rather than dump the entire set of documentation into the book, we'll leave most of the details in the blueprint document and on Apiary for you to read on your own.

The purpose of this chapter isn't to teach you how to make a game server, but to teach you the process of building a service in the Go language, so details like the rules of Go and actual game implementation will be secondary to things like Test-Driven Development and setting up a service scaffold, which we'll cover next.

## Scaffolding a Microservice

In a perfect world, we would start with a completely blank slate and go directly into testing. The problem with ideal, perfect worlds is they rarely ever exist. In our case, we want to be able to write tests for our RESTful endpoints.

The reality of the situation is we can't really write a test for RESTful endpoints unless we know what kind of functions we're going to be writing per endpoint. To figure this out, and to get a basic scaffolding for our service set up, we're going to create two files.

The first file, main.go (Listing 5.2), contains our main function, and creates and runs a new server. We want to keep our main function as small as possible because the main function is usually notoriously hard to test in isolation.

Listing 5.2  **main.go**

```
package main

import (
  "os"
  service "github.com/cloudnativego/gogo-service/service"
)

func main() {
  port := os.Getenv("PORT")
  if len(port) == 0 {
    port = "3000"
  }

  server := service.NewServer()
  server.Run(":" + port)
}
```

The code in Listing 5.2 invokes a function called NewServer. This function returns a pointer to a Negroni struct. Negroni is a third-party library for building routed endpoints on top of Go's built-in net/http package.

It is also important to note the bolded line of code. External configuration is crucial to your ability to build cloud native applications. By allowing your application to accept its bound port from an environment variable, you're taking the first step toward building a service that will work in the cloud. We also happen to know that a number of cloud providers automatically inject the application port using this exact environment variable.

Listing 5.2 shows our server implementation. In this code we're creating and configuring Negroni in **classic** mode, and we're using Gorilla Mux for our routing library. As a rule, we treat any third party dependency with skepticism, and must justify the inclusion of everything that isn't part of the core Go language.

In the case of Negroni and Mux, these two play very nicely on top of Go's stock `net/http` implementation, and are extensible pieces of middleware that don't interfere with anything we might want to do in the future. Nothing there is mandatory; there is no "magic", just some libraries that make our lives easier so we don't spend so much time writing boilerplate with each service.

For information on Negroni, check out the GitHub repo https://github.com/codegangsta/negroni. And for information on Gorilla Mux, check out that repo at https://github.com/gorilla/mux. Note that these are the same URLs that we import directly in our code, which makes it extremely easy to track down documentation and source code for third-party packages.

Listing 5.3 shows the `NewServer` function referenced by our `main` function and some utility functions. Note that `NewServer` is exported by virtue of its capitalization and functions like `initRoutes` and `testHandler` are not.

Listing 5.3  **server.go**

```
package service

import (
        "net/http"

        "github.com/codegangsta/negroni"
        "github.com/gorilla/mux"
        "github.com/unrolled/render"
)

// NewServer configures and returns a Server.
func NewServer() *negroni.Negroni {

        formatter := render.New(render.Options{
                IndentJSON: true,
        })

        n := negroni.Classic()
        mx := mux.NewRouter()

        initRoutes(mx, formatter)
```

```
        n.UseHandler(mx)
        return n
}

func initRoutes(mx *mux.Router, formatter *render.Render) {
        mx.HandleFunc("/test", testHandler(formatter)).Methods("GET")
}

func testHandler(formatter *render.Render) http.HandlerFunc {

        return func(w http.ResponseWriter, req *http.Request) {
                formatter.JSON(w, http.StatusOK,
                    struct{ Test string }{"This is a test"})
        }
}
```

The most important thing to understand in this scaffolding is the `testHandler` function. Unlike regular functions we've been using up to this point, this function returns an anonymous function.

This anonymous function, in turn, returns a function of type `http.HandlerFunc`, which is defined as follows:

```
type HandlerFunc func(ResponseWriter, *Request)
```

This type definition essentially allows us to treat any function with this signature as an HTTP handler. You'll find this type of pattern used throughout Go's core packages and in many third-party packages.

For our simple scaffolding, we return a function that places an anonymous struct onto the response writer by invoking the `formatter.JSON` method (this is why we pass the formatter to the wrapper function).

The reason this is important is because all of our RESTful endpoints for our service are going to be wrapper functions that return functions of type `http.HandlerFunc`.

Before we get to writing our tests, let's make sure that the scaffolding works and that we can exercise our test resource. To build, we can issue the following command (your mileage may vary with Windows):

```
$ go build
```

This builds all the Go files in the folder. Once you've created an executable file, we can just run the GoGo service:

```
$ ./gogo-service
[negroni] listening on :3000
```

When we hit `http://localhost:3000/test` we get our test JSON in the browser, and we see that because we've enabled the classic configuration in Negroni, we get some nice logging of HTTP request handling:

```
[negroni] Started GET /test
[negroni] Completed 200 OK in 212.121µs
```

Now that we know our scaffolding works, and we have at least a functioning web server capable of handling simple requests, it's time to do some real Test-Driven Development.

# Building Services Test First

It's pretty easy to talk about TDD, but, despite countless blogs and books extolling its virtues, it is still pretty rare to find people who practice it regularly. It is even rarer still to find people who practice it without cutting corners. Cutting corners in TDD is the worst of both worlds—you're spending the time and effort on TDD but you're not reaping the benefits of code quality and functional confidence.

In this section of the chapter, we're going to write a method for our service in test-first fashion. If we're doing it right, it should feel like we're spending 95% of our time writing tests, and 5% of our time writing code. The size of our test should be *significantly* larger than the size of the code we're testing. Some of this just comes from the fact that it takes more code to exercise all possible paths through a function under test than it does to write the function itself. For more details on this concept, check out the book *Continuous Delivery* by Jez Humble & David Farley.

Many organizations view the effort to write tests as wasteful, claiming that it does not add value and actually increases time-to-market. There are a number of problems with this myopic claim.

It is true that TDD will, indeed, slow initial development. However, let's consider a new definition of the term development:

> development(n) : The period where the features of the application are being added without the so-called burden of a running version of it in production.
>
> Dan Nemeth

With this definition in mind when we look at the entire life cycle of an application, only for a very small portion of that time is the application ever in this state of "development".

Investment in testing will pay dividends throughout the entire life cycle of the application, but especially in production where:

- Uptime is a must.
- Satisfying change/feature requests is urgent.
- Debugging is costly, difficult, and oftentimes approaching impossible.

To get started on our own TDD journey of service creation, let's create a file called handlers_test.go (shown in Listing 5.4). This file is going to test functions written in the handlers.go file. If your favorite text editor has a side-by-side or split-screen mode, this would be a great time to use it.

We're going to be writing a test for the HTTP handler invoked when someone POSTs a request to start a new match. If we check back with our Apiary documentation, we'll see that one of the requirements is that this function return an HTTP status code of *201 (Created)* when successful.

Let's write a test for this. We'll call the function TestCreateMatch and, as with all Go unit tests using the basic unit testing package, it will take as a parameter a pointer to a testing.T struct.

## Creating a First, Failing Test

In order to test our server's ability to create matches, we need to invoke the HTTP handler. We could invoke this manually by fabricating all of the various components of the HTTP pipeline, including the request and response streams, headers, etc. Thankfully, though, Go provides us with a test HTTP server. This doesn't open up a socket, but it does all the other work we need it to do, which lets us invoke HTTP handlers.

There is a lot going on here, so let's look at the full listing (Listing 5.4) for the test file in our first iteration, which, in keeping with TDD ideology, is a *failing* test.

Listing 5.4   **handlers_test.go**

```
package main

import (
        "bytes"
        "fmt"
        "io/ioutil"
        "net/http"
        "net/http/httptest"
        "testing"

        "github.com/unrolled/render"
)

var (
        formatter = render.New(render.Options{
                IndentJSON: true,
        })
)
```

```go
func TestCreateMatch(t *testing.T) {
        client := &http.Client{}
        server := httptest.NewServer(
            http.HandlerFunc(createMatchHandler(formatter)))
        defer server.Close()

        body := []byte("{\n  \"gridsize\": 19,\n  \"players\": [\n    {\n
\"color\": \"white\",\n        \"name\": \"bob\"\n    },\n    {\n
\"color\": \"black\",\n        \"name\": \"alfred\"\n    }\n  ]\n}")

        req, err := http.NewRequest("POST",
                server.URL, bytes.NewBuffer(body))
        if err != nil {
                t.Errorf("Error in creating POST request for createMatchHandler: %v",
                err)
        }
        req.Header.Add("Content-Type", "application/json")

        res, err := client.Do(req)
        if err != nil {
                t.Errorf("Error in POST to createMatchHandler: %v", err)
        }

        defer res.Body.Close()

        payload, err := ioutil.ReadAll(res.Body)
        if err != nil {
                t.Errorf("Error reading response body: %v", err)
        }

        if res.StatusCode != http.StatusCreated {
                t.Errorf("Expected response status 201, received %s",
                        res.Status)
        }

        fmt.Printf("Payload: %s", string(payload))
}
```

Here's another reason why we like Apiary so much: if you go to the documentation for the *create match* functionality and click on that method, you'll see that it can actually generate sample client code in Go. Much of that generated code is used in the preceding test method in Listing 5.3.

The first thing we do is call `httptest.NewServer`, which creates an HTTP server listening at a custom URL that will serve up the supplied method. After that, we are using most of Apiary's sample client code to invoke this method.

We have two main assertions here:

- We do not receive any errors when executing the request and reading the response bytes
- The response status code is *201 (Created)*.

If we were to try and run the test above, we would get a compilation failure. This is true TDD, because we haven't even written the method we're testing (`createMatchHandler` doesn't exist yet). To get the test to compile, we can add a copy of our original scaffold test method to our **handlers.go** file as shown in Listing 5.5:

Listing 5.5     **handlers.go**

```
package main

import (
        "net/http"

        "github.com/unrolled/render"
)

func createMatchHandler(formatter *render.Render) http.HandlerFunc {
        return func(w http.ResponseWriter, req *http.Request) {
                formatter.JSON(w,
                  http.StatusOK,
                  struct{ Test string }{"This is a test"})
        }
}
```

Now we can see what happens when we try and test this. First, to test we issue the following command:

```
$ go test -v $(glide novendor)
```

We should see the following output:

```
Expected response status 201, received 200 OK
```

Now we've written our first failing test! At this point, some of you may be starting to doubt these methods. If so, please bear with us; we promise that by the end of the chapter you will have seen the light.

Let's make this failing test a passing one. To make it pass, *all* we do is make the HTTP handler return a status of 201. We don't write the full implementation, we don't add complex logic. The *only* thing we do is make the test pass. It is vitally important to the process that *we only write the minimum code necessary to make the test pass*. If we write code that isn't necessary for the test to pass, we're no longer in *test-first* mode.

To make the test pass, change the formatter line in `handlers.go` to as follows:

```
formatter.JSON(w, http.StatusCreated, struct{ Test string }{"This is a test"})
```

We just changed the second parameter to `http.StatusCreated`. Now when we run our test, we should see something similar to the following output:

```
$ go test -v $(glide novendor)
=== RUN    TestCreateMatch
--- PASS: TestCreateMatch (0.00s)
PASS
ok       github.com/cloudnativego/gogo-service       0.011s
```

## Testing the Location Header

The next thing that we know our service needs to do in response to a *create match* request (as stated in our Apiary documentation) is to set the *Location* header in the HTTP response. By convention, when a RESTful service creates something, the *Location* header should be set to the URL of the newly created thing.

As usual, we start with a failing test condition and then we make it pass.

Let's add the following assertion to our test:

```
if _, ok := res.Header["Location"]; !ok {
  t.Error("Location header is not set")
}
```

Now if we run our test again, we will fail with the above error message. To make the test pass, modify the `createMatchHandler` method in `handlers.go` to look like this:

```
func createMatchHandler(formatter *render.Render) http.HandlerFunc {
        return func(w http.ResponseWriter, req *http.Request) {
                w.Header().Add("Location", "some value")
                formatter.JSON(w, http.StatusCreated,
                        struct{ Test string }{"This is a test"})
        }
}
```

Note that we didn't add a *real* value to that location. Instead, we just added *some* value. Next, we'll add a failing condition that tests that we get a valid location header that contains the `matches` resource and is long enough so that we know it also includes the GUID for the newly created match. We'll modify our previous test for the location header so the code looks like this:

```
        loc, headerOk := res.Header["Location"]
        if !headerOk {
                t.Error("Location header is not set")
        } else {
                if !strings.Contains(loc[0], "/matches/") {
                        t.Errorf("Location header should contain '/matches/'")
                }
```

```
                if len(loc[0]) != len(fakeMatchLocationResult) {
                        t.Errorf("Location value does not contain guid of new match")
                }
        }
}
```

We've also added a constant to the test called `fakeMatchLocationResult`, which is just a string that we also pulled off of Apiary representing a test value for the location header. We'll use this for test assertions and fakes. This is defined as follows:

```
const (
    fakeMatchLocationResult = "/matches/5a003b78-409e-4452-b456-a6f0dcee05bd"
)
```

## Epic Montage—Test Iterations

Since we have limited space in this book, we don't want to dump the code for every single change we made during every iteration where we went from red (failing) to green (passing) light in our testing.

Instead, we'll describe what we did in each TDD pass we made:

- Wrote a failing test.

- Made the failing test pass.

- Checked in the results.

If you want to examine the history so you can sift through the changes we made line-by-line, check out the commit history in GitHub. Look for commits labelled "TDD GoGo service Pass *n*" where *n* is the testing iteration number.

We've summarized the approaches we took for each failed test and what the resolution was to make the test pass in the following list of steps, so cue up your favorite Hollywood hacker movie montage background music and read on:

1. **TDD Pass 1.** We created the initial setup required to host a test HTTP server that invokes our HTTP handler method (the method under test). This test initially failed because of compilation failure—the method being tested did not yet exist. We got the test to pass by dumping the test resource code into the `createMatchHandler` method.

2. **TDD Pass 2.** Added an assertion that the result included a *Location* header in the HTTP response. This test initially failed, so we added a placeholder value in the location header.

3. **TDD Pass 3.** Added an assertion that the *Location* header was actually a properly formatted URL pointing at a match identified by a GUID. The test initially failed, so we made it pass by generating a new GUID and setting a proper location header.

4. **TDD Pass 4.** Added an assertion that the *ID* of the match in the response payload matched the GUID in the location header. This test initially failed and, to make it pass, we had to add code that un-marshaled the response payload in the test. This meant we actually had to create a struct that represented the response payload on the server. We stopped returning "this is a test" in the handler and now actually return a real response object.

5. **TDD Pass 5.** Added an assertion that the repository used by the handler function has been updated to include the newly created match. To do this, we had to create a repository interface and an in-memory repository implementation.

6. **TDD Pass 6.** Added an assertion that the grid size in the service response was the same as the grid size in the match added to the repository. This forced us to create a new struct for the response, and to make several updates. We also updated another library, gogo-engine, which contains minimal Go game resolution logic that should remain mostly isolated from the service.

7. **TDD Pass 7.** Added assertions to test that the players we submitted in the new match request are the ones we got back in the service JSON reply and they are also reflected accordingly in the repository.

8. **TDD Pass 8.** Added assertions to test that if we send something other than JSON, or we fail to send reasonable values for a new match request, the server responds with a *Bad Request* code. These assertions fail, so we went into the handler and added tests for JSON un-marshaling failures as well as invalid request objects. Go is pretty carefree about JSON de-serialization, so we catch most of our "bad request" inputs by checking for omitted or default values in the de-serialized struct.

Let's take a breather and look at where things stand after this set of iterations. Listing 5.6 shows the one handler that we have been developing using TDD, iterating through successive test failures which are then made to pass by writing code. To clarify, *we never write code unless it is in service of making a test pass*. This essentially guarantees us the maximum amount of test coverage and confidence possible.

This is a really hard line for many developers and organizations to take, but we think it's worth it and have seen the benefits exhibited by real applications deployed in the cloud.

Listing 5.6  **handlers.go (after 8 TDD iterations)**

```
package service

import (
        "encoding/json"
        "io/ioutil"
        "net/http"

        "github.com/cloudnativego/gogo-engine"
        "github.com/unrolled/render"
)

func createMatchHandler(formatter *render.Render, repo matchRepository)
    http.HandlerFunc {
        return func(w http.ResponseWriter, req *http.Request) {
            payload, _ := ioutil.ReadAll(req.Body)
            var newMatchRequest newMatchRequest
```

```
    err := json.Unmarshal(payload, &newMatchRequest)
    if err != nil {
      formatter.Text(w, http.StatusBadRequest,
        "Failed to parse create match request")
      return
    }
    if !newMatchRequest.isValid() {
      formatter.Text(w, http.StatusBadRequest,
        "Invalid new match request")
      return
    }

    newMatch := gogo.NewMatch(newMatchRequest.GridSize,
      newMatchRequest.PlayerBlack, newMatchRequest.PlayerWhite)
    repo.addMatch(newMatch)
    w.Header().Add("Location", "/matches/"+newMatch.ID)
    formatter.JSON(w, http.StatusCreated,
      &newMatchResponse{ID: newMatch.ID,
              GridSize: newMatch.GridSize,
                PlayerBlack: newMatchRequest.PlayerBlack,
                PlayerWhite: newMatchRequest.PlayerWhite})
  }
}
```

While Go's formatting guidelines generally call for an 8-character tab, we've condensed some of that to make the listing a little more readable here.

We have about 20 lines of code in a single function, and we have about 120 lines of code in the two test methods that exercise that code. This is exactly the type of ratio we want. Before we even open a single HTTP test tool to play with our service, we want to have 100% confidence and know exactly how our service should behave.

Based on the tests that we've written thus far, and the code in Listing 5.6, can you spot any testing gaps? Can you see any scenarios or edge cases that might trip up our code that we have not yet accounted for in testing?

There are two glaring gaps that we see:

1. This service is not stateless. If it goes down, we lose all of our in-progress games. This is a known issue, and we're willing to let it slide because we have a crystal ball, and we know that Chapter 7 will address data persistence.

2. There are a number of abuse scenarios against which we are not guarding. Most notably, there is nothing to stop someone from rapidly creating game after game until we exceed our memory capacity and the service crashes. This particular abuse vector is a side-effect of us storing games in memory and us violating a cardinal rule of cloud native: statelessness. We're not going to write tests for this either because, as mentioned in #1, these conditions are temporary and writing DDoS-guarding code is a rabbit hole we want to avoid in this book.

We'll correct some of these as we progress throughout the book, but others, like guarding against all of the edge cases, are really going to be your responsibility as you build production-grade services.

# Deploying and Running in the Cloud

Now that we've used Go to build a microservice while following *the way of the cloud*, we can put that effort to good use and deploy our work to the cloud. The first thing we're going to need is *a cloud*. While there are a number of options available to us, in this book we favor Cloud Foundry's PCF Dev and Pivotal Web Services (PWS) as deployment targets because they're both extremely easy to get started with and PWS has a free trial that *does not* require a credit card to get started.

## Creating a PWS Account

Head over to http://run.pivotal.io/ to create an account with Pivotal Web Services. Pivotal Web Services is platform powered by Cloud Foundry that lets you deploy your applications in their cloud and take advantage of a number of free and paid services in their marketplace.

Once you've created an account and logged in, you will see the dashboard for your organization. An organization is a logical unit of security and deployment. You can invite other people to join your organization so you can collaborate on cloud projects, or you can keep all that cloudy goodness to yourself.

On the home page or dashboard for your organization, you will see a box giving you some helpful information, including links pointing you to the *Cloud Foundry CLI*. This is a command-line interface that you can use to push and configure your applications in *any* cloud foundry (not just PWS).

Download and install the CF CLI and make sure it works by running a few test commands such as `cf apps` or `cf spaces` to verify that you're connected and working. Remember that you have 60 days to play in the PWS sandbox without ever having to supply a credit card, so make sure you take full advantage of it.

For information on what you can do with the CF CLI, check out the documentation here http://docs.run.pivotal.io/devguide/cf-cli/.

## Setting up PCF Dev

If you're more adventurous, or you simply like to tinker, then **PCF Dev** is the tool for you. Essentially, **PCF Dev** is a stripped-down version of Cloud Foundry that provides application developers all of the infrastructure necessary to deploy an application into a CF deployment, but without all of the production-level stuff that would normally prevent you from running a cloud on your laptop.

PCF Dev utilizes a virtual machine infrastructure (you can choose between VMware or VirtualBox) and a tool called *vagrant* to spin up a single, self-contained virtual machine that will play host to PCF Dev and your applications.

You can use PCF Dev to test how well your application behaves in the cloud without having to push to PWS. We've found it invaluable for testing things like service bindings and doing testing that falls somewhere between automated integration testing and full acceptance testing.

At the time this book is being written, PCF Dev is still in its early stages and, as a result, the instructions for installing and configuring the various releases are likely to change.

To get set up with PCF Dev, go to https://docs.pivotal.io/pcf-dev/.

The beauty of PCF Dev is that once you have the pre-requisites installed, you can simply issue the start command and everything you need will be brought up for you on your local virtualization infrastructure. For example, on OS X, you start your foundation with the ./start-osx script.

Using the exact same Cloud Foundry CLI that you used to communicate with your PWS cloud, you can retarget that CLI to your new MicroPCF installation:

```
$ cf api api.local.pcfdev.io --skip-ssl-validation
Setting api endpoint to api.local.pcfdev.io...
OK


API endpoint:   https://api.local.pcfdev.io (API version: 2.44.0)
Not logged in. Use 'cf login' to log in.
```

Make sure you login as the instructions indicate (the default username and password are *admin* and *admin*), and you can then issue standard Cloud Foundry CLI commands to communicate with your newly started local, private CF deployment:

```
$ cf apps
Getting apps in org local.pcfdev.io-org / space kev as admin...
OK
```

## Pushing to Cloud Foundry

Now that you've got the CF CLI installed and you can choose whether your CLI is targeting the PWS cloud or your local PCF Dev installation, you can push your application and run it in the cloud.

While you can manually supply all of the various options that you need to push your application to the cloud, it's easier (and more compatible with the CD pipeline work we'll be doing later in the book) to create a **manifest** file, like the one in Listing 5.7.

Listing 5.7    **manifest.yml**

```
applications:
- path: .
  memory: 512MB
  instances: 1
  name: your-app-name
  disk_quota: 1024M
  command: your-app-binary-name
  buildpack: https://github.com/cloudfoundry/go-buildpack.git
```

With this manifest file in the main directory of your application, you can simply type the following command and your application will be deployed in the cloud.

```
$ cf push
```

As we'll also illustrate later in the book, you can even configure your Wercker pipeline to automatically deploy your application to the Cloud Foundry of your choice at the end of a successful build for continuous delivery.

### A Note on the Go Buildpack

Buildpacks are designed to merge your application code with the underlying requirements necessary to run your app. The Java buildpack contains the JDK and the JRE, the Node buildpack contains `node`, etc. While the Go buildpack might suffice for tinkering, it is far too easy to violate the "single immutable artifact" rule with it. It's also possible that someone will commit a change to the buildpack that breaks your code or pipeline. As you'll see later in the book, when we deploy real apps, we are going to favor deploying our Docker images to the cloud directly from Docker Hub. The choice of buildback vs. Docker is entirely up to you and your organization and often boils down to simple personal preference.

## Summary

In this chapter we illustrated the basics of building microservices in Go. We took a look at the code you need in order to set up basic routes and handlers, but more importantly, we showed you how to build this code *test-first*.

Further, we walked you through getting your code deployed into the cloud. The rest of the book is going to get more technical and explore more in-depth topics, so you may want to take a moment to review any of the content of this chapter you didn't quite understand before continuing on.

This would also be a great time to tinker a bit and create your own ***hello world*** services, deploy them to PWS and play with starting, stopping, and scaling your applications. You may also want to browse the *marketplace* in PWS to get an idea of the types of incredibly powerful services, including databases, message queues, and monitoring, that are available to the applications you deploy there.

6

# Using Backing Services

*"Push your business technology into the cloud and get back to focusing on your core competencies."*

Tom Cochran, Deputy Coordinator for Platforms, US Dept. of State

So far everything we've done has been to build a single service, but the real world consists of more than just a service that emits the JSON equivalent of "hello world." In the real world, you have services that depend on each other; you have an entire ecosystem of dependent and related services.

In this chapter, we'll explore techniques for designing service ecosystems. We will then take a look at how to build service ecosystems in a test-first manner. It's one thing to be able to test an individual service, but we'll also show you how to use TDD on services that communicate with other services, and we'll look at some design pattern options for dealing with sharing data structures across multiple services.

Finally, we'll deploy multiple services to the cloud and discuss various techniques for externally configuring or discovering the URLs of services that communicate with each other.

At a high level, we're going to cover the following topics in this chapter:

- Designing service ecosystems.

- How TDD fits in with dependent and backing services.

- Patterns for sharing schemas and data structures among services.

- Service bindings and external configuration.

- Dynamic, runtime service discovery.

## Designing Service Ecosystems

Though it might make our lives easier to think so, services rarely ever exist in a vacuum. Services need authorization, they need authentication, they need long-term data stores and short-term caches, and they need document generators and widget makers and hoozit factories.

Services are a needy lot, and we need to embrace that notion when designing and building service ecosystems, because developing services in a vacuum will cost us dearly when it comes time to flip the switch in production.

Unfortunately, Figure 6.1 shows what many people think most service ecosystems look like.

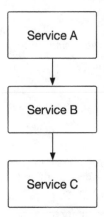

Figure 6.1   An Unrealistic Service Dependency Graph

In this myopic view of the world, you can always identify the service that depends upon no other services and work your way back up the hierarchy. There is a clear top and bottom, and an obvious dependency chain.

A false sense of security comes from looking at a diagram like this. We assume that we can work on Service C, then B, then A, and we can have teams that only ever have to talk to one other team. This world is *much* too simple a place.

Another problem with hierarchies like Figure 6.1 is that we tend to make assumptions about them. When we test, we assume that things are going to work because there are so few downstream side-effects and we leave everything to chance. If we're being diligent about following the *way of the cloud*, then we test everything and leave nothing to chance.

Figure 6.2 shows a more realistic view of a service hierarchy. As complicated as this looks, it's still *much* simpler than many enterprise service ecosystems.

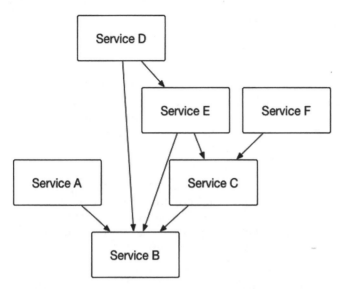

Figure 6.2    A More Realistic Service Dependency Graph

How do you even get started building something like this? From a methodology standpoint, the answer is to use *API First*. The only thing keeping a system like the one in Figure 6.2 from turning into an unmanageable mess is strict adherence to API contracts, and clear governance around release cadence and versioning.

As you go through the rest of this chapter, you'll see some specific code techniques for building services like this without having to sacrifice test quality and still approaching service development as a test-first activity. We'll also answer questions like: *how do services find each other?* and *where do credentials and other configuration values go?*

## Building Dependent Services Test-First

In the previous chapter, we went through some of the steps and discipline necessary to build services using Test-Driven Development. Eventually, the rhythm of writing failing tests and then converting them to passing tests by writing *just* enough code to make the build go green will become second nature.

After writing code like this for years, doing it any other way feels unnatural and, more importantly, unreliable. Without writing code test-first, we have no confidence in our code, no matter how good we are or how many books we've written.

This habit breeds confidence that you haven't just ticked some box on a test coverage report. Anyone can write tests with high coverage, but it requires a bit more thought and good habits to write tests that leave you feeling confident that your application does what it's supposed to do.

In this section of the chapter, we're going to build a service, and then we're going to build a service that depends on that service. A service that depends on another is no different than any other service, with the exception that somewhere in its request handler there is code that invokes another service.

The trick here is being able to do this properly in a test-first fashion without tightly coupling the services. For the samples we're going to build in this chapter, we're going to create a *catalog* service and a *fulfillment* service. The catalog service simulates a service that supports a web UI for an e-commerce site, while the fulfillment service simulates a service that might be exposed by a warehouse infrastructure or a third party shipper, indicating quantity remaining in stock and average shipping time.

In this sample, the catalog service returns details about products, but also queries the fulfillment service about that same product, returning an augmented data set to the caller. Make no mistake: this sample falls into the overly simplistic, contrived dependency graph shown in Figure 6.1. However, developing the right set of disciplines building the simple example will help prepare you for building real-world, complex microservice ecosystems.

## Creating the Fulfillment Service

The first step in this process will be to create the fulfillment service. Since this service depends on no other services, the decision to start here is obvious. For real applications, we don't always have that luxury. In that case, you should probably be using some standard like API Blueprint to allow related services to be built in parallel while still adhering to strong public API contracts.

We're going to use the same scaffolding that we've used for our other services, which includes a main.go file and a service sub-package. The *service* package contains a server.go file, a handlers.go file, and the tests for our HTTP request handlers in handlers_test.go. You can take a look at the github repository for the fulfillment service at https://github.com/cloudnativego/backing-fulfillment.

Since we're using TDD, the first thing we're going to do is write a test, which is shown in its entirety in Listing 6.1 (as usual, the tabs have been altered from the original code to make it more readable in print).

Listing 6.1  **handlers_test.go**

```
package service

import (
        "encoding/json"
        "io/ioutil"
        "net/http"
        "net/http/httptest"
        "testing"

        "github.com/codegangsta/negroni"
        "github.com/gorilla/mux"
        "github.com/unrolled/render"
)
```

```go
var (
        formatter = render.New(render.Options{
                IndentJSON: true,
        })
)


func TestGetFullfillmentStatusReturns200ForExistingSKU(t *testing.T) {
        var (
                request  *http.Request
                recorder *httptest.ResponseRecorder
        )

        server := NewServer()

        targetSKU := "THINGAMAJIG12"

        recorder = httptest.NewRecorder()
        request, _ = http.NewRequest("GET", "/skus/"+targetSKU, nil)
        server.ServeHTTP(recorder, request)

        var detail fulfillmentStatus

        if recorder.Code != http.StatusOK {
        . t.Errorf("Expected %v; received %v", http.StatusOK, recorder.Code)
        }
        payload, err := ioutil.ReadAll(recorder.Body)
        if err != nil {
          t.Errorf("Error parsing response body: %v", err)
        }
        err = json.Unmarshal(payload, &detail)
        if err != nil {
          t.Errorf("Error unmarshaling response to fullfillment status: %v", err)
        }

        if detail.QuantityInStock != 100 {
          t.Errorf("Expected 100 qty in stock, got %d", detail.QuantityInStock)
        }
        if detail.ShipsWithin != 14 {
          t.Errorf("Expected shipswithin 14 days, got %d", detail.ShipsWithin)
        }
        if detail.SKU != "THINGAMAJIG12" {
          t.Errorf("Expected SKU THINGAMAJIG12, got %s", detail.SKU)
        }
}
```

There are a number of assertions in this test:

- We receive a *200* from the/skus/*{sku}* resource.

- We can parse the body of that response.

- The body of that response can be converted into a `fulfillmentStatus` struct.

- The details of that response are the fakes that we expect, since we're not building a fully functioning service.

Recalling from the previous chapter, a test like this isn't written in a single sitting. Instead, you write one assertion that fails, make that assertion pass, then write another assertion that fails, rinse and repeat.

We followed this pattern when building this test, but to spare you the chore of having to sift through pages and pages of iterative code, the complete test is shown above in Listing 6.1.

The code under test, the single request handler for the fulfillment service, is shown in Listing 6.2. Keep in mind that we are deliberately building a service that returns artificial or fabricated values, so that's exactly what we're testing. If we were to move this to a more production-like set of functionality, we would do so by first writing assertions that prove that we're not using bogus values. These assertions would then fail, and we'd have to make our service "more real" in order to get the test suite to go green again.

Listing 6.2   **handlers.go**

```go
package service

import (
  "net/http"

  "github.com/gorilla/mux"
  "github.com/unrolled/render"
)

// getFullfillmentStatusHandler simulates actual fulfillment by supplying
// bogus values for QuantityInStock
// and ShipsWithin for any given SKU. Used to demonstrate a backing service
// supporting a primary service.
func getFullfillmentStatusHandler(formatter *render.Render) http.HandlerFunc {
  return func(w http.ResponseWriter, req *http.Request) {
        vars := mux.Vars(req)
        sku := vars["sku"]
        formatter.JSON(w, http.StatusOK, fulfillmentStatus{
                SKU:            sku,
                ShipsWithin:    14,
                QuantityInStock: 100,
        })
  }
}
```

```
func rootHandler(formatter *render.Render) http.HandlerFunc {
        return func(w http.ResponseWriter, req *http.Request) {
                formatter.Text(w,
                  http.StatusOK,
                  "Fulfillment Service, see (url) for API.")
        }
}
```

This function makes our tests pass by creating a fabricated fulfillment result, using the supplied SKU as the only dynamic value. We always return products that ship within 2 weeks and that have 100 items in stock.

Finally, we set this route up so we can test it in a browser or RESTful client with the following initRoutes function:

```
func initRoutes(mx *mux.Router, formatter *render.Render) {
        mx.HandleFunc("/skus/{sku}",
          getFullfillmentStatusHandler(formatter)).Methods("GET")
}
```

We should be confident that our fulfillment simulator works as designed because we can run our tests, but if we want we can run this and manually hit the endpoint as the following trace shows (we issued a GET request for the SKU WIDGET42), we can use the following commands (assuming we've already pulled latest from Git and done a glide install to populate the vendor directory):

```
$ go build
$ ./fulfillment-service
[negroni] listening on :3001
[negroni] Started GET /skus/WIDGET42
[negroni] Completed 200 OK in 163.614µs
```

## Creating the Catalog Service

Now that we've got our fulfillment simulator service in a state where we have unit tests that assure we have good coverage and confidence and we've tested it manually, we can move on to creating the catalog service.

Our catalog service is also a simulator in that we're going to return fabricated values, with one exception: some of the data we return from the catalog service will come from a separate call o the fulfillment service.

Issuing a GET to the product catalog service for a given SKU will return some fabricated values, then invoke the fulfillment service for that same SKU.

The code in Listing 6.3 shows that we're testing our catalog service in exactly the same fashion that we tested our fulfillment service. As mentioned, our test assertions are all based on the expectation that we're returning fabricated values.

Listing 6.3   **handlers_test.go**

```go
package service
import (
  "encoding/json"
  "io/ioutil"
  "net/http"
  "net/http/httptest"
  "testing"
  "github.com/codegangsta/negroni"
  "github.com/unrolled/render"
)

var (
  formatter = render.New(render.Options{
        IndentJSON: true,
  })
)

func TestGetDetailsForCatalogItemReturnsProperData(t *testing.T) {
  var (
        request  *http.Request
        recorder *httptest.ResponseRecorder
  )

  server := MakeTestServer()

  targetSKU := "THINGAMAJIG12"

  recorder = httptest.NewRecorder()
  request, _ = http.NewRequest("GET", "/catalog/"+targetSKU, nil)
  server.ServeHTTP(recorder, request)

  var detail catalogItem

  if recorder.Code != http.StatusOK {
        t.Errorf("Expected %v; received %v", http.StatusOK, recorder.Code)
  }
  payload, err := ioutil.ReadAll(recorder.Body)
  if err != nil {
        t.Errorf("Error parsing response body: %v", err)
  }
  err = json.Unmarshal(payload, &detail)
  if err != nil {
        t.Errorf("Error unmarshaling response to catalog item: %v", err)
  }
```

```go
    if detail.QuantityInStock != 1000 {
        t.Errorf("Expected 100 qty in stock, got %d", detail.QuantityInStock)
    }
    if detail.ShipsWithin != 99 {
        t.Errorf("Expected shipswithin 14 days, got %d", detail.ShipsWithin)
    }
    if detail.SKU != "THINGAMAJIG12" {
        t.Errorf("Expected SKU THINGAMAJIG12, got %s", detail.SKU)
    }
    if detail.ProductID != 1 {
        t.Errorf("Expected product ID of 1, got %d", detail.ProductID)
    }
}

func MakeTestServer() *negroni.Negroni {
  fakeClient := fakeWebClient{}
  return NewServerFromClient(fakeClient)
}


type fakeWebClient struct{}

func (client fakeWebClient) getFulfillmentStatus(sku string)
  (status fulfillmentStatus, err error) {
  status = fulfillmentStatus{
        SKU:             sku,
        ShipsWithin:     99,
        QuantityInStock: 1000,
  }
  return status, err
}
```

To make this test pass, we're going to need to create our handler in a way that allows us to either use a *real* client that consumes the fulfillment service, or a *fake* client that just returns mocked up values. Listing 6.4 shows how we accomplish this.

Listing 6.4   **handlers.go**

```go
package service
import (
        "fmt"
        "net/http"

        "github.com/gorilla/mux"
        "github.com/unrolled/render"
)
```

```go
// getAllCatalogItemsHandler returns a fake list of catalog items
func getAllCatalogItemsHandler(formatter *render.Render) http.HandlerFunc {
  return func(w http.ResponseWriter, req *http.Request) {
        catalog := make([]catalogItem, 2)
        catalog[0] = fakeItem("ABC1234")
        catalog[1] = fakeItem("STAPLER99")
        formatter.JSON(w, http.StatusOK, catalog)
  }
}

// getCatalogItemDetailsHandler returns a fake catalog item. The key takeaway here
// is that we're using a backing service to get fulfillment status for the individual
// item.
func getCatalogItemDetailsHandler(formatter *render.Render,
    serviceClient fulfillmentClient) http.HandlerFunc {
  return func(w http.ResponseWriter, req *http.Request) {
        vars := mux.Vars(req)
        sku := vars["sku"]
        status, err := serviceClient.getFulfillmentStatus(sku)
        if err == nil {
                formatter.JSON(w, http.StatusOK, catalogItem{
                        ProductID:       1,
                        SKU:             sku,
                        Description:     "This is a fake product",
                        Price:           1599, // $15.99
                        ShipsWithin:     status.ShipsWithin,
                        QuantityInStock: status.QuantityInStock,
                })
                } else {
                        formatter.JSON(w, http.StatusInternalServerError,
                    fmt.Sprintf("Fulfillment Client error: %s", err.Error())))
                }
        }
}

func rootHandler(formatter *render.Render) http.HandlerFunc {
        return func(w http.ResponseWriter, req *http.Request) {
                formatter.Text(w, http.StatusOK,
  "Catalog Service, see http://github.com/cloudnativego/backing-catalog for API.")
        }
}

func fakeItem(sku string) (item catalogItem) {
        item.SKU = sku
        item.Description = "This is a fake product"
```

```
        item.Price = 1599
        item.QuantityInStock = 75
        item.ShipsWithin = 14
        return
}
```

As you can see, we've got two values in this payload that should definitely be populated by our backing service, `ShipsWithin` and `QuantityInStock`. With this test passing, we can move on to the next iteration.

This is a spot where you typically see a philosophical rift form among people when it comes to testing patterns. In the world of magic and injection and countless libraries, you might create some mock object and then the mock records what is and isn't invoked, and you can even specify what the mock should return under given situations.

While there's nothing particularly wrong with that method, it's an awful lot of ceremony and work for something that we can do simply in Go with little more than an interface and taking serendipitous advantage of Go's implicit interfaces, or what we call *will-it-blend typing*[1].

What we do is create a fulfillment client. This client, when *real*, will make an HTTP call to the backing service. When faked (supplied by a test), this client will just return whatever value we deem appropriate. By rigging our server and our handler such that they expect to be passed such a client, we can now make it very easy to communicate with a backing service.

Let's take a look at the real implementation of the HTTP client in Listing 6.6. In this code you can see the declaration of the `fulfillmentClient` interface, which just indicates the one method we want to be common between our test fake and our real client.

### Apiary and Client Code Generation

Invoking HTTP methods and obtaining the result is a chore that we have to do all the time. One thing that makes writing this code a little easier is if you're looking at an API in Apiary, you can view and execute sample code that consumes a particular API endpoint. This is extremely handy in generating client wrappers in any language, including Go.

The code in Listing 6.6 makes a simple HTTP call and de-serializes the response of that call into a `fulfillmentStatus` struct.

### Listing 6.6   fulfillment-client.go

```
package service

import (
        "encoding/json"
        "fmt"
```

---

1  As we discussed earlier, *will-it-blend typing* is slightly more informative than the common "duck typing" term that comes from the phrase, "If it walks like a duck, and talks like a duck, it's a duck."

```
        "io/ioutil"
        "net/http"
)

type fulfillmentClient interface {
        getFulfillmentStatus(sku string) (status fulfillmentStatus, err error)
}
type fulfillmentWebClient struct {
        rootURL string
}
func (client fulfillmentWebClient) getFulfillmentStatus(sku string)
 (status fulfillmentStatus, err error) {
        httpclient := &http.Client{}

        skuURL := fmt.Sprintf("%s/%s", client.rootURL, sku)
        fmt.Printf("About to request SKU details from backing service: %s\n", skuURL)
        req, _ := http.NewRequest("GET", skuURL, nil)

        resp, err := httpclient.Do(req)

        if err != nil {
                fmt.Printf("Errored when sending request to the server: %s\n",
                 err.Error())
                return
        }

        defer resp.Body.Close()
        payload, _ := ioutil.ReadAll(resp.Body)

        err = json.Unmarshal(payload, &status)
        if err != nil {
                fmt.Println("Failed to unmarshal server response.")
                return
        }

        return status, err
}
```

If we hard-code the URL of the backing service (we'll fix this shortly) as shown in the snippet below,

```
func NewServer() *negroni.Negroni {

        formatter := render.New(render.Options{
                IndentJSON: true,
        })
```

```
        n := negroni.Classic()
        mx := mux.NewRouter()
        webClient := fulfillmentWebClient{
                rootURL: "http://localhost:3001/skus",
        }

        initRoutes(mx, formatter, webClient)

        n.UseHandler(mx)
        return n
}

func initRoutes(mx *mux.Router, formatter *render.Render, webClient fulfillmentClient) {
        mx.HandleFunc("/catalog",
          getAllCatalogItemsHandler(formatter)).Methods("GET")
        mx.HandleFunc("/catalog/{sku}",
          getCatalogItemDetailsHandler(formatter, webClient)).Methods("GET")
}
```

then we can force the fulfillment service to start on port 3001 using an environment variable, then start the catalog service. We can then hit the catalog service, and we'll see the following output in our console:

```
[negroni] Started GET /catalog/THINGY
[negroni] Completed 200 OK in 2.122473ms
```

And we'll *also* see the following output in the console output of our fulfillment service as well, proving that the catalog service is indeed using the fulfillment service:

```
[negroni] Started GET /skus/THINGY
[negroni] Completed 200 OK in 79.226µs
```

Taking a step back, we can evaluate what we've done so far:

- We built a service that depends on no other services. We built this service using TDD methodology.

- We built another service test-first, and we returned fake values, mocking the existing functionality of the supporting service.

- Once we had our passing tests, we created a service client abstraction. We used a real HTTP client in live code, and used fake data in our test code, all of which was possible without the use of code generation, mocks, aspects, or unnecessary ceremony.

- We started up both services, each running on a unique port, and ensured that one service called the other in response to a product catalog request.

# Sharing Structured Data Among Services

Throughout this chapter you've seen a number of examples where one service consumes data exposed by another service. In our case, we have a fulfillment service that exposes a very small structure representing the warehouse fulfillment status of a particular SKU. This status contains information such as how long it will be before the item ships, and how many of that item we have left in stock.

If you have been paying close attention, you'll notice that there is something happening here that, depending on how we deal with it, could result in everything from elegant code, to smelly code, to downright horrible code.

The fulfillment service needs to maintain a struct that represents fulfillment status so that it can be manipulated by the service and serialized as JSON. The catalog service needs to be able to maintain a struct that represents this same status so that it can consume the JSON exposed by the fulfillment service and add that information to the catalog item detail results.

At the core, we have a *model sharing* issue. Traditionally, there are three main ways to deal with this problem, and we'll discuss those here and when we think you might want to use each approach.

## Client Imports Server Package

In this solution to the problem, we just change the `fulfillmentStatus` struct to `FulfillmentStatus` (thereby exporting the type), and have the catalog service import the fulfillment service package. This gives the catalog service direct access to the fulfillment status data type.

On the surface, this often looks like a good idea. We maximize code reuse, we don't have a single line of duplicated code, and we aren't susceptible to drift between fulfillment and catalog definitions of the same entity.

While this might *look* like a great solution, there are some potentially hazardous side-effects. The biggest of these is that we now have access to *everything* that the fulfillment service has exposed as an exported type. This also means we're now tightly coupled and if the fulfillment package changes anything, it could potentially cause compilation or runtime failures in the catalog service, even if the change didn't have anything to do with the public contract between the two.

It is our opinion that you should try and avoid this solution at all costs. As authors and developers, we went through our combined histories of developing service ecosystems, and allowing a client to directly reference the code of a server has *never* led to anything good and, in many cases, has led to disastrous failure.

## Client Duplicates Server Structure

This is the option that we have chosen to go with in the samples for this chapter. In this scenario, both the fulfillment and the catalog service have private definitions of the `fulfillmentStatus` struct and the accompanying JSON serialization tags.

A lot of developers and architects will look at this choice and scream bloody murder. *How dare you copy and paste the same thing twice! Ten lines of completely duplicated code cannot be allowed to walk this earth, for it is an abomination!*

### Duplication of Code

Believe it or not, we've had this very debate with others many times in the past. Not over 10 lines of code, but over *three*. All too often people forget the intent of a pattern while adhering too strictly to its rules.

You do not want internal changes to the *fulfillment* service to cause you to make internal changes to the *catalog* service. If the catalog service is pointing at the HEAD (most recent) version of the fulfillment service's struct (which it would be, depending on how careful you've been in maintaining your dependencies), you are at the mercy of whatever they're doing internally even if it doesn't change the public contract.

To summarize, the server and client both have two entirely different internal definitions of a structure that is part of the *public, versioned* API. This allows the server and client to maintain their own release cadence, and to allow for variance in how the internals are written. For example, it is entirely possible to represent the same JSON structure using many different Go structures. How you choose to represent your data structures should be based on how *your service* needs to deal with that data, and should *never* be influenced by how the other side of the contract deals with that data *internally*.

To further bolster this as our favored option, here is a quote from Sam Newman's *Building Microservices* book:

> The evils of too much coupling between services are far worse than the problems caused by code duplication.
>
> Sam Newman

## Client And Server Import Shared Package

Now we have our third option. We've agreed that having a client directly reference the internals of a server is a bad thing, which can lead to ugly phrases like *tier bleeding* or *anti-corruption layer violation*. So with this option we decide to fix this, and we extract the bits of shared data structure out of both the client and the server and we move it into a Switzerland-style neutral territory that can be used by both packages. This is the perfect solution, right?

No. This pattern has all the downsides of the first option, but has cleverly disguised itself as something that might be an elegant solution. In reality, this solution is just playing a shell game where it tries to hide the bad code smell. It is possible, with a clever combination of public and private structs, to cleanly have a shared dependency among multiple services that exchange data, but history tells us that this usually ends poorly.

If you can avoid this pattern, you should. The only safe way to ensure that you are truly creating an agile ecosystem of collaborating services is to guarantee that they are as loosely coupled as possible, and that means not sharing any struct definitions between them.

When you factor in **Conway's Law**, which asserts a direct correlation between team structure and microservice boundaries, you have to account for the very real possibility that the client and server will not be maintained by the same people, adding a degree of friction to the maintenance of the third option.

In a past project, I had attempted to share simple Java classes (POJOs) between a RESTful server and the Android client communicating with this server. This turned out to be an endless nightmare that manifested itself in bizarre runtime failures and periodic data corruption. You should let our mistakes be your guide and avoid this pattern like the inevitable zombie apocalypse plague.

## Using Service Bindings to Externalize URLs and Metadata

In the previous section, we created two services: a catalog service and a fulfillment service. In this sample, the catalog service knew where to find the fulfillment service because we hardcoded the URL directly in the `server.go` file.

This is not the way our applications should work in production, and this is certainly not a cloud-friendly solution. What we really want is to *externalize* our configuration, and have our application get the URLs and other metadata for backing services from the *environment*.

If you look back at some of our examples, you'll see that we allow the server port used for our services to be overridden by an environment variable called PORT. This is externalized configuration and, as a happy coincidence, is a value that is automatically supplied to our applications by Cloud Foundry or PCF Dev.

Now we want to allow for the URL of the fulfillment service to be overridden via the environment. In our case, we're going to push our applications to a Cloud Foundry[2] installation, and we'll create something called a **user-provided service**[3] to bind a URL property to the catalog application that points to the fulfillment service.

If you haven't yet set up either a local copy of PCF Dev or created a free account with Pivotal Web Services[4], you should probably do that now before continuing, as this section of the chapter deals directly with using Cloud Foundry service bindings to get service URLs.

---

2   Pivotal Web Services, a public Cloud Foundry service, can be found at http://run.pivotal.io/.

3   Documentation on User-Provided Services can be found at https://docs.pivotal.io/pivotalcf/devguide/services/user-provided.html.

4   http://run.pivotal.io/.

We've updated our usual scaffolded `server.go` in the Catalog service to allow the URL of the fulfillment client to come from our environment—specifically, a Cloud Foundry environment. Listing 6.7 shows the changes we've made.

Listing 6.7     **server.go**

```go
package service

import (
        "fmt"

        "github.com/cloudfoundry-community/go-cfenv"
        "github.com/cloudnativego/cf-tools"
        "github.com/codegangsta/negroni"
        "github.com/gorilla/mux"
        "github.com/unrolled/render"
)

// NewServerFromCFEnv decides the URL to use for a webclient
func NewServerFromCFEnv(appEnv *cfenv.App) *negroni.Negroni {
    webClient := fulfillmentWebClient{
        rootURL: "http://localhost:3001/skus",
    }

    val, err := cftools.GetVCAPServiceProperty("backing-fulfill", "url", appEnv)
    if err == nil {
        webClient.rootURL = val
    } else {
        fmt.Printf("Failed to get URL property from bound service: %v\n", err)
    }
    fmt.Printf("Using the following URL for fulfillment backing service: %s\n",
        webClient.rootURL)

    return NewServerFromClient(webClient)
}

// NewServerFromClient configures and returns a Server.
func NewServerFromClient(webClient fulfillmentClient) *negroni.Negroni {
  formatter := render.New(render.Options{
        IndentJSON: true,
  })

  n := negroni.Classic()
  mx := mux.NewRouter()

  initRoutes(mx, formatter, webClient)
```

```
  n.UseHandler(mx)
  return n
}
func initRoutes(mx *mux.Router, formatter *render.Render, webClient fulfillmentClient) {
  mx.HandleFunc("/", rootHandler(formatter)).Methods("GET")
  mx.HandleFunc("/catalog", getAllCatalogItemsHandler(formatter)).Methods("GET")
  mx.HandleFunc("/catalog/{sku}",
    getCatalogItemDetailsHandler(formatter, webClient)).Methods("GET")
}
```

We start off by assuming that the localhost URL is going to be the default. Next we're using an open source package called cf-env that gives us an abstraction around a Cloud Foundry environment that we initialize in the main.go file. We then use a package we created for this book called cf-tools. This package has a method called GetVCAPServiceProperty that lets us query a named property of a named bound service, and return the value in the idiomatic Go pattern of getting a result and an error.

If we get a meaningful result querying the url property of a bound user-provided service named backing-fulfill then we replace the default fulfillment URL with that one.

We can create this user-provided service with the following Cloud Foundry CLI command:

```
cf create-user-provided-service backing-fulfill -p "url"
```

The CLI will ask us for the value of the URL and we can give the URL of the application that we pushed to CF. Because all of our CD pipelines result in Docker Hub images, we can then push these applications with a simple push command:

```
cf push -o cloudnativego/backing-catalog
```

This works because each application has a manifest.yml file that you can see in our GitHub repository. For example, here's the manifest file for the fulfillment service:

```
applications:
- path: .
  memory: 512MB
  instances: 1
  name: backing-fulfillment
  disk_quota: 1024M
```

If you're playing along with the home game and using Pivotal Web Services (PWS), then you'll likely need to change the name of the application since that also creates a route with the same name, and routes are shared globally among all users of PWS. Since we tested this section of the chapter with Pivotal Web Services, we already laid claim to the route backing-fulfillment. cfapps.io.

Once we've created the service, and we have the fulfillment and catalog applications running in our cloud, we can bind it to our catalog application:

```
cf bind-service backing-catalog backing-fulfill
```

This command binds a service named `backing-fulfill` to an application named `backing-catalog`. With the CF command-line tools, the application name is almost always the first argument to every command that involves an application.

Now that we've created the service and bound it to the catalog application, we can re-stage the catalog application so that it will be started aware of the new environment variables. When it starts, we'll see the following message in the application log emitted by CF:

```
2016-01-16T16:15:48.96-0500 [APP/0]      OUT Using the following URL for
fulfillment backing service: http://fulfillment.cfapps.io/skus
```

So far so good. With both the fulfillment and catalog applications up and running in our cloud, we can hit the `/catalog/` URL (e.g. `backing-catalog.cfapps.io/catalog/BOB`) with any SKU we like. In the case below, we used *BOB* as a SKU. Everything worked as you would expect, and if we watch the `fulfillment` logs in real time, we'll see that the catalog service has made a fulfillment status request for that same SKU (we've changed some of the output to keep readers from trying to hack my account):

```
$ cf logs fulfillment
Connected, tailing logs for app fulfillment in org (redacted) / space (redacted)
 as (redacted)...
2016-01-16T16:17:53.69-0500 [RTR/0]      OUT fulfillment.cfapps.io -
[16/01/2016:21:17:53 +0000] "GET /skus/BOB HTTP/1.1" 200 0 64 "-" "Go-http-client/1.1"
10.10.2.12:39519 x_forwarded_for:"54.84.112.162" x_forwarded_proto:"http" vcap_
request_id:b21bdeee-1403-4cd1-44ad-16e083ea3f37 response_time:0.002252901 app_
id:fc79464e-ab53-42a1-90b0-afbb99f888d7
2016-01-16T16:17:53.69-0500 [APP/0]      OUT [negroni] Started GET /skus/BOB
2016-01-16T16:17:53.69-0500 [APP/0]      OUT [negroni] Completed 200 OK in 115.318µs
2016-01-16T16:18:19.33-0500 [HEALTH/0]   OUT Exit status 0
```

# Discovering Services

Up to this point in the chapter, the service ecosystems we have discussed have all operated on the concept of **bound resources**. This means that a service gets bound to another service, and that's how one service becomes aware of the URL, credentials, and metadata required to consume the other.

Whether this binding occurs automatically through manifests, is done by a continuous delivery pipeline, or is done manually by operators, the fact remains that the binding is still explicit and fixed.

This pattern works great and, in many cases, organizations prefer the kind of tight controls they can exert over this. In this scenario, the URLs exposed to applications are part of an explicit decision made by someone in the organization.

On the other hand, sometimes people want a more dynamic ecosystem of services. People who enjoy a little more flexibility in their environments might want to be able to discover services at runtime. Runtime discovery also comes with the added benefit of being able to detect whether or not a service is up and running.

## Dynamic Service Discovery

In the explicit bindings world, you can't just drop an application into an environment and expect it to work. Fixed bindings mean pre-requisites that can fail. If you're dynamically discovering services, things work a little differently.

Let's say you have two services: a game server and a user profile service. The game server depends on the user profile service. First, you deploy the user profile service to some environment (a Cloud Foundry space, Heroku, AWS, etc.). As soon as the user profile service comes up, it will **register** itself with the service discovery system. The service advertises to some subset of the world that it is up and ready for business.

Next, you deploy your game server. The game server also registers itself with the discovery sub-system, advertising that it is up and running. When the game server attempts to talk to the user profile service, it asks the registry for the service's metadata. It doesn't get the service's URL from an explicit binding, it gets it from the registry.

With dynamic discovery, backing services like the user profile service can be moved, they can go down and come back up under a new URL, and you can expose multiple versions, all without having to re-bind or re-start any of the applications that consume that service.

Further, with a service registry, you can also keep tabs on which services are up and running at a glance, without having to explicitly invoke a **health check** endpoint on every service. This is possible because services that communicate with the registry can emit **heartbeats** to that registry and, if a heartbeat stops, then not only do the consuming applications know about it, but you can also notify administrators if the service doesn't heal itself within some period of time.

## Service Discovery with Netflix's Eureka

After all this talk of how amazing service discovery systems are, you might be thinking, "It would be fantastic if there were an open source service discovery system just ready for me to use!"

As with so many other things in life, Netflix comes to the rescue. Netflix has open sourced a whole suite of the software it uses to maintain its massive infrastructure. One such product in Netflix's arsenal is *Eureka*, their service discovery system.

For more information on the Eureka project, we always like to start at the source, which in this case would be at https://github.com/Netflix/eureka. At its core, the Eureka server supports service registration and discovery, but there are many other features that might also come in handy.

The barrier to entry in playing with new products like Eureka is often pretty high and can even discourage people from experimenting. We have to figure out how to download the product (is it just source, or is there an installer?), then we need to set up all the pre-requisites, which might conflict with things we already have installed on our workstation. Then we probably have to spend some time configuring the server, and all of a sudden the joy of tinkering with a new product feels an awful lot like hard work.

If all you want to do is experiment with some basic features, and just get a Eureka server up and running, the easiest thing to do is just run a Docker image. We've mentioned a few times how Docker is an invaluable tool in your toolbox, and this is exactly the type of situation that goes from untenable to easy in a matter of seconds.

To run the Eureka server, we used a command like this one:

```
docker run -p 8080:8080 netflixoss/eureka:1.3.1
```

The -p parameter just maps port 8080 from inside the Docker image to port 8080 on the outside of the image. The default for the Eureka server is to use port 8080, so this mapping makes sense. When we start this up, we get a *ton* of spam. After waiting a few minutes for things to quiet down and for all of the server's startup tasks to happen, we're actually ready to go.

Our Docker machine's IP was 192.168.99.100 when we ran the test, so that's going to be part of the URL of our Eureka server. If your IP is different, you'll need to change the Go code.

So now that the server is running, what do we do with it? Well, if we were using Java, we would have access to the officially supported client libraries. But, there are very few features in Netflix's OSS suite that aren't just RESTful endpoints, so it's fairly straightforward to write a client for their well-documented APIs.

One such client for Eureka is *fargo*, which can be found here: https://github.com/hudl/fargo. The author of this project claims that the client is not yet complete, but it works well enough for us to play with our Eureka server.

In Listing 6.8, we use the *fargo* library to register an application instance, and then query Eureka to see if our application has been registered. Eureka separates the concept of applications and instances so that it can be used to register multiple instances of the same app (ideal for elastically scaled cloud applications), and supports regular updates to the status record as well as heartbeats so Eureka can keep track of which instances are slow or seemingly dead.

Listing 6.8 **fargo.go**

```
package main

import (
        "fmt"

        "github.com/hudl/fargo"
)
func main() {
  // For a real app, you'd bind a user-provided service with eureka
  // credentials and URL.
  c := fargo.NewConn("http://192.168.99.100:8080/eureka/v2")

  i := fargo.Instance{
        HostName:        "i-6543",
        Port:            9090,
        App:             "TESTAPP",
```

```
        IPAddr:            "127.0.0.10",
        VipAddress:        "127.0.0.10",
        SecureVipAddress:  "127.0.0.10",
        DataCenterInfo:    fargo.DataCenterInfo{Name: fargo.MyOwn},
        Status:            fargo.UP,
    }

    c.RegisterInstance(&i)
    f, _ := c.GetApps()

    for key, theApp := range f {
        fmt.Println("App:", key, " First Host Name:", theApp.Instances[0].HostName)
    }

    app, _ := c.GetApp("TESTAPP")
    fmt.Printf("%v\n", app)
}
```

We use the NewConn method to create a new connection to Eureka using the IP address of our Docker machine and the port we mapped when we ran the server. Next, we create an application instance and register it with the server. Finally, we test that we can iterate through all the applications as well as pull application data individually.

This is a sample of the output we get when iterating through the list of registered apps:

```
App: TESTAPP  First Host Name: i-6543
```

Before moving on to the next chapter, you should take a look at this code and play around a bit with Eureka, registration, and querying registered instances.

### Getting Eureka's URL

In our sample, we hard-coded the URL for the Eureka server, which is not going to fly in production. If our application were destined for a Cloud Foundry installation, then we would use bound services as we've already illustrated in this chapter to bind a Eureka instance to our application. Otherwise, we would just rely on simple environment variables.

## Reader Exercise

In this exercise, you'll take everything you've learned in this book so far and put it all to practical use. We highly recommend that you take the time to go through this exercise, because it will start building the muscle memory needed to rapidly and effectively build and deploy services in a complex ecosystem.

In this exercise, you'll be adapting the catalog and fulfillment services so that they register themselves with Eureka, and modifying the catalog service so that it gets the URL of the fulfillment service from the Eureka registry.

For this part of the reader exercise, you can hard-code the information you use when you register your services with Eureka. While there are many different approaches to complete the exercise, the following is a high-level list of some recommended steps:

1. Use GitHub to create forks of the `backing-catalog` and `backing-fulfillment` repositories we created for this chapter. This makes it easy to track your work, compare it with the original, and have your work stay within a valid Go workspace.

2. Using the sample code for the *fargo* library as a reference, modify the fulfillment service so that it registers itself when it starts up. You'll want to get Eureka's URL from a bound user-provided service.

3. Modify the catalog service so that it registers itself when it starts up. Also get Eureka's URL from a bound user-provided service. *Hint*: you can bind the same service to both applications so long as those apps are in the same *space*.

4. Modify the catalog service so that it uses *fargo* to ask Eureka for the fulfillment service's host information.

## Bonus Activity

Take the exercise you just completed and modify it so that registered host information is not hard-coded. Update the code so that you use the `cf-env` library to query your application's own route information so that you can register your application as it starts up in Cloud Foundry (either PCF Dev or Pivotal Web Services will work).

Your updated catalog service should be able to discover and connect to the fulfillment service deployed within your cloud without any explicit binding other than to the Eureka server.

> ### Hint
>
> Take a look at the documentation and tests for the cf-env project: https://github.com/cloudfoundry-community/go-cfenv. Here you'll see how you can use the environment object to query an application's name and host name. Don't worry about ports, because Cloud Foundry is going to expose all of your apps on port 80 (or 443 for SSL).

# Summary

In this chapter we took our first steps off the shore of microservices and into the larger ocean, an ocean in which countless other services live. We talked about patterns and practices for when (and when not) to share data between services, and how to communicate with, configure, and discover backing services.

This was all necessary because, as we'll see in the coming chapters, microservices never exist in a vacuum. If we truly want to learn how to build cloud native services that can scale independently and participate in robust ecosystems, we need the concepts we discussed in this chapter.

# 7

# Creating a Data Service

*"Any fool can write code that a computer can understand. Good programmers write code that humans can understand."*

Martin Fowler

When people talk about database access, certain programming languages seem to automatically be part of the vernacular. Everyone just assumes that Java and C# can talk to virtually any database out there, and if they can't, you probably didn't need that database anyway.

We have actually had people ask us, "Can Go talk to a database?" without a hint of irony. Somewhere out on the Internet there lies a conspiracy to convince people that Go is useful for little more than command-line utilities and specialized tasks, and that you should leave the "real work" to other languages.

We couldn't disagree more, and one of our core motivations in writing this book is to convince anyone who will listen that this idea is a myth and a vicious rumor.

In this chapter we're going to make some changes to our Go-playing microservice. If you'll recall from chapter 5, we built this service using an in-memory repository backed by a slice of matches. In this chapter, we'll create an alternative repository based on MongoDB.

The topics covered in this chapter are:

- Creating a repository in MongoDB (test-first!).
- Updating the Go service to use the new repository.
- Integration testing with a database.

# Creating a MongoDB Match Repository

In this section we're going to go through the process of extending our trivial service sample so that it can become truly stateless. To do this, we're going to create an implementation of a repository that communicates with a MongoDB database.

## Why MongoDB?

If you aren't familiar with MongoDB, you might want to take a few minutes to read some of the high-level overviews. At its core, MongoDB is a *document* database. It allows you to store and retrieve JSON documents. Unlike a traditional relational database, no two documents within the same collection have to have the same schema. Some people love this flexibility, others consider it the kiss of death. We will allow you to decide. For details, documentation, and a wealth of other related links, check out https://www.mongodb.org/.

Note that you will *not* need to install a copy of MongoDB in your developer environment to play along with this chapter because we've embraced Wercker and Docker already. Everything we need will be provided by freely available Docker Hub images.

In Chapter 5, we created a service that allows clients to add and query individual matches for the game of Go. This service was *stateful*, and maintained the list of matches in-memory. This meant that if the process died or was restarted, all of the current matches in that server would be lost. More importantly, if we scaled that process out to multiple instances, each instance would have its own private state.

While that model was useful for learning and experimentation, it is untenable for real-world applications.

## Updating the Repository Pattern

The pattern we used in Chapter 5 was to create an interface called matchRepository. Then, we passed an inMemoryMatchRepository to all of our route handlers. This allowed us to unit test the route handlers to ensure they invoked the right methods on the repository, and it allowed us to unit test the in-memory match repository in isolation.

To refresh our memory, this is the match repository interface from Chapter 5:

```
type matchRepository interface {
        addMatch(match gogo.Match) (err error)
        getMatches() []gogo.Match
        getMatch(id string) (match gogo.Match, err error)
}
```

We then created an in-memory version of this repository that used a simple slice of Match structs from the gogo-engine project. As we progress through this section of the chapter, we'll be creating a MongoDB implementation of this interface.

> ## Success by Accident
>
> If you have a keen eye, then you noticed that some aspects of the in-memory repository, like being able to retain the state of matches that have been updated with new moves, only work by *accident*. This works because we're storing pointers to objects in memory, so the repository automatically sees changes to game boards. Once we go stateless, we will quickly notice that there is a deficiency in our repository interface in that there is no explicit update method. We'll correct this as soon as we start writing our tests by writing a failing test that catches this bug.

## Communicating with MongoDB in Go

We have a very strict policy of evaluating every single external dependency we take in our Go projects. We need to explicitly decide that we aren't going to write this ourselves, and that it makes our lives simple enough and unblocks our critical path enough that it warrants the use of the dependency. Many teams aren't nearly as strict about this sort of thing, and we know it is largely a personal decision.

Personally, we feel that if we take a dependency on something, *we own* that dependency. For better or worse, it is part of our codebase.

In this case, it would be hard to argue that we should write our own MongoDB driver. We might want to extend or wrap what already exists, but we would rarely ever choose to re-invent such a complex wheel as a database driver.

If you look at MongoDB's site, they list the only officially supported Go driver as a project called mgo, the documentation for which can be found at https://godoc.org/labix.org/v2/mgo.

Using mgo revolves around creating and utilizing **sessions**. To create a session in mgo, we use the Dial function. As you continue to learn Go and you explore the source code for other networking libraries, you will find that the use of the Dial function is a fairly idiomatic pattern.

```
session, err := mgo.Dial(url)
```

Once we have a session, we can use this session to create new documents or query existing documents as shown in the following snippet:

```
result := Person{}
err = c.Find(bson.M{"name": "Buckshank"}).Select(bson.M{"phone": 0}).One(&result)
if err != nil {
  panic(err)
}
```

In this sample, we're querying a collection (indicated by the variable c) looking for documents that have a name property that we're looking for. We select the person's phone number if we find them.

There are some quirks to using the mgo driver, especially when using it in the cloud. For example, in some cases the connection to the database may drop or the virtual machine behind the database's host name or IP address may move from one coast of the country to the other. In situations like this, we need to be able to detect a stale connection and wake it up.

For this reason among others, we've developed a package called cfmgo that we have used internally at Pivotal for some of our Go services that needed to communicate with MongoDB. You can decide not to use our library and work directly with mgo or you can use our library. Better yet, in the spirit of open source, you could contribute to our library to make it better!

The cfmgo package also has a number of wrappers and shortcuts for binding Cloud Foundry services to your application, such as the marketplace version of MongoDB. We've also implemented a wrapper pattern which allows for a uniform data structure to be exposed if you like, wrapping successful and failed queries in the same structured envelope. You can find cfmgo and its documentation at https://github.com/cloudnativego/cfmgo.

## Writing a MongoDB Repository Test-First

Since we've already written unit tests for the in-memory repository, a decent starting point would be to create tests that assert the same behavior as the in-memory repository, but using MongoDB instead.

Before we get into the code, it is probably worth devoting a small tangent to the often daunting task of unit testing a database repository. When we unit test our HTTP handlers, we are asserting that they receive, parse, and forward the payloads to the appropriate place. The HTTP handler unit test doesn't care if the target of the forwarding (in our case, the repository) works properly because there is an assumption that the repository has also been unit tested.

Therefore, when unit testing the repository, we need to assert that the various high-level repository methods translate into the proper lower-level invocations. However, it is *not* our responsibility to test that those lower level functions behave as designed, because the database driver authors (in theory) will have created their own tests for that.

The only time we care about end-to-end functional testing is in an **integration** test, which we'll cover later in this chapter.

Armed with the information that we only need to test that the repository methods are simply wrappers for the appropriate lower-level database connectivity functions, we can start creating unit tests.

Taking the naming convention and original purpose of our in-memory repository test, we can guess that we'll probably want the following tests for the MongoDB repository:

- TestAddMatchShowsUpInMongoRepository—ensure that adding a match to the repository invokes the appropriate low-level functions.

- TestGetMatchRetrievesProperMatchFromMongo—ensure that we can retrieve an individual match from the repository.

- TestGetNonExistentMatchReturnsError—ensure that our repository has higher-level error handling in place to return an error when we try and fetch a non-existent match.

As you look at the code, you'll notice that we don't actually write tests that assert that if I look for a document of ID *some-id* among a collection of other documents, that it will actually give me the appropriate document. This is because in order to do so, we would have to create a whole implementation of a BSON-based query engine just to add it to our fake. If you get to a point where you feel like you're re-writing an entire library just to test your usage of the library, that's a smell and you need to re-evaluate your technique.

So here we decided to choose practicality over ideology. We will ensure that we exercise this use case in the full integration test, but to get that extra 1% test coverage, we would have to fabricate a piece of software that is more error-prone than the already fully tested component from within the MongoDB library.

To build our tests, we're going to use the real `cfmgo.Connect` method, but we're going to pass a completely fake connection dialer generated with the `FakeNewCollectionDialer` method we'll create later.

Listing 7.1 shows our unit tests.

Listing 7.1   **mongorepository_test.go**

```go
package main

import (
        "testing"

        "github.com/cloudnativego/cfmgo"
        "github.com/cloudnativego/gogo-engine"
        "github.com/cloudnativego/gogo-service/fakes"
)

var (
        fakeDBURI = "mongodb://fake.uri@addr:port/guid"
)

func TestAddMatchShowsUpInMongoRepository(t *testing.T) {
  var fakeMatches = []matchRecord{}
  var matchesCollection = cfmgo.Connect(
        fakes.FakeNewCollectionDialer(fakeMatches),
        fakeDBURI,
        MatchesCollectionName)

  repo := newMongoMatchRepository(matchesCollection)

  match := gogo.NewMatch(19, "bob", "alfred")
  err := repo.addMatch(match)
  if err != nil {
        t.Errorf("Error adding match to mongo: %v", err)
  }
```

```
    matches, err := repo.getMatches()
    if err != nil {
        t.Errorf("Got an error retrieving matches: %v", err)
    }
    if len(matches) != 1 {
        t.Errorf("Expected matches length to be 1; received %d", len(matches))
    }
}

func TestGetMatchRetrievesProperMatchFromMongo(t *testing.T) {
    fakes.TargetCount = 1
    var fakeMatches = []matchRecord{}
    var matchesCollection = cfmgo.Connect(
        fakes.FakeNewCollectionDialer(fakeMatches),
        fakeDBURI,
        MatchesCollectionName)

    repo := newMongoMatchRepository(matchesCollection)
    match := gogo.NewMatch(19, "bob", "alfred")
    err := repo.addMatch(match)
    if err != nil {
        t.Errorf("Error adding match to mongo: %v", err)
    }

    targetID := match.ID
    foundMatch, err := repo.getMatch(targetID)
    if err != nil {
        t.Errorf("Unable to find match with ID: %v... %s", targetID, err)
    }

    if foundMatch.GridSize != 19 || foundMatch.PlayerBlack != "bob" {
        t.Errorf("Unexpected match results: %v", foundMatch)
    }
}

func TestGetNonExistentMatchReturnsError(t *testing.T) {
    fakes.TargetCount = 0
    var fakeMatches = []matchRecord{}
    var matchesCollection = cfmgo.Connect(
        fakes.FakeNewCollectionDialer(fakeMatches),
        fakeDBURI,
        MatchesCollectionName)

    repo := newMongoMatchRepository(matchesCollection)

    _, err := repo.getMatch("bad_id")
    if err == nil {
```

```
            t.Errorf("Expected getMatch to error with incorrect match details")
    }

    if err.Error() != "Match not found" {
            t.Errorf("Expected 'Match not found' error; received: '%v'", err)
    }
}
```

In each one of these tests, we create a new instance of a real cfmgo.Collection, but we pass in our fake collection dialer that allows us to provide some basic fake collections as a backing store. We then invoke the repository method under test and make some assertions that give us a good indication that the appropriate low-level MongoDB functions are being invoked.

Listing 7.2 contains the source code for our fake connection dialer. Again, remember that our job isn't to simulate a real MongoDB database, it is just to provide enough fake entry points to test that our repository invokes the right low-level methods. For example, our Find method doesn't actually look at any of the search criteria... because to do so we would be testing functionality in the fake and not something truly important to us.

Listing 7.2    **fakes/fake.go**

```
package fakes

import (
        "encoding/json"
        "strconv"

        "github.com/cloudnativego/cfmgo"
        "gopkg.in/mgo.v2"
)

var TargetCount int = 1

//FakeNewCollectionDialer -
func FakeNewCollectionDialer(c interface{})
    func(url, dbname, collectionname string) (col cfmgo.Collection, err error) {
  b, err := json.Marshal(c)
  if err != nil {
        panic("Unexpected Error: Unable to marshal fake data.")
  }

  return func(url, dbname, collectionname string)
      (col cfmgo.Collection, err error) {
        col = &FakeCollection{
                Data: b,
        }
        return
  }
}
```

```go
//FakeCollection -
type FakeCollection struct {
  mgo.Collection
  Data   []byte
  Error error
}

//Close -
func (s *FakeCollection) Close() {

}

//Wake -
func (s *FakeCollection) Wake() {

}

//Find -- finds all records matching given selector
func (s *FakeCollection) Find(params cfmgo.Params, result interface{})
     (count int, err error) {
  count = TargetCount
  err = json.Unmarshal(s.Data, result)

  return
}

//FindAndModify -
func (s *FakeCollection) FindAndModify(selector interface{}, update interface{},
    result interface{}) (info *mgo.ChangeInfo, err error) {
  return
}

//UpsertID -
func (s *FakeCollection) UpsertID(id interface{}, result interface{})
   (changeInfo *mgo.ChangeInfo, err error) {
  var col []interface{}
  err = json.Unmarshal(s.Data, &col)
  if err != nil {
        return
  }

  col = append(col, result)
  b, err := json.Marshal(col)
  if err != nil {
        return
  }
```

```
    s.Data = b
    changeInfo = &mgo.ChangeInfo{
        Updated:    1,
        Removed:    0,
        UpsertedId: id,
    }
    return changeInfo, nil
}

//FindOne -
func (s *FakeCollection) FindOne(id string, result interface{}) (err error) {
    i, err := strconv.Atoi(id)
    if err != nil {
        return
    }
    var col []interface{}
    err = json.Unmarshal(s.Data, &col)
    if err != nil {
        return
    }
    b, err := json.Marshal(col[i])
    if err != nil {
        return
    }
    err = json.Unmarshal(b, result)
    return
}
```

# Integration Testing a Mongo-Backed Service

Integration testing is a difficult thing. There is no easy button, there's no quick fix, and no matter how much experience you have doing it, it still requires forethought, discipline, and effort.

However, this shouldn't discourage you, because there are a number of tools and techniques that we can use to soften the blow and make writing integration tests a valuable part of our development workflow.

## Integrating with a Transient MongoDB Database

The hardest part of integration testing is, of course, *integration*. In our case, we're adding MongoDB persistence to our microservice that supports playing the game of Go (this can be found at https://github.com/cloudnativego/gogo-service). This service requires a real MongoDB database in order to function properly. How do you set up a temporary MongoDB database?

With traditional enterprise database drivers in other languages, people often integration test with an in-memory version of a database that uses the same kind of JDBC driver. This looks like it works, and it usually does, until you encounter scenarios where the in-memory version works fine and the real backing store (e.g. Postgres or mySQL) doesn't support what you're doing, and the app fails. Worse, your app fails in production, and it does so in subtle ways.

A real integration test should use a real database server. Thankfully, we don't have to install a database server on our local workstations to support this. Our continuous delivery tool of choice, Wercker, allows us to spin up backing services inside Docker containers during our automated build. All of these backing service Docker images are connected to the image in which our application tests are run via environment variables.

This means we can use Wercker and Docker to fire up an empty MongoDB database every time we build our application, during which time we can make a series of RESTful calls against our service API, which will flow all the way to our real MongoDB database. Once the build is done, the database disappears. We can run this test locally with the Wercker CLI and we can run it automatically after every single `git commit`.

First, we just add two lines to our `wercker.yml` file to indicate that our build requires the MongoDB service:

```
services:
  - mongo
```

When this service starts up, Wercker will automatically create several environment variables that our application can use to communicate with this service. Wercker will link the Docker container in which our build is taking place with the Docker container in which the MongoDB service is running.

By their nature, integration tests take longer to execute and they require a bunch of resources. We don't want our integration test to run every time we execute `go test` to double-check our unit tests. To facilitate this, we'll put the integration test in a directory that starts with an underscore, which will hide it from Go unless we explicitly point it at the directory.

Now we can add an integration test step to our `wercker.yml`:

```
- script:
    name: integration tests
    code: |
        export VCAP_SERVICES=`vcapinate -path=./integrations/vcap.yml`
        export VCAP_APPLICATION={}
        godep go test ./integrations/_test -v -race
```

You don't have to worry about the `vcapinate` command yet. This is a tool that we've written that makes it easy to convert a set of environment variables like the ones provided by Wercker into a format recognizable by Platform as a Service providers like Cloud Foundry. We fetch this tool inside the Wercker build, but if you want to use it outside of Wercker, you can find it inside our `cf-tools` GitHub repo: https://github.com/cloudnativego/cf-tools/tree/master/ vcapinate.

It might look like we're adding some unnecessary complexity here, but it isn't that bad, and it's worth it. The benefit is that we can run our application locally, in a Docker container, and in the cloud.

The `vcap.yml` file just provides configuration input to the `vcapinate` tool that builds the `VCAP_SERVICES` environment variable. For more information on service bindings and this environment variable and how it works in Cloud Foundry, check out https://docs.run.pivotal .io/devguide/deploy-apps/environment-variable.html#VCAP-SERVICES.

In the snippet below, we've added newlines to make it easier to read. If you want the real file, we suggest you take it from GitHub rather than typing what's below in the `vcap.yml`:

```
---
userprovided:
- name: mongodb
  credentials:
    url: mongodb://{{.MONGO_PORT_27017_TCP_ADDR}}:{{.MONGO_PORT_27017_TCP_PORT}}/
      some-guid-string
```

When a Wercker build is running with a MongoDB service active, it provides the `MONGO_*` environment variables, as documented here on Wercker's site: http://devcenter.wercker.com/ docs/services/. Note that this configuration and these environment variable substitutions are only for our Wercker build, and they won't be necessary when we're deploying to Cloud Foundry, which will be covered in the next section.

We've also added some code to `server.go` so that we detect the presence of the Cloud Foundry `VCAP_SERVICES` environment variable and, if we find a bound MongoDB service, we attach the service to a real MongoDB instance rather than the in-memory repository. Here's our newly added `initRepository` function for reference:

```
func initRepository() (repo matchRepository) {
  appEnv, _ := cfenv.Current()
  dbServiceURI, err := cftools.GetVCAPServiceProperty(dbServiceName, "url", appEnv)
  if err != nil || dbServiceURI == "" {
    if err != nil {
      fmt.Printf("\nError retrieving database configuration: %v\n", err)
    }
    fmt.Println("MongoDB was not detected; configuring inMemoryRepository...")
    repo = newInMemoryRepository()
    return
  }
  matchCollection := cfmgo.Connect(cfmgo.NewCollectionDialer, dbServiceURI,
   MatchesCollectionName)
  fmt.Printf("Connecting to MongoDB service: %s...\n", dbServiceName)
  repo = newMongoMatchRepository(matchCollection)
  return
}
```

## Writing an Integration Test

Now that we've gotten some of the basic infrastructure out of the way, we can focus on the actual integration test. Our service exposes RESTful methods that allow us to create new matches, add moves to existing matches, query match details, and query the list of all matches. The API is a little bit naive for a massive-scale game server, but it suits our needs for demonstration purposes.

It helps to write a script of what it looks like to test the functionality we want exercised before writing the code. In our case, this is what we want our test to do:

1. Issue a GET to /matches after starting with an empty database and assert that we get an empty array and no errors.

2. Add a new match via POST to /matches. Assert that we get an HTTP 201 reply and a valid JSON response.

3. GET /matches again and assert that we have one match in the response.

4. Add a second match via POST to /matches. Assert that we get a valid reply.

5. GET /matches/{id of first match}, assert that the details are as expected.

6. Add a move to the first match via POST to /matches/{id}/moves. Assert we get an HTTP 201 reply and a valid JSON response.

7. Query first and second match details. Assert that the first match has the right move on its game board, and the second match does *not*.

8. Add a move to the second match.

9. Query first and second match details. Assert that the second match has the right move on its board, and the first match does *not*.

10. For a real-world app, go back and add a bunch of negative cases to prove that bad input is handled properly, repeated identical requests work properly, etc.

There are probably a few other scenarios we could run for this integration test, but many of them would run the risk of becoming scenario testing for the gogo game engine itself, and not tests of our service functionality and its persistence layer.

Listing 7.3 shows most of the code for the integration test. We left out the code for the utility functions but you can, as always, find that code on GitHub. Additionally, we left out some of the raw JSON payloads for the book, but those are also available on GitHub.

Listing 7.3  **integrations/_test/integration_test.go**

```
func TestIntegration(t *testing.T) {
  // Get empty match list
  emptyMatches, err := getMatchList(t)
  if len(emptyMatches) > 0 {
    t.Errorf("Expected get match list to return an empty array; received %d",
        len(emptyMatches))
  }
```

```
// Add first match
matchResponse, err := addMatch(t, firstMatchBody)
if matchResponse.PlayerBlack != "Hingle McCringleberry" {
  t.Errorf("Didn't get expected black stone player name from creation, got '%s'",
    matchResponse.PlayerBlack)
}

matches, err := getMatchList(t)
if err != nil {
    t.Errorf("Error getting match list, %v", err)
}
if len(matches) != 1 {
    t.Errorf("Expected 1 active match, got %d", len(matches))
}
if matches[0].PlayerWhite != "L'Carpetron Dookmarriott" {
    t.Errorf("Player white name was wrong, got %s", matches[0].PlayerWhite)
}

// Add second match
matchResponse, err = addMatch(t, secondMatchBody)
if matchResponse.PlayerBlack != "J'Dinkalage Morgoone" {
  t.Errorf("Didn't get expected black stone player name from creation, got '%s'",
    matchResponse.PlayerBlack)
}

matches, err = getMatchList(t)
if err != nil {
    t.Errorf("Error getting match list, %v", err)
}
if len(matches) != 2 {
    t.Errorf("Expected 2 active match, got %d", len(matches))
}
if matches[1].PlayerWhite != "Devoin Shower-Handel" {
    t.Errorf("Player white name was wrong, got %s", matches[1].PlayerWhite)
}

// Get match details (first match)
firstMatch, err := getMatchDetails(t, matches[0].ID)
if firstMatch.GridSize != 19 {
    t.Errorf("Expected match gridsize to be 19; received %d",
  firstMatch.GridSize)
}

secondMatch := matches[1]

// Add Move
addMoveToMatch(t, firstMatch.ID, []byte("(cut for print chapter)");
```

```
updatedFirstMatch, err := getMatchDetails(t, firstMatch.ID)
if err != nil {
    t.Errorf("Error getting match details, %v", err)
}
if updatedFirstMatch.GameBoard[3][10] != 2 {
    t.Errorf("Expected gameboard position 3,10 to be 2, received: %d",
        updatedFirstMatch.GameBoard[3][10])
}

originalSecondMatch, err := getMatchDetails(t, secondMatch.ID)
if originalSecondMatch.GameBoard[3][10] != 0 {
    t.Errorf("Expected gameboard position 3,10 to be 0, received: %d",
        originalSecondMatch.GameBoard[3][10])
}

addMoveToMatch(t, secondMatch.ID, []byte("(cut for print chapter)"))

updatedFirstMatch, err = getMatchDetails(t, firstMatch.ID)
if updatedFirstMatch.GameBoard[3][10] != 2 {
    t.Errorf("Expected gameboard position 3,10 to be 2, received: %d",
        updatedFirstMatch.GameBoard[3][10])
}

updatedSecondMatch, err := getMatchDetails(t, secondMatch.ID)
if updatedSecondMatch.GameBoard[3][10] != 1 {
    t.Errorf("Expected gameboard position 3,10 to be 1, received: %d",
        updatedSecondMatch.GameBoard[3][10])
}
}
```

With this integration test in place, and our `wercker.yml` updated, we can use our `buildlocal`
script to execute a Wercker build and our integration test. We've cut out most of the output
except for the parts pertaining to the integration test execution. We strongly encourage you to
get the latest code from GitHub and try this yourself:

```
$ ./buildlocal
--> Executing pipeline
--> Running step: setup environment
--> Running step: wercker-init
--> Running step: setup-go-workspace
--> Running step: go get
--> Running step: go build
--> Running step: env
--> Running step: go test
--> Running step: integration tests
```

```
Connecting to MongoDB service: mongodb...
=== RUN    TestIntegration
[negroni] Started GET /matches
[negroni] Completed 200 OK in 1.655502ms
        Queried Match List OK
[negroni] Started POST /matches
[negroni] Completed 201 Created in 8.447573ms
        Added Match OK
[negroni] Started GET /matches
[negroni] Completed 200 OK in 1.317576ms
        Queried Match List OK
[negroni] Started POST /matches
[negroni] Completed 201 Created in 1.032064ms
        Added Match OK
[negroni] Started GET /matches
[negroni] Completed 200 OK in 1.037217ms
        Queried Match List OK
[negroni] Started GET /matches/0b2b3f3d-d3cb-4ae5-9a05-8a84f3416a98
[negroni] Completed 200 OK in 1.159048ms
        Queried Match Details OK
[negroni] Started POST /matches/0b2b3f3d-d3cb-4ae5-9a05-8a84f3416a98/moves
[negroni] Completed 201 Created in 3.722095ms
        Added Move to Match OK
[negroni] Started GET /matches/0b2b3f3d-d3cb-4ae5-9a05-8a84f3416a98
[negroni] Completed 200 OK in 1.237185ms
        Queried Match Details OK
[negroni] Started GET /matches/c8c76740-70a8-4732-9127-0be77764b797
[negroni] Completed 200 OK in 1.189956ms
        Queried Match Details OK
[negroni] Started POST /matches/c8c76740-70a8-4732-9127-0be77764b797/moves
[negroni] Completed 201 Created in 2.356393ms
        Added Move to Match OK
[negroni] Started GET /matches/0b2b3f3d-d3cb-4ae5-9a05-8a84f3416a98
[negroni] Completed 200 OK in 1.468825ms
        Queried Match Details OK
[negroni] Started GET /matches/c8c76740-70a8-4732-9127-0be77764b797
[negroni] Completed 200 OK in 1.000479ms
        Queried Match Details OK
--- PASS: TestIntegration (0.03s)
PASS
ok      github.com/cloudnativego/gogo-service/integrations/_test   1.045s
--> Running step: copy files to wercker output
--> Steps passed: 35.81s
--> Pipeline finished: 36.92s
```

If this test passes, then we should have a very high degree of confidence that our service does what it is supposed to do, that the MongoDB repository wrapper works properly, and that all the other minor details such as persistence, marshaling, and converting data across tiers all works as planned.

Of course, there is no substitute for actually running your application in a real-world scenario, so that's what we're going to do next.

## Running in the Cloud

At this point we have an integration test that runs within Wercker that provides us with a good measure of confidence about how well our application will perform. However, we still need to deploy and run our application in the cloud so we can put it through real-world testing.

If you have your Cloud Foundry command-line client configured to point either to your Pivotal Web Services account or your local installation of MicroPCF, then you're almost ready to go.

### Configuring a Backing Service

In Pivotal Web Services, you can browse the **marketplace** for the services you'd like to add to your space. Once a service has been added to a space, it can be bound to an application either manually or automatically by being declared within a manifest.

Figure 7.1 shows my *gogo* space in PWS, configured with an instance of MongoDB.

Figure 7.1  Pivotal Web Services Space Contents
Source: http://run.pivotal.io

With a space set up for our application, we can create a `manifest.yml` file which will tell our Cloud Foundry CLI how to push the application. In the code for the application, we've written the app to rely upon a backing service named mongodb, so we'll write our manifest to make this reliance mandatory:

```
applications:
- path: .
  memory: 512MB
  instances: 1
  name: gogo-service
  disk_quota: 1024M
  command: gogo-service
  buildpack: https://github.com/cloudfoundry/go-buildpack.git
  services:
   - mongodb
```

If we attempt to push our application to Cloud Foundry and a service named mongodb doesn't already exist, then the push will fail. We know from experimentation and documentation that the MongoDB service comes with a credentials property called url, which contains the host name, port, user name, password, and all other necessary connection details for our private instance of MongoDB.

At this point we can open a terminal window in our application's root directory and issue the following command:

```
cf push
```

This will create an application called gogo-service that is compiled in the cloud using the Go buildpack, and automatically bound to a service named mongodb. Note that since we've already created an application in Pivotal Web Services with the route gogo-service.cfapps.io, you may encounter an error message asking that you change your application's name since this one is already taken.

### A Note on the Go Buildpack

You are free to decide what approach works best for pushing to the cloud. However, throughout the course of writing this book and pushing real Go applications to the cloud manually as well as through build pipelines, we have become less fond of the buildpack model. There is just too much opportunity to get an inconsistent push using a buildpack versus pushing an immutable artifact like a Docker image (yes, we know it's also possible for those to change out from underneath you, but less so than if a buildpack re-vendors your dependencies incorrectly).

Experiment with using a buildpack and with removing the buildpack from the manifest and pushing a Docker Hub image so you can decide for yourself which method best suits your needs.

Now you can open your favorite interactive REST tool (our favorite is the **Postman** plugin for Chrome) and issue requests to create matches, add moves, and query match details. You'll see that even if you stop and start your application, or scale it to *n* number of instances, the data persists within your MongoDB instance.

Figure 7.2 below shows us using the MongoLab dashboard application to inspect some details of our database. You can reach this dashboard simply by clicking the *manage* link on your MongoDB service in Pivotal Web Services. If you are using your own locally run copy of MongoDB via Docker image for PCF Dev, then you'll need to point a MongoDB administration tool at your local instance.

Figure 7.2   MongoLab Dashboard for Managed PWS Service

Source: PWS (run.pivotal.io)

## Summary

As much as we all love communicating solely over HTTP, assuming that everything we need will always be satisfied by simple REST calls, sometimes we need to communicate with databases.

In this chapter, we took a look at how to perform some basic tasks in Go like building a unit-tested database repository, incorporating that with our RESTful server code, and using Wercker and HTTP to integration test everything in a predictable, isolated environment.

Finally, we took a look at how we can take advantage of cloud-based databases and robust service marketplaces, and deployed our service to the cloud.

# 8

# Event Sourcing and CQRS

*"Reality is merely an illusion, albeit a very persistent one."*

Albert Einstein

As much as our inner geek would like to think so, building microservices isn't all about the code. While code and tech stacks are certainly a large part of what we're doing, some problems are best solved by getting out of the weeds and looking at them from an architectural standpoint.

In this chapter we're going to talk about some architectural designs that deal with massive scale. Many people think that if you simply comply with the 12 factors, you automatically have a cloud native application that can scale infinitely. We disagree.

Cloud native applications need to be able to support enormous scale. If you're going to deploy something on the Internet and expect thousands, or millions, of people to use it, your architecture needs to be prepared for this and sometimes just dialing up the number of instances of your application isn't good enough.

We're going to talk about two patterns, **Event Sourcing** and **CQRS**, that are all about solving the problem of reacting and responding to enormous volume and throughput. The topics we're going to cover are:

- Introduction to Event Sourcing.
- Introduction to Command Query Responsibility Segregation (CQRS).
- Building an advanced ES+CQRS code sample.
  - Building a command handler service.
  - Building an event processor.
  - Building a query handler service.

# Reality is Event Sourced

Of all the topics we get to chat about with colleagues and customers, none are more interesting than the discussions we have around Event Sourcing. Some people have never heard of it, other people swear by it, and a lot of people have been doing it for years without knowing there was a name for it.

The easiest way to understand Event Sourcing is with an analogy. Take the brain, for example. You may not have thought about it like this before, but the human mind is an event processing system. A part of your mind is responsible for receiving stimuli from the five senses. These events are then re-ordered (more on that in a bit) and submitted to another part of your brain *where reality is constructed.*

Have you ever stopped to wonder how, if light travels faster than sound, and it takes your eyes longer to process visual signals than your ears process audio, your brain manages to synchronize the audio and visual to give you a cohesive reality? Even more interesting is that, depending on the stimulus, it can take a few hundred milliseconds from receipt of the event until the cognitive portion of your brain is able to act on that information. A classic example of this is that a fast-kicked soccer ball can be past the goalie and in the net before her brain even gets the signal that something important happened.

Reality as you perceive it as actually nothing more than a function of inputs your sensory system received *in the past.* No matter how smart or alert you are, the reality on which you operate is actually lagging behind the sensory input you receive. You're living in the past and there's nothing you can do about it.

What does this have to do with building software? Oddly enough, *everything.* What it shows us is that *reality is event-sourced.* Reality is a function performed on a stream of inbound events. If we make the the small analogous leap that the *reality* within any given application is that application's *current state*, then we start to see how Event Sourcing isn't just some new fad way of dealing with input, it is *the* way of dealing with input.

Re-written mathematically, we can state that a function that takes a sequence of events returns a state:

```
f(event, ...) = state
```

In traditional state management approaches, we are often maintaining some in-memory construct that represents all of our state. Stimulus comes in and we mutate this state on demand, with little to no concern for event ordering or how the state is mutated. This model gets us into trouble at scale.

In an Event Sourcing system, every time we receive an event, we can apply it to a previously calculated state, and produce a new state:

```
f(state₁, event, ...) = state₂
```

Don't worry if this doesn't quite click at the moment; we'll be going into more detail on this pattern throughout the chapter.

Event Sourcing has a number of advantages that are also often cited by its detractors as what makes it "hard". The following is a list of some of the key tenets of an event-sourced system.

One of the reasons many people claim Event Sourcing is hard (or that it failed outright) is that they did not treat these tenets as laws that can never be broken. Without that discipline, event-sourced apps turn out to be horrible messes.

## Idempotent

*Event-sourced business logic must be idempotent[1].*

In a truly event-sourced system, `f(e,...)` will always equal `state` for the same sequence of events... *always*. This isn't just a side-effect of Event Sourcing, this is the single most absolute rule of Event Sourcing. If you are going to build an event-sourced system then *your business logic must be deterministic*.

This is also one reason why so many people who enjoy functional programming like the Event Sourcing pattern.

When you execute this deterministic business logic multiple times against the same input stream, the resultant state must always be the same. There isn't a typeface bold enough to stress how important this rule is. Without this, everything else you attempt to do, including CQRS (discussed shortly), will fail. And trust us when we say that when Event Sourcing fails, it does so in spectacular, often explosive ways.

## Isolated

*Event-sourced business logic must never rely upon data from outside the event stream.*

There is a subtle requirement to Event Sourcing that often contributes to failure. Failures like this are frequently catastrophic, but caused by tiny, obscure details. Developers suffering through these situations often become vocal detractors of the Event Sourcing pattern. It's like assembling an IKEA cabinet without using the instructions and then blaming the cabinet when it falls apart.

Business logic is rarely ever executed in a vacuum. Applications use reference data all the time and, more importantly, applications regularly make use of external cached information, even if the developers don't think of it that way.

You simply cannot do this in an event-sourced system. Let's take the canonical example of a stock trading application. You've converted it into an event-sourced system and you are computing the state of the application by running your business logic against a stream of stock trades. Everything looks great until your application recovers from a crash and replays the event stream to rebuild its state. You then notice that the resulting transactions are all wrong, and you're losing money and updating your resume as you make a hasty exit from the building.

---

1  https://en.wikipedia.org/wiki/Idempotence

What's happened is the business logic evaluating the event stream is actually using data from *outside* the stream to compute results, such as the *current* stock price of a symbol. This means that the stock price used in state computation can change upon multiple evaluations of the same stream. This in turn violates the *idempotent* rule of Event Sourcing, which we've already described as the single most important and inviolable rule of this pattern.

Every piece of information needed by your application to process events must be contained in the events themselves. This is often a *very* hard requirement to satisfy, depending on the application or the team building it, but it is a *requirement* nonetheless. A common pattern for dealing with this is *injecting* notifications of external data change as events into the stream. Since these change notifications are in the stream, and the stream is properly sequenced, you can then re-run your logic against the stream and get the expected results.

> ### The Wall Clock is External Data...and Terrible
>
> If your application has business logic in it that makes decisions based upon time of day (this happens *a lot* in financial applications; e.g., "is the market open or closed?") then time *cannot* be allowed to remain external to the stream. If time is allowed to be external, then your tests (or crash recoveries!) will perform differently depending on the time of day they are run. This is why nearly every event-sourced system you will encounter is absolutely ruthless about ensuring that there is a meaningful timestamp on every event, and business logic *never* accesses the "wall clock" or *time as it exists outside the event stream*. If you need time, you can maintain it in your computed state as the *last known report of the current time*, which would come in off of received events.

## Testable

*Event-sourced applications, when built properly, can be some of the most well-tested applications.*

One of our favorite aspects of event-sourced applications is that in many cases they are an absolute joy to test. At the core of your application is a function that processes a list of inputs, and returns some state. This function needs to be idempotent and it is *restricted* to only use information in the event stream when computing state.

You can't ask for a more test-friendly environment. In fact, most of the cruft and ceremony that you usually find around other ugly tests goes away here. You probably won't need complicated mocking frameworks or to set up fake objects in memory to support stream-external data because the functions you're testing will be properly isolated and idempotent.

## Replayable and Recoverable

*Event-sourced applications are often optimized for supporting replay and recovery.*

If you're building an event-sourced application and you've been following *the way of the cloud*, and adhering to all the other guidelines of cloud native applications, then you might be wondering how the pattern of Event Sourcing fits in with the requirement that applications be stateless.

Assuming that the event stream is durable, event-sourced applications are often written so that the first thing they do when they start up is process the stream so that state can be computed. This is decent, but there are better, more cloud-friendly options that we'll discuss in the CQRS section.

Regardless of whether you're using CQRS, if you have a durable event stream then your application can recover from a crash and, more importantly, can quickly get into a steady state after startup when being scaled out.

Another benefit of replay ability that is often overlooked is in auditing as well as troubleshooting. If something went wrong in your application in production, you can grab the event stream that caused the problem, run it through in a test environment, and examine the application to figure out what happened. There are very few running production applications these days that can claim this kind of visibility and flexibility.

## Big Data

*Event-sourced applications often generate enormous amounts of data.*

As you can probably guess, event-sourced systems can often produce an enormous amount of data. Depending on how many events you have, how often they arrive, and how big the data payload is per event, you can easily run into the realm of so-called "big data" very quickly. In the next section illustrating some samples of Event Sourcing, we'll talk about some use cases that can easily produce millions of events per day, or even millions per hour.

This fact is neither intrinsically good nor bad, but it is one you need to be aware of when approaching Event Sourcing. The cloud, and on-demand infrastructure, can definitely help you deal with the data volume, but it's something you want to put some design and architecture effort into, and not simply "throw more capacity" at the problem.

# Embracing Eventual Consistency

We've established that reality is event-sourced, and that your brain is actually a few milliseconds behind what's really happening. Your mind has to make sense of and properly sequence incoming events before it can construct reality. In short, your reality is **eventually consistent**.

The classic scenario we use to explain eventual consistency goes something like this: Imagine that you've been using a social media application on your phone and you add a comment to someone else's post. That person is looking at their post in a web browser, and they get a notification that you added a comment, but when they go to take a look at your incredibly witty riposte, it's not there! The comment appears to have fallen through the cracks.

You are crushed, saddened that all the effort you put into the world's most amazing Internet reply went unnoticed! Then, just when you are about to succumb to despair, your friend refreshes the browser window and they can now bask in the glow of your amazing commentary!

What happened? *Eventual consistency* happened. In exchange for the guarantee that your comment will *eventually* show up everywhere, the architects of that service have made design decisions that favor reliability and massive scale over instantaneous data availability worldwide. In many cases this is the best design for the job.

Contrary to what you might think at the time, your world will not end if it takes about 2 seconds before the amazing prose you typed on your phone makes its way to your friend's browser.

When an application is designed to handle an event stream, it is often designed to do so in a "fire and forget" manner. The events arrive asynchronously from varied sources and are then processed asynchronously, probably by a completely separate component. This decoupling allows the event receivers to scale out separately from the event processors. It also allows receivers, journalers, and processors to all have their own reliability models. This is embracing the microservices model to achieve massive scale.

A few seconds later, when your friend's social media feed automatically updates, it will *probably* see the changes that resulted from the inbound event stream, but it could take a little longer than that. This is perfectly acceptable, because this architecture allows your infrastructure to have geographically optimized event receivers, or edge services deployed to optimize mobile response time. If your mobile device had to sit and wait until it received acknowledgements that your post had made its way to all of your friends' feeds, the entire system would be so slow as to be completely unusable.

Not all event-sourced applications need to embrace this kind of asynchronous, loosely coupled, eventually consistent model. However, the sooner you embrace the concept of eventual consistency and how it goes hand in hand with Event Sourcing and the type of massive scale it enables, the easier it will be to start building these applications in the cloud.

## Introducing Command Query Responsibility Segregation

Command Query Responsibility Segregation (CQRS) is a fancy pattern name that means decoupling the input and the output of your system. In a classic monolithic application, you have endpoints that write to a database and endpoints that read from it. The same database is used for both, and you typically don't get a reply from the write endpoints until an acknowledgement or transaction commit is received from the database.

As we've discussed so far, this type of application still works in many scenarios, but in the type of scenario we're discussing in this chapter, it's simply untenable. At massive scale, with high inbound event throughput and complex event processing requirements, you can't afford to run slow queries for reads nor can you afford to sit and wait for processing to take place every time you get a new inbound event. You also don't want the high load of one component of your system to slow down an otherwise healthy component.

Take a look at Figure 8.1 below, a sample illustration for how to model an event-sourced system that separates the responsibility of command and query.

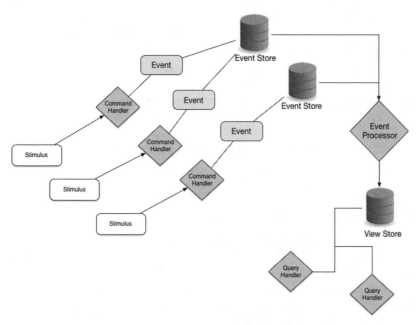

Figure 8.1    Event Flow in Event Sourcing and CQRS Pattern

We call the inbound receipt of stimulus a **command** and, for obvious reasons, we call a read operation a **query**. It should be clear from this diagram that there is absolutely no direct dependency between either the command or the query portions of this application. In fact, you can probably infer that these two functions are likely going to be performed by completely different services.

The flow from stimulus to query in Figure 8.1 works as follows:

1. Some external stimulus invokes a command handler. This could be a bit of data from a remote sensor, or a response to a button press in a mobile application, or virtually anything else.

2. The command handler is responsible for creating an event. By convention (and for good reason), the events are typically named as nouns that occur in the past tense. For example, a `StockPriceChangedEvent` or a `GpsCoordinateChangedEvent` or `AlarmTriggeredEvent`.

3. This event is then stored in the **event store**. There can be any number of intervening technologies between creation and storage. In fact, most production-grade implementations of this pattern are likely to have **message queues** involved to guarantee that any event that is created will be stored properly.

4. The event processor responds to the receipt of inbound events and does whatever aggregation or calculations are necessary in order to *create new data* that is destined

for the query handlers. This data is absolutely tailor-fit to the specific purpose of feeding queries. This is essentially a *computed reality*, available for query. This isn't a transient cache, this is a durable view or warehouse.

5. When requests come in to the query handlers, they then make extremely fast and *simple* requests to the view store. In many scenarios, there might be a caching layer between the view store and the query handlers to even further speed up query response times.

In the next section, we will walk through some fairly typical use cases for Event Sourcing and CQRS that can be implemented with an architecture like the one depicted in Figure 8.1.

# Event Sourcing Use Cases

We've briefly discussed the use case of a stock trading application and how it could make use of Event Sourcing to make it more testable, more reliable, and in general more equipped to run in the cloud.

A few more potential use cases for Event Sourcing are outlined below to give you a better idea of how this pattern isn't just a niche idea that a few random people are using, but rather a pattern that is being applied with great success in virtually every industry.

## Weather Monitoring

Let's say you have monitoring devices set up all across the country. You've got thousands of them set up, some on hilltops, some at sea level, in metropolitan areas and out in the countryside.

You might be getting a stream of events that includes changes in barometric pressure, temperature, wind speed, direction, and humidity. Each of these devices could be emitting multiple data points per second. So now you have tens or hundreds of thousands of pieces of data coming into your stream per second.

This is a classic example of why CQRS not only makes sense from a performance standpoint, but from a design perspective as well. Consumers of this weather service don't need access to the lowest level of detail all the time, they just want to know the current values for any given sensor. If they need to dig into the details and history, they can, but the queries would be optimized for getting current weather conditions.

Additionally, the system could be running complex meteorological algorithms in the background that are used to satisfy higher-level queries that might detect aggregate conditions like potential storm formations or alarm conditions.

Regardless of your preference for cloud native, you would likely never build a system like this without Event Sourcing and CQRS.

## Connected Cars

Newer Tesla vehicles support a feature called *autopilot*. The car uses an assortment of sensors to gather information about its surroundings in order to help the driver do things like stay in the lane and maintain a standard distance from the car ahead. It even has a camera that can read speed limit signs on the side of the road.

This system is a **learning** system. The entire fleet of Tesla vehicles out on the road is constantly sending information back to Tesla so that it can learn and improve the autopilot. This learning is then sent back to the cars so that they get better, and can take more informed readings, and further the virtuous cycle of autopilot and machine learning.

Now you might be able to imagine the kind of volume that makes Event Sourcing not just useful, but essential. Hundreds of thousands of cars worldwide, each sending *massive* amounts of sensor capture information to Tesla constantly. Tesla then needs to capture each of these hundreds of thousands of event streams without losing any of that data or running out of capacity, and perform incredibly complicated machine learning algorithms on that data, as well as support queries for things like the last known position and current status of individual cars to support the Tesla mobile app.

Try and imagine even attempting to build this system using an old-school monolith that stored everything in memory or in a traditional database, without the ability to rapidly scale horizontally. Just the transaction throughput alone would be enough to completely crush a web application built without ES, CQRS, and eventual consistency.

## Social Media Feed Processing

This one probably seems fairly obvious. You can consider a social media feed to be an event stream. Social activity such as new posts, new comments, likes, friend requests, and request accepts and denies are all events in the stream.

An event-sourced application could then be consuming these streams, recording data that it needs to record, and performing processing on those streams to make aggregate or calculated information available for queries. You might use such a system to gauge sentiment around a particular hashtag or to generate recommendations or predictions based on activity streams.

# Code Sample: Managing a Drone Army

As a reward for having sat through a large amount of theory and exposition, we're going to build an app that manages a drone army. The only thing we'll be missing are sharks with lasers (you can add those as a reader exercise).

In this application, we will have command handlers that accept commands to generate events that correspond to things like position, speed change, and remaining battery of individual drones. These events will be dropped into our event store and then processed asynchronously by our drone event processor. Finally, the output of the event processing will be stored in our view store and made available to our query handlers, allowing application clients to get the current status of any drone in our army.

While we won't implement this to keep things easier to manage for the book, you can probably imagine that we might also want a command handler that accepts a command changing a drone's current target. This handler would create an event like `TargetChangedEvent`. The event processor would then react to this event and dispatch a command directly to a drone, telling it to change target, rather than creating any information in the query views.

For some data, like drone position, we can just store the last received position in the view store. Other calculations can also be done asynchronously, like calculating the number of minutes of flight time remaining for each drone. This could be a simple calculation, or it could use an algorithm like Tesla uses to calculate an estimated remaining charge based on the last $n$ minutes of consumption information (which we could get from the last $x$ reports of remaining battery).

It is calculations and asynchronous processing like this that makes CQRS and Event Sourcing so appealing, and gives us the ability to dynamically scale any portion of our architecture on demand. If we need to add some extra, heavy-duty calculation that didn't exist before, we can just drop another microservice into the ecosystem that examines our inbound event stream.

In the next few sections of the chapter we will build a command handler, an event processor, and a query handler. All of these will be loosely coupled and independently scalable. While our trivial sample won't do complex aggregations or calculations in the event processor, we hope that you'll be able to use this sample as a template for the more complex work you might be doing in your own projects. We can only hope that you are indeed planning to take over the world with microservices written in Go and deployed to the cloud.

Also keep in mind that the final sample at the end of the book also makes more complex use of the Event Sourcing and CQRS patterns.

# Creating a Command Handler Service

In this section of the chapter, we're going to build the first of the three main components of our Event Sourcing sample—the *command handler* service. The role of this service is to accept incoming commands, convert them into events, and place them onto a queue for asynchronous processing by the event processor.

Rather than starting with our first failing test like we would normally do, this time we're going to do a little spike to acquaint ourselves with RabbitMQ. Since this is the first time we've done any kind of messaging middleware coding in the book, it's worth spending a few minutes with a canonical "hello world" sample to get our feet wet and to familiarize ourselves with the technology.

## Introduction to RabbitMQ

RabbitMQ is an open-source message broker that implements the Advanced Message Queueing Protocol (AMQP). Among the many reasons why we chose RabbitMQ are its simplicity, remarkably short ramp-up time, and its inherent affinity for the cloud. We're also huge fans of OTP (Open Telecom Platform) and Erlang, two technologies used to write RabbitMQ.

Everything in this introduction can be found in our github repository https://github.com/cloudnativego/rabbit-hello. In this simplest of examples, we're going to start up a RabbitMQ server using Docker, then we're going to put a message on a queue with one Go application and receive it using another. If you're using Pivotal Web Services as your cloud deploy target, you'll be pleased to see that there is a RabbitMQ tile in the marketplace there.

To spin up a RabbitMQ server and ensure that the right ports are exposed on our Docker machine's IP address, we use the following command (all on one line; any newlines are for print-friendliness only):

```
docker run -d --hostname my-rabbit --name some-rabbit -p 8080:15672
-p 4369:4369 -p 5672:5672 rabbitmq:3-management
```

Note that we're using an image tagged 3-management. This not only gives us the RabbitMQ server, but it exposes an administrative console on the internal port 15672 (which we've mapped to port 8080 because we're lazy and typing a five-digit port number is simply unacceptable).

Next, we'll use the send.go from the RabbitMQ tutorials found in the RabbitMQ documentation, shown in Listing 8.1 to enqueue a simple message.

Listing 8.1  **send.go**

```go
package main

import (
        "fmt"
        "log"

        "github.com/streadway/amqp"
)

func failOnError(err error, msg string) {
        if err != nil {
                log.Fatalf("%s: %s", msg, err)
                panic(fmt.Sprintf("%s: %s", msg, err))
        }
}

func main() {
        conn, err := amqp.Dial("amqp://guest:guest@192.168.99.100:5672/")
        failOnError(err, "Failed to connect to RabbitMQ")
        defer conn.Close()

        ch, err := conn.Channel()
        failOnError(err, "Failed to open a channel")
        defer ch.Close()
```

```
    q, err := ch.QueueDeclare(
            "hello", // name
            false,    // durable
            false,    // delete when unused
            false,    // exclusive
            false,    // no-wait
            nil,      // arguments
    )
    failOnError(err, "Failed to declare a queue")

    body := "hello"
    err = ch.Publish(
            "",        // exchange
            q.Name, // routing key
            false,  // mandatory
            false,  // immediate
            amqp.Publishing{
                    ContentType: "text/plain",
                    Body:          []byte(body),
            })
    log.Printf(" [x] Sent %s", body)
    failOnError(err, "Failed to publish a message")
}
```

At this point, if you're struggling with some of the concepts here, we highly recommend taking a few coffee breaks to go sift through the RabbitMQ tutorials and overviews of basic concepts. The flow for sending a message with this library works like this:

1. Connect to an AMQP server with the `Dial` function.

2. Get a `Channel` from your `Connection`.

3. Declare the `Queue` you're going to use and set options using the channel.

4. Create the body of your message.

5. Publish that message on the channel.

Note that when you publish a message on a channel, you're only specifying the *name* of the queue. This implies that you could potentially write your code in a way that assumes the queues already have been created. We strongly recommend *against* this approach. Safe, defensive programming that assumes nothing is always the best way to go, especially when your backing services are in the cloud.

With RabbitMQ running in the background (you might have to modify the IP address in the code sample to match your Docker environment), we can run the sample:

```
$ go run send.go
2016/02/08 07:13:10  [x] Sent hello
```

At this point, there's a message sitting in the queue in RabbitMQ. If we killed the server we would lose the message. Don't worry, though, there are countless options for configuring RabbitMQ, queues, and messages to set up durability and resilience however you like. Outside the scope of this book, **exchanges** are also an incredibly powerful feature that let you spread delivery of messages to multiple queues at once, among many other things.

Receiving a message is very similar to sending, and uses much the same preamble including connecting, obtaining a channel, and declaring a queue. The difference is that in this case, we're going to receive messages on this queue rather than send:

```
msgs, err := ch.Consume(
            q.Name, // queue
            "",     // consumer
            true,   // auto-ack
            false,  // exclusive
            false,  // no-local
            false,  // no-wait
            nil,    // args
    )
    failOnError(err, "Failed to register a consumer")

    forever := make(chan bool)

    go func() {
            for d := range msgs {
                    log.Printf("Received a message: %s", d.Body)
            }
    }()

    log.Printf(" [*] Waiting for messages. To exit press CTRL+C")
    <-forever
```

Instead of the `Publish` method, we use the `Consume` method. Then we create a simple **goroutine** (https://golang.org/doc/effective_go.html#goroutines) that runs forever, eternally awaiting the arrival of messages. When one does arrive, we output the body.

```
$ go run receive.go
2016/02/08 07:13:37  [*] Waiting for messages. To exit press CTRL+C
2016/02/08 07:13:37 Received a message: hello
```

Since we already had a message sitting on the queue, we get one immediately upon running our receiver. If we open up the admin console (http://*your docker IP*:8080) and click on *queues*, we can see that we have created the ***hello*** queue, as shown in Figure 8.2.

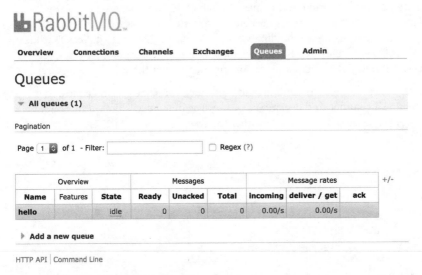

Figure 8.2    RabbitMQ Admin Console—Queues

Source: http://192.168.99.100:8080/

## Building the Command Handler Service

The job of our command handler is to receive incoming commands, convert them into an endpoint-agnostic *event* format, and then submit them to the appropriate queue. At this point, the command handler washes its hands of the request and moves on.

It is this extremely fine-grained responsibility that makes this pattern so scalable. It's also one reason people like to complain about it: because of the number of services you have to create to get a simple "hello world" in place. Of course, we're building something to support massive, real-world volume, so complaining about its lack of ideal support for "hello world" is a bit ridiculous.

You can find the full source code for the command handler sample in GitHub at https://github .com/cloudnativego/drones-cmds. Because of the size and relative complexity of this sample, we're not going to spend as much time showing you every single line of code, or all the tests. We're going to highlight the most important parts and then let you go explore the GitHub repositories on your own.

Listing 8.2 shows an example command handler. All of the command handlers in the project follow this basic format.

Listing 8.2  **Command Handlers**

```
func addTelemetryHandler(formatter *render.Render,
  dispatcher queueDispatcher) http.HandlerFunc {
  return func(w http.ResponseWriter, req *http.Request) {
        payload, _ := ioutil.ReadAll(req.Body)
        var newTelemetryCommand telemetryCommand
        err := json.Unmarshal(payload, &newTelemetryCommand)
        if err != nil {
                formatter.Text(w, http.StatusBadRequest,
                        "Failed to parse add telemetry command.")
                return
        }
        if !newTelemetryCommand.isValid() {
                formatter.Text(w, http.StatusBadRequest,
                        "Invalid telemetry command.")
                return
        }

        evt := dronescommon.TelemetryUpdatedEvent{
                DroneID:           newTelemetryCommand.DroneID,
                RemainingBattery: newTelemetryCommand.RemainingBattery,
                Uptime:            newTelemetryCommand.Uptime,
                CoreTemp:          newTelemetryCommand.CoreTemp,
                ReceivedOn:        time.Now().UnixNano(),
        }
        dispatcher.DispatchMessage(evt)
        formatter.JSON(w, http.StatusCreated, evt)
  }
}
```

The first thing we do upon receipt of a command is to pull that command off the request body and unmarshal it into a usable struct. In the case of Listing 8.2, it's going to be a telemetryCommand struct, which looks like this:

```
type telemetryCommand struct {
        DroneID          string 'json:"drone_id"'
        RemainingBattery int    'json:"battery"'
        Uptime           int    'json:"uptime"'
        CoreTemp         int    'json:"core_temp"'
}
```

If we are able to unmarshal this, then we invoke the isValid function that we've anchored to the telemetryCommand struct. This gives us a clean way of ensuring that the command has all the pre-requisite fields and that they are formatted properly. Each one of our command types has a corresponding isValid function (which you can see in the service/types.go file).

Next, we create a TelemetryUpdatedEvent from the incoming command. Remember, in the command handler we're not supposed to do any kind of processing, so this is just a straight conversion with the addition of a timestamp (see earlier in the chapter about the importance of timestamping our events). If we had other external data we needed to pull in (such as current status of our plans for world domination, remaining funds, etc.) we would augment the event with that information in the command handler.

Finally, the last responsibility of our command handler is to dispatch the newly created event to the appropriate queue. This is done by calling `dispatcher.DispatchMessage(evt)`. Each handler is passed in its own dispatcher, so the request handler doesn't have to figure out the *where* or the *how* of dispatching. This also makes unit testing our handlers much easier because we can pass in fake dispatchers with ease.

That's it! If we've set everything up correctly, we now have a service that drops events onto RabbitMQ queues when it receives commands via HTTP POST.

If we look at the `manifest.yml` file for the `drones-cmds` project, we'll see that it requires a `rabbit` service. This means that we've created a service instance from the marketplace (either using PCF Dev or Pivotal Web Services or an enterprise PCF) to give us access to a RabbitMQ instance, and we've named it **rabbit**.

Before moving on to the discussion of the event processor, you might want to sift through the code in GitHub. Of particular interest might be the integration test, which submits a bunch of commands via HTTP POST and then monitors the Wercker-supplied RabbitMQ instance for events, asserting that the events we expected made it onto their respective queues.

This service, like all our other samples, is automatically built by Wercker and deployed to Docker Hub (so you can run it locally with `docker run`), and you can push that same Docker image to the cloud.

## Building the Event Processor

The event processor has one job, as its name makes fairly obvious: *process events*. When this service starts up it will sit and listen on the three queues being used. Each time it gets an event it is going to process the event and then put the event in an event store.

In a much more complicated, real-world sample, the event processor would be doing calculations based on slices of time or aggregations or groupings. It might also be doing two different kinds of writes: one to the event store so that every event is archived, and another write to the view store that supports the query handler service (we often refer to this ultimate destination as *reality* or a *reality service*).

In our case we're going to try and keep the example as simple as possible so you can see how all of the pieces of event sourcing and CQRS fit together and so that you can potentially use this code as a template for building out your own ES/CQRS pattern. To keep things simple, we're not going to do any aggregations and we're only going to write to a store designed to support the query service. You'll be able to see all of the various points within this solution that you could extend to add this functionality easily.

All of the code for the event processor can be found on GitHub at https://github.com/cloudnativego/drones-events.

One of the interesting things about the event processor is that it doesn't really have a public API. It doesn't need any kind of RESTful stimulus from the outside world to do its job—it's just listening for events to arrive on a queue.

Because we're deploying this service to the cloud, we need it to be up and running all the time and we also want it to play nice within the microservice ecosystem. At this point we can choose to run the service as a **task** (no HTTP endpoints) where we simply tell the platform not to hit it with a health check, or we can put up a simple HTTP endpoint for our own ease of local testing as well as to make less flexible platforms happy.

In our case, we just exposed some basic text on the root (/) resource in case we're deploying to a cloud that doesn't support tasks or circumventing HTTP health checks.

Take a look at the `NewServer` function in Listing 8.3.

Listing 8.3    **NewServer() for Event Processor**

```
// NewServer configures and returns a Server.
func NewServer() *negroni.Negroni {
  formatter := render.New(render.Options{
        IndentJSON: true,
  })

  n := negroni.Classic()
  mx := mux.NewRouter()

  initRoutes(mx, formatter)

  n.UseHandler(mx)

  alertChannel := make(chan dronescommon.AlertSignalledEvent)
  telemetryChannel := make(chan dronescommon.TelemetryUpdatedEvent)
  positionChannel := make(chan dronescommon.PositionChangedEvent)

  repo := initRepository()
  dequeueEvents(alertChannel, telemetryChannel, positionChannel)
  consumeEvents(alertChannel, telemetryChannel, positionChannel, repo)
  return n
}
```

This should look *a lot* like all of the other `NewServer` functions we've written so far in this book. There are a couple of interesting additions, however.

First, we are creating three Go **channels**. Go channels are constructs that allow us to do coordinated asynchronous processing without all the baggage of multi-threading we get from other languages. For more information on Go channels, consult your favorite Go language reference.

We're going to use these channels as a *pipeline* of sorts. We're going to dequeue events from AMQP (RabbitMQ) and place them on these channels. As events arrive on these channels, we're going to consume them with our event processor, which will ultimately store the most recent events in our query store, a MongoDB instance.

As you may have guessed, the vast majority of all work being done by this service can be found in the dequeueEvents and consumeEvents functions.

Listing 8.4 shows the dequeueEvents function:

### Listing 8.4  dequeueEvents()

```
func dequeueEvents(alertChannel chan common.AlertSignalledEvent,
                   telemetryChannel chan common.TelemetryUpdatedEvent,
                   positionChannel chan common.PositionChangedEvent) {
    fmt.Printf("Starting AMQP queue de-serializer...")
    appEnv, _ := cfenv.Current()
    amqpURI, err := cftools.GetVCAPServiceProperty("rabbit", "url", appEnv)
    if err != nil {
            fmt.Println("No Rabbit/AMQP connection details supplied.
ABORTING. No events will be dequeued!!!")
        return
    }
    fmt.Printf("dialing %s\n", amqpURI)
    conn, err := amqp.Dial(amqpURI)
    if err != nil {
            fmt.Printf("Failed to connect to rabbit, %v\n", err)
    }
    ch, err := conn.Channel()
    if err != nil {
            fmt.Printf("Failed to open AMQP channel %v\n", err)
    }

    alertsQ, _ := ch.QueueDeclare(
            alertsQueueName, false, false, false, false, nil,
    )

    positionsQ, _ := ch.QueueDeclare(
            positionsQueueName, false, false, false, false, nil,
    )

    telemetryQ, _ := ch.QueueDeclare(
            telemetryQueueName, false, false, false, false,nil,
    )
```

```
alertsIn, _ := ch.Consume(
        alertsQ.Name, "", true, false, false, false,nil,
)
positionsIn, _ := ch.Consume(
        positionsQ.Name, "", true, false, false, false, nil,
)

telemetryIn, _ := ch.Consume(
        telemetryQ.Name, "", true, false, false, false, nil,
)

go func() {
        for {
          select {
            case alertRaw := <-alertsIn:
                dispatchAlert(alertRaw, alertChannel)
            case telemetryRaw := <-telemetryIn:
                dispatchTelemetry(telemetryRaw, telemetryChannel)
            case positionRaw := <-positionsIn:
                dispatchPosition(positionRaw, positionChannel)
          }
        }
  }()
}
```

The basic flow of this code is we declare our queues, we consume events from the queues, and then we use a Go select statement in an infinite loop to pull messages off the queues and dispatch them to the appropriate channels. One thing we have to do in the act of dispatching is convert the raw AMQP message into one of our event structs, as shown in the dispatchAlert function below:

```
func dispatchAlert(alertRaw amqp.Delivery, out chan common.AlertSignalledEvent) {
  var event common.AlertSignalledEvent
  err := json.Unmarshal(alertRaw.Body, &event)
  if err == nil {
        out <- event
  } else {
        fmt.Printf("Failed to de-serialize raw alert from queue, %v\n", err)
  }
  return
}
```

If the conversion from raw AMQP format to a strongly typed event works, we then send the event to the channel, where the other goroutine is waiting, defined in the `consumeEvents` function shown in Listing 8.5 below.

Listing 8.5    **consumeEvents()**

```
func consumeEvents(alertChannel chan common.AlertSignalledEvent,
  telemetryChannel chan common.TelemetryUpdatedEvent,
  positionChannel chan common.PositionChangedEvent, repo eventRepository) {
  go func() {
        fmt.Println("Started event consumer goroutine")
        for {
                select {
                case alert := <-alertChannel:
                        processAlert(repo, alert)
                case telemetry := <-telemetryChannel:
                        processTelemetry(repo, telemetry)
                case position := <-positionChannel:
                        processPosition(repo, position)
                }
        }
  }()
}
```

This is a pretty simple function. It waits for incoming messages, again using a `select` statement, and processes them accordingly. This is where you could inject additional levels of complexity depending on what kind of complex processing you need done. In our case, the processing consists of just "upserting" (updating or inserting) the most recently received event into our MongoDB repository.

In a more advanced and properly separated sample (like the one at the end of the book), you might actually submit the calculated state to a *reality* microservice rather than communicating directly with a MongoDB database. This allows the event stores and reality/query stores to scale independently of the event processor.

A sample of this logic is shown in the `processAlert` function:

```
func processAlert(repo eventRepository, alertEvent common.AlertSignalledEvent) {
  fmt.Printf("Processing alert %+v\n", alertEvent)

  repo.UpdateLastAlertEvent(alertEvent)
}
```

One of the huge advantages of doing event processing this way is if a single instance of the event processor gets bogged down, we can simply scale up to multiple event processor services because our workload is being dispatched from queues, and we can set up our RabbitMQ server so that it won't give the same message to two different consumers.

Looking at the `manifest.yml` for the event processor service, we see that we require two backing services:

- `rabbit`
- `mongoevent-rollup`

It's worth noting that the RabbitMQ service used by the event processor is *the same* as the one used by the command handler. If it weren't, we would never see messages produced by the command handler, as they would be stored in a separate, isolated instance of Rabbit.

Looking forward into the future, we know that the event processor and the query handler are going to share the same MongoDB service (`mongoevent-rollup`) so that the query service will be able to see the most recently stored and processed events.

> ### Anti-Pattern Alert!
>
> The idea that the event processor and the query handler both communicate with the same MongoDB database violates a critical rule of microservices: *never use databases as an integration tier*. We're only doing this to reduce the complexity of the sample. In a real-world application, the event processor would consume services for writing to the event store and to computed state (reality).
>
> It's also worth pointing out that this is a bone of contention among microservice developers. Some think it's fine for two services to share the same database, others (like us) think it is anathema to everything that is good and pure about the universe. We will leave you to make this decision on your own.

## Integration Testing the Event Processor

The main goal behind the integration test for this service is to ensure that it is properly handling incoming events and placing the appropriate values in the MongoDB repository. To do this, we start up our server with a manufactured set of bound services (via our `vcapinate` tool and Wercker service images). Once running, we submit various events to the queues, wait for the processor to complete, and then query the repository to make sure the events made it safely.

If you want to see the code for the integration test, you can find it at https://github.com/cloudnativego/drones-events/blob/master/integrations/_test/integration_test.go.

# Creating the Query Handler Service

Once we're done creating the command handler and the event processor, the hard part is done. The query handler is the "dumbest" of all three of our services in this chapter. It does nothing but query the most recent alert, telemetry, and position events from MongoDB.

The queries that it will be doing were already written when we created a MongoDB repository in the event processor project (the code for which is in GitHub; we didn't show it in the chapter).

This is all very simple code that we've written a number of times before in the book. The following snippet shows the request handler that returns the last received telemetry update for a given drone:

```
func lastTelemetryHandler(formatter *render.Render,
  repo eventRepository) http.HandlerFunc {
  return func(w http.ResponseWriter, req *http.Request) {
        droneID := getDroneID(req)
        fmt.Printf("Looking up last telemetry event for drone %s\n", droneID)
        event, err := repo.GetTelemetryEvent(droneID)
        if err == nil {
                formatter.JSON(w, http.StatusOK, &event)
        } else {
                formatter.JSON(w, http.StatusInternalServerError, err.Error())
        }
  }
}
```

We know we're going to need to extract the drone ID from the request for every single handler in this service, so we've extracted that functionality into the following function:

```
func getDroneID(req *http.Request) (droneID string) {
        vars := mux.Vars(req)
        droneID = vars["droneId"]
        return
}
```

We've declared the droneId parameter as part of the route pattern for our REST endpoints, as shown in the code from the server initialization function:

```
func initRoutes(mx *mux.Router, formatter *render.Render, repo eventRepository) {
  mx.HandleFunc("/drones/{droneId}/lastTelemetry",
    lastTelemetryHandler(formatter, repo)).Methods("GET")
  mx.HandleFunc("/drones/{droneId}/lastAlert",
    lastAlertHandler(formatter, repo)).Methods("GET")
  mx.HandleFunc("/drones/{droneId}/lastPosition",
    lastPositionHandler(formatter, repo)).Methods("GET")
}
```

That's essentially all there is to the query service. It is designed specifically to be as dumb as possible, so that it can respond to extremely high volumes of requests to support high throughput and low latency. In more complicated or advanced implementations, the query service is often supported by a caching service.

# Summary

This chapter is one of the larger and more complex ones in the book. As fun as it would be to conquer the planet with an army of quadcopter drones powered by the Go language, the problem domain was just for illustrative purposes.

We started off with definitions for Event Sourcing and the Command Query Responsibility Segregation (CQRS) patterns and a discussion of eventual consistency. We talked about why these patterns are useful, and how they have a particular harmony with building massive-scale, cloud native applications.

We created a service that accepts incoming commands, converts them into events, and dispatches them to queues. We created an event processing service that reads events from queues and processes them, performing whatever calculations are necessary (though our calculations were a simple capture of the most recent event) and storing appropriate events in the view store. Finally, we created a query service that allows consuming services or applications to query the current state of things, which is not unlike inspecting a snapshot of reality.

Properly separating these services and their concerns allows us to scale, update, and deploy individual components of the system while all the other components continue to run with zero downtime.

# 9

# Building a Web Application with Go

*"There are two ways of constructing a software design: One way is to make it so simple that there are obviously no deficiencies, and the other way is to make it so complicated that there are no obvious deficiencies. The first method is far more difficult."*

C.A.R. Hoare, 1980 Turing Award Winner

A web application is nothing more than a service. The attribute that makes this service different from others is the implicit contract between it and a web browser that requires at least one of the service's resources to respond with HTML.

Surrounded by frameworks and libraries that add myriad flavors of magic and abstraction to our work, the concept of *web application* often carries with it negative connotations. In some circles, just saying the phrase "web app" automatically brings to mind images of difficult to maintain monoliths. It doesn't have to be this way.

In some languages, you don't even get to use the same libraries or APIs for building a website that you use for building a service. This furthers the misconception that a website is somehow a more bloated, intrinsically monolithic creature.

In this chapter, we're going to:

- Create a fully functioning website in Go.
- Show how to serve static files and assets.
- Incorporate our existing microservice knowledge to expose RESTful endpoints to JavaScript clients.
- Learn how to use server-side templating.
- Learn how to process HTML forms.
- Build and deploy a website to the cloud with Wercker.

## Serving Static Files and Assets

There are a million different kinds of web applications that do a million different things, but one task that every web application needs to do is serve up files. Even if the only file you're going to serve is a `favicon.ico` file, you've got to expose some files to client browsers.

Most modern web applications use Cascading Style Sheets (CSS), JavaScript files, images, and even special fonts and styles for glyph libraries like Font Awesome[1], one of our favorite libraries in our toolbox.

If you've made the transition from microservice to web application in other languages before, you might expect to have to throw out all your existing code and start over again with a new set of libraries and APIs. Thankfully, this is not the case in Go.

To start serving static files (which can include HTML files), let's first create a somewhat organized directory structure:

- `static-content`
  - `js`
  - `images`
  - `css`

We can put HTML files in the `static-content` directory, JavaScript in the `js` directory, and so on. To get started serving static files, we can re-use the template we've been using with the `main.go` and `server.go` pair. We can actually copy `main.go` wholesale without any change.

Listing 9.1 shows our `server.go`, where we map the virtual URL "/" to the `static-content` directory.

Listing 9.1  **server.go**

```
package main

import (
        "net/http"

        "github.com/codegangsta/negroni"
        "github.com/gorilla/mux"
)

// NewServer configures and returns a Server.
func NewServer() *negroni.Negroni {
  n := negroni.Classic()
  mx := mux.NewRouter()

  initRoutes(mx)
```

---

1  Font Awesome can be found at https://fortawesome.github.io/Font-Awesome/.

```
    n.UseHandler(mx)
    return n
}

func initRoutes(mx *mux.Router, formatter *render.Render) {
    webRoot = os.Getenv("WEBROOT")
    if len(webRoot) == 0 {
        root, err := os.Getwd()
        if err != nil {
            panic("Could not retrieve working directory")
        } else {
            webRoot = root
        }
    }
    mx.PathPrefix("/").Handler(http.FileServer(http.Dir(webRoot + "/assets/")))
}
```

As you can see, we've basically added just one line to our usual code that configures RESTful routes on services. We're nesting a couple of functions that warrant an explanation:

- `http.Dir`—A `Dir` implements a `FileSystem` at the given path using the underlying operating system's implementation. In this case, we're exposing the `assets` directory beneath our application root.

- `http.FileServer`—A `FileServer` returns a handler that responds to HTTP requests with the contents of the exposed file system.

- `mux.Router.PathPrefix`—Adds a path prefix to the route matcher.

Go ahead and create an `assets` directory below the directory containing `main.go` and `server.go`. Don't add anything to this directory yet, and build and run your web application.

First, see what happens when files are missing and explore whether or not you can browse directories by default using the methods we've shown. Next, start adding things like HTML files and stylesheets.

By changing your `initRoutes` function from previous service examples to use just a single function call, you've created a basic web application. It doesn't get much simpler than that!

# Supporting JavaScript Clients

Being able to serve up simple files is the foundation on which all websites are built, but we need more functionality to be able to create real web applications. These days, you would be hard-pressed to find a website that doesn't use JavaScript. Specifically, you are unlikely to find a piece of software claiming to be a web application that isn't exposing RESTful endpoints for the consumption of JavaScript dispensed by that application.

The first step toward this goal is to be able to serve up JavaScript files. We've got that covered in the `assets` directory we created in the preceding section. Next, we need an HTML file that makes use of this script.

The HTML in Listing 9.2 is about as basic as it gets. We are including jQuery and a JavaScript file called `hello.js` that we are going to be serving up locally by our web server.

In the main portion of the page, we have two paragraphs. These have been given CSS classes so that we can write some JavaScript that will modify the contents of those paragraph elements with data retrieved from our server.

While this is a fairly simple and somewhat contrived sample, it will hopefully give you an idea of how easy it is to perform standard web application tasks that other people might try and convince you can only be done in other languages.

Listing 9.2  **index.html**

```html
<html>
<head>
  <link rel="stylesheet" href="css/main.css" />
  <script src="https://ajax.googleapis.com/ajax/libs/jquery/1.10.2/jquery.min.js">
  </script>
  <script src="js/hello.js"></script>
</head>
<body>
  Sample Go Application! <br/>
  <div>
    <p class="greeting-id">The ID is </p>
    <p class="greeting-content">The content is </p>
  </div>
</body>
</html>
```

We're not quite ready to run anything because we don't have our JavaScript written yet. If you're familiar with jQuery, the code in Listing 9.3 should be pretty easy to read.

Listing 9.3  **hello.js**

```javascript
$(document).ready(function() {
    $.ajax({
        url: "/api/test"
    }).then(function(data) {
        $('.greeting-id').append(data.id);
        $('.greeting-content').append(data.content);
    });
});
```

This JavaScript performs an Ajax call against a RESTful endpoint (/api/test) as soon as the JavaScript document object is finished loading. It then takes the data retrieved from that endpoint and appends it to the paragraph elements we created in Listing 9.2. This illustrates one of the huge advantages of JavaScript: you don't need to explicitly marshal JSON into something. JavaScript Object Notation (JSON) actually started in JavaScript, so it deals with JSON data returned from RESTful endpoints natively.

Exposing an endpoint should be old hat to us by now after several chapters of working with services. First, let's create a handlers.go like we've done several times before, as shown in Listing 9.4:

Listing 9.4  **handlers.go**

```go
package main

import (
  "net/http"

  "github.com/unrolled/render"
)

type sampleContent struct {
  ID      string 'json:"id"'
  Content string 'json:"content"'
}

func testHandler(formatter *render.Render) http.HandlerFunc {
  return func(w http.ResponseWriter, req *http.Request) {
        formatter.JSON(w, http.StatusOK,
          sampleContent{ID: "8675309", Content: "Hello from Go!"})
  }
}
```

And we can modify our server.go file to map the /api/test endpoint to this handler in our initRoutes function:

```go
mx.HandleFunc("/api/test", testHandler(formatter)).Methods("GET")
```

Now if we build our web application and run it, we will automatically serve up the index.html file we created. This will then run the JavaScript, which hits our service endpoint to get data, and then manipulates the paragraph elements.

Figure 9.1 shows what this page looks like in Chrome.

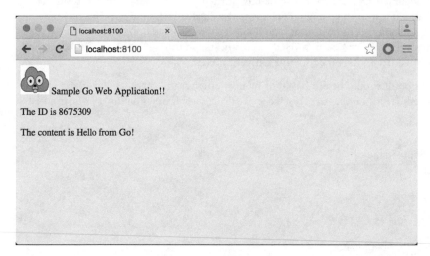

Figure 9.1    Web Application Written in Go, Using JavaScript and a REST Service

We can watch the console output of our web application to see the Negroni trace showing that the JavaScript is actually hitting our service endpoint in order to produce the page shown in Figure 9.1.

## Using Server-Side Templates

In the previous section, we went through an example of how to serve up an HTML page that has JavaScript on it, and the JavaScript on that page interacted with service endpoints exposed by the Go application.

This is how we think most people want to build modern web applications: an incredibly thin veneer that exposes HTML, where most of the work is done by a front-end framework like AngularJS that communicates with services.

While this scenario may be ideal, there are still going to be times when, no matter how hard you try, you can't get around the need to expose server-side data in the HTML being rendered.

For example, you might have a secure website, and you want to create some JavaScript variables that contain the name of the currently logged-in user. You also might have read some cookie values or other data that you want to be in the HTML before the page's JavaScript loads.

This actually turns out to be fairly simple as well. For the full sample using templates, check out https://github.com/cloudnativego/web-application-template.

The `main.go` file for this sample is identical to all the others. All the work we're going to do is in Listing 9.5, the `server.go` file.  In this sample, instead of exposing the data to be rendered dynamically via service endpoint, we're going to inject a reference to that object into a template processor so that the HTML can be manipulated *before* being sent to the client browser.

Listing 9.5    **server.go**

```go
package main

import (
  "net/http"
  "text/template"

  "github.com/codegangsta/negroni"
  "github.com/gorilla/mux"
)

// NewServer configures and returns a Server.
func NewServer() *negroni.Negroni {
  n := negroni.Classic()
  mx := mux.NewRouter()

  initRoutes(mx)

  n.UseHandler(mx)
  return n
}

func initRoutes(mx *mux.Router) {
  mx.PathPrefix("/images/").Handler(http.StripPrefix("/images/",
    http.FileServer(http.Dir("./assets/images/"))))
  mx.PathPrefix("/css/").Handler(http.StripPrefix("/css/",
    http.FileServer(http.Dir("./assets/css/"))))
  mx.HandleFunc("/", homeHandler)
}

type sampleContent struct {
  ID      string 'json:"id"'
  Content string 'json:"content"'
}

var t *template.Template

func init() {
  t = template.Must(template.ParseFiles("assets/templates/index.html"))
}
```

```
func homeHandler(w http.ResponseWriter, req *http.Request) {
    data := sampleContent{ID: "8675309", Content: "Hello from Go!"}
    t.Execute(w, data)
}
```

As we did in the previous example, we're using `PathPrefix` to expose virtual directories of files like the `images` and `css` directories. The important function to look at here is the `homeHandler` function.

In this function, we create an instance of `sampleContent`, like we did in the previous example. But then we call the `Execute` method on our template struct (the `t` variable). This template is initialized in the package's `init` function.

> ### Warning
> You need to pay close attention to the use of the `init` function. This function is called to initialize a package, and is guaranteed to execute before your application's main function. However, if you have multiple packages with multiple `init` functions, you cannot guarantee the order in which they will execute. In other words, never put something in a package initializer that requires that some other package initializer has run.

Listing 9.6 shows the HTML that contains the template processing tags that allow us to inject data prior to sending to the browser. It looks almost identical to the last one, with the exception of the substitution syntax.

Listing 9.6    **index.html**

```
<html>
<head>
  <link rel="stylesheet" href="/css/main.css"/>
</head>
<body>
  <img src="/images/cng.png" height="48" width="48" />
  Sample Go Web Application!!
  <div>
    <p class="greeting-id">The ID is {{ .ID }}</p>
    <p class="greeting-content">The content is {{ .Content }}</p>
  </div>
</body>
</html>
```

Now if we run this application, we'll see we get output that looks almost exactly like our previous JavaScript sample, except that we didn't use any JavaScript and we didn't consume a RESTful endpoint.

As more web applications move toward the single-page application model using frameworks like Angular, React, etc., the need for server-side templating isn't as important as it was in the past.

# Processing Forms

Back in the glory days of building powerful web applications, form processing was the pinnacle of development. If you knew how to parse and validate forms, then you were an invaluable member of the web development team.

Go makes it incredibly simple to handle form values, which are just exposed as the `Form` property on the `request` struct. Form values are handled as a map of strings to a slice of strings (`map[string][]string`).

If you want to process the data that has been submitted from a form, then you simply need to access this collection and react accordingly.

The reason why we're not going to include a code sample of doing this manual type of form processing is that processing form values like this goes against some of the patterns we're going to be showing you later in the book.

If you use a framework like React to build extremely powerful, highly interactive pages within your application, then you will be using it to validate user input and you will be submitting that input to a RESTful endpoint exposed via the Go application, and *not* allowing the user to use the old-school form post method.

If you absolutely have to do manual form processing, then just access the `Form` map on the request struct, as shown in this sample handler that just dumps the form key-value pairs to the console:

```
func processFormHandler(w http.ResponseWriter, r *http.Request) {
    r.ParseForm()
    for k, v := range r.Form {
        fmt.Printf("Key %s, Val %s", k, strings.Join(v, ""))
    }
    fmt.Fprintf(w, "Form handled.\n")
}
```

> **Note**
>
> You cannot access the `Form` property without first calling either `ParseForm` or `ParseMultipartForm`, depending on what type of form you're receiving as input.

# Working with Cookies and Session State

As old fashioned as it might seem to have to deal with cookies, they are still used by the vast majority of session state management systems today. If you need to separate one browser from another and remember what someone has done since they logged into your site, you are likely using a cookie to do this. Even if you don't *know* you're using cookies (see our incessant nattering about *magic* throughout the book), you're still using cookies.

Thankfully, dealing with cookies is easy in Go, and cookies are already part of the `net/http` package, so we don't even need to go looking for a third-party package to do the job.

Cookies are written to the response and read from the request. It is the job of the browser to gather up the cookies that are relevant for the site to which it is making a request, and include those with every request to the site as appropriate. When a response comes back from the web application with a cookie, the browser must then write that cookie.

Every browser stores cookies in a different way, and this method even varies across operating systems for the same browser. While we can usually assume that cookie storage on the user's disk is secure and other sites and malicious users can't access that information, we need to be vigilant.

A good plan is to never store confidential or sensitive information in a cookie. For obvious reasons, don't store things like user credentials in cookies and, if you must store uniquely identifying information, make sure it's something that can do no harm if it falls into the wrong hands. Many good schemes write an identifier to the cookie that is randomly generated specifically for the cookie, and that ID is only mapped to useful information on the server after being received from an authenticated request.

As mentioned earlier, the unique identifiers in these cookies are often used to identify transient information like session state.

## Writing Cookies

Writing a cookie is a very easy process. The `Cookie` struct from the `net/http` package is defined as follows:

```go
type Cookie struct {
        Name   string
        Value string

        Path       string    // optional
        Domain     string    // optional
        Expires    time.Time // optional
        RawExpires string     // for reading cookies only

        // MaxAge=0 means no 'Max-Age' attribute specified.
        // MaxAge<0 means delete cookie now, equivalently 'Max-Age: 0'
        // MaxAge>0 means Max-Age attribute present and given in seconds
        MaxAge   int
        Secure   bool
        HttpOnly bool
        Raw      string
        Unparsed []string // Raw text of unparsed attribute-value pairs
}
```

At its core, a cookie is a name/value pair. You can further customize and tweak cookies to do all sorts of interesting things, but those things are well-documented elsewhere and have little to no bearing on how cloud native a particular application might be.

We can write a handler such that when we hit a RESTful endpoint with a web browser, we will get a cookie. Such a handler might look like this:

```go
func cookieWriteHandler(formatter *render.Render) http.HandlerFunc {
  return func(w http.ResponseWriter, req *http.Request) {
        expiration := time.Now().Add(2 * 24 * time.Hour)
        cookie := http.Cookie{Name: "sample",
          Value: "this is a cookie", Expires: expiration}
        http.SetCookie(w, &cookie)
        formatter.JSON(w, http.StatusOK, "cookie set")
  }
}
```

As you can see, writing a cookie boils down to just one function call: setCookie.

## Reading Cookies

Reading a cookie is just as easy as writing it. You can access a slice of all cookies for a given request with the Cookies function, or you can attempt to access a single cookie, as shown in this handler:

```go
func cookieReadHandler(formatter *render.Render) http.HandlerFunc {
  return func(w http.ResponseWriter, req *http.Request) {
        cookie, err := req.Cookie("sample")
        if err == nil {
                fmt.Fprint(w, cookie.Value)
        } else {
                fmt.Fprintf(w, "failed to read cookie, %v", err)
        }
  }
}
```

In this handler, we attempt to retrieve a cookie named sample and display its value in the browser. Finally, we can test this out by hitting a /cookies/write endpoint first and then hittin /cookies/read to see the value. We rig up these endpoints as follows:

```go
mx.HandleFunc("/cookies/write", cookieWriteHandler(formatter)).Methods("GET")
mx.HandleFunc("/cookies/read", cookieReadHandler(formatter)).Methods("GET")
```

# Build and Deploy with Wercker

So far we've been working with an extremely basic web application. It exposes access to static files like JavaScript, HTML files, CSS, and images. We've also seen how to modify that same service so that it can expose an API to be consumed by JavaScript running in that application's pages.

This is great, but this is only the beginning. It is a tiny nugget around which you'll likely want to build a much bigger application. Before doing that, you should make sure that your app is in a continuous delivery pipeline.

For that, as with all of the applications in this book, we're going to use Wercker. You can see the Wercker build definition for this sample at https://app.wercker.com/#applications/ 56a4f473212b43b24e0badbb, and the GitHub source code at https://github.com/cloudnativego/ web-application.

We've used Glide to manage this application's dependencies, which gives us version-locked vendored dependencies when we use Wercker to build. Before we switch modes from spiking on learning web application techniques to building real features, we're going to want to put in tests of our resources.

The following is a snippet of the build pipeline section of our `wercker.yml` file:

```
build:

  steps:
    - setup-go-workspace

    - script:
        name: go get
        code: |
          cd $WERCKER_SOURCE_DIR
          go version
          go get -u github.com/Masterminds/glide
          go get -u github.com/cloudnativego/cf-tools/vcapinate
          export PATH=$WERCKER_SOURCE_DIR/bin:$PATH
          glide install

    # Build the project
    - script:
        name: go build
        code: |
          go build

    # Test the project
    - script:
        name: go test
        code: |
          go test -v $(glide novendor)

    - script:
        name: copy files to wercker output
        code: |
          cp -R ./ ${WERCKER_OUTPUT_DIR}
```

With this in place, you can actually run this application as a self-contained Docker image with the following command:

```
$ docker run -p 8100:8100 cloudnativego/web-application:latest
[negroni] listening on :8100
```

If this is the first time you've downloaded the image, you'll see some console output showing the various slices of the Docker image being downloaded to your local cache.

## Summary

A properly designed web application is nothing more than a microservice that exposes static file endpoints as well as traditional service-style endpoints. There is nothing intrinsically cloud native or cloud "non-native" about the concept of a web application, but there are ways to do web apps very wrong in the cloud.

This chapter provided you with some lightweight examples of how you can combine your now-growing knowledge of building services in Go with the ability to serve up static files, template-processed files, and assets like JavaScript and images. Finally, we showed you how you can set up your Docker and Wercker configurations to automatically build and deploy web applications.

This web foundation will come in handy when you get to later sections of the book where we discuss concepts like security, web sockets, and patterns and libraries like React and Flux.

# 10

# Security in the Cloud

*"Security is always excessive until it's not enough."*

Robbie Sinclair, Head of Security, Country Energy, NSW Australia

Security is hard. It's messy, it's ugly, it's time consuming, and it's far less interesting to write code for than the rest of our application. As a result, most security-related coding tasks are often left until the last minute. When the last minute has arrived, people are usually scrambling to get the release out the door, and they need to make tradeoffs. Should we fix bugs or add new features? Since the security stuff hasn't even been started yet, it gets qualified as new features, and, in Hollywood jargon, gets *left on the cutting-room floor*.

It doesn't have to be this way. More importantly, it *cannot* be this way. If you're thinking of building applications for the cloud, you're thinking of building apps that can scale to support massive volume, apps that have instances running in multiple locations in the world, apps that are provisioned and started automatically without human intervention. You simply cannot leave security as an afterthought when building applications like this.

In this chapter we'll talk about:

- Options and implementation for securing a web application.
- How to secure microservices.
- A note on privacy and data security.
- A reader exercise to build more muscle memory around developing secure services.

## Securing a Web Application

In this section of the chapter we're going to take a look at securing web applications. While there's nothing inherently cloud native about security, there are some things to avoid and some patterns to embrace when securing web applications that you intend to deploy in the cloud.

## Web Application Security Options

At times it may seem like there is an infinite supply of different ways to secure your applications. There are dozens of technologies and each of those usually has several variations and multiple libraries and language APIs. The following list is far from complete, but gives you some idea of the options available:

- **HTTP Basic Auth**—Simple user name and password are hashed and sent to the web server by the client. While SSL prevents the password from being snooped, there are still a number of other vulnerabilities associated with Basic Auth, including browsers caching passwords, passwords being transmitted on every request, etc.

- **Forms** (Cookies)—This involves a web page (rather than the browser) prompting for credentials. The page then does some authentication of those and grants a cookie in response. There are also security issues when this approach is used in isolation.

- **Windows Authentication**—Historically this option has been preferred for applications being used for Intranet and enterprise sites, even if they are deployed on internal or private clouds. This is *not* a cloud native security option for a number of reasons.

- **SAML** (ADFS, AD Azure, Shibboleth, etc.)—*Security Assertion Markup Language* is a bearer token technology that involves identity providers that grant SAML tokens and applications that validate them and examine the claims asserted within. SAML is an industry standard used mostly for **identity federation**[1] and there are a number of APIs and server products available for multiple languages and operating systems.

- **OAuth/OpenID**—OAuth is an open standard for authorization and is extremely common among websites that allow users to log in with third-party credentials, such as Facebook, Google, Twitter, etc. There are a number of extremely good reasons to use OAuth and we will be using it in this chapter.

- **Custom**—Those who are unwilling to learn from the mistakes of the past are doomed to recode them again in the future.

> **Warning**
>
> Do not ever choose a security mechanism that relies on the existence of features, key stores, or user account information in the underlying operating system. You can rely on these things, so long as you expect them to be external or backing services. Your security implementation needs to work *without regard for the virtual host on which it runs*.

Throughout the rest of this chapter we'll be developing two code samples: a secured web application and a secured microservice.

To start with, we're going to use OAuth for our web application authorization mechanism. There are a number of reasons for this choice, including:

---

1  https://en.wikipedia.org/wiki/Federated_identity

- It makes no assumption about underlying OS or installed features.

- It is designed specifically for allowing disparate systems on the web to share authorization claims.

- It is simple and easy to use.

- It is a solid and proven technology.

- Availability of simple, easy-to-use Go libraries.

- Availability of free, open source identity provider server software.

- Access to cloud-based identity providers like Google, Auth0, and StormPath.

## Setting up an Auth0 Account

OAuth doesn't work without a service to grant a JWT (JSON Web Token, a URL-safe JSON format for expressing claims that can be transferred between parties). Identity providers are responsible for validating a user's identity and granting a JWT in response to a valid identity. Your application can then crack open the JWT and gain access to user information necessary for maintaining a user profile without ever having asked your user for a password.

You could use Google Web Applications to set up an identity provider. You could also use the open source UAA service from Cloud Foundry or the Pivotal Cloud Foundry Single-Sign-On tile. For the purposes of this book, to keep things as simple as possible with as few swipes of a credit card as possible, we're going to use a service called **Auth0**. Auth0 is a cloud security provider.

We can configure an Auth0 account to maintain a private database of users (including allowing users to self-register!), or we can configure which third party identities it will accept on behalf of our website. In this way we can configure our site to allow logins from Twitter, LinkedIn, Facebook, Google, and many other applications. Or, as we'll do in the sample for this book, we'll choose a private database.

To create an Auth0 account, head over to http://auth0.com and read up on the services they provide. Like all the services we've used for this book, you can sign up without having to supply a credit card.

You can use whatever source of user identity you like and the code samples in the rest of this chapter will work without requiring a single change. This is another one of the many reasons we like using external identity providers for cloud applications. Once you are logged in, you'll be able to see a dashboard like the one in Figure 10.1. Auth0 gives you extensive metrics, dashboards, and controls over your authentication system.

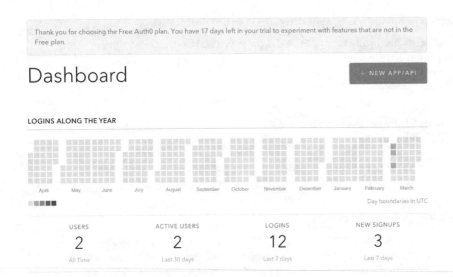

Figure 10.1   Auth0 Dashboard

Source: http://auth0.com

## Building an OAuth-Secured Web App

Now that we have an Auth0 account set up, all we really need to do is create a web application that works with it. This means that when we encounter an unauthenticated request, we need to redirect over to Auth0 to get a valid token.

If we get a request that contains a token, then we need to crack open the token and expose that user information to our handler methods somehow. There is a lot going on in this sample so we're going to try and keep it as simple as possible so we can focus on the really important pieces.

You can find the full source code for this application at https://github.com/cloudnativego/secureweb. The first thing we need to do is set up a server. We've done this a number of times throughout the book so much of the code in Listing 10.1 shouldn't be a surprise.

Listing 10.1   **server/server.go**

```go
package server

import (
        "net/http"

        "github.com/astaxie/beego/session"
        "github.com/cloudfoundry-community/go-cfenv"
        "github.com/cloudnativego/cf-tools"
        "github.com/codegangsta/negroni"
        "github.com/gorilla/mux"
)
```

```go
type authConfig struct {
        ClientID     string
        ClientSecret string
        Domain       string
        CallbackURL  string
}

func NewServer(appEnv *cfenv.App) *negroni.Negroni {
  authClientID,_ := cftools.GetVCAPServiceProperty("authzero", "id", appEnv)
  authSecret,_:= cftools.GetVCAPServiceProperty("authzero", "secret", appEnv)
  authDomain,_:= cftools.GetVCAPServiceProperty("authzero", "domain", appEnv)
  authCallback,_:= cftools.GetVCAPServiceProperty("authzero", "callback",
                  appEnv)

  config := &authConfig{
        ClientID:     authClientID,
        ClientSecret: authSecret,
        Domain:       authDomain,
        CallbackURL:  authCallback,
  }

  sessionManager, _ := session.NewManager("memory",
   '{"cookieName":"gosessionid","gclifetime":3600}')
  go sessionManager.GC()

  n := negroni.Classic()
  mx := mux.NewRouter()

  initRoutes(mx, sessionManager, config)

  n.UseHandler(mx)
  return n
}

func initRoutes(mx *mux.Router, sessionManager *session.Manager,
  config *authConfig) {
  mx.HandleFunc("/", homeHandler(config))
  mx.HandleFunc("/callback", callbackHandler(sessionManager, config))
  mx.Handle("/user", negroni.New(
        negroni.HandlerFunc(isAuthenticated(sessionManager)),
        negroni.Wrap(http.HandlerFunc(userHandler(sessionManager))),
  ))
  mx.PathPrefix("/public/").Handler(http.StripPrefix("/public/",
   http.FileServer(http.Dir("public/"))))
}
```

In the preceding listing, the first thing you may have noticed that differs from our previous samples is the use of a session state manager. Here we're using a third-party library to enable a cookie-keyed session state system. We're going to use this session state to remember the information we take off an authentication token so we can use that information when rendering web pages.

Not included in the listings in the book is the source code for the callback handler, which we copied directly from Auth0's samples. You can find that code in our GitHub repository.

> ### Session State Warning
>
> To keep this sample focused on security, we used the simplest possible session state management we could, an in-memory cache. A production application needs to scale to multiple instances, which is incompatible with this type of session state. Your production-grade apps will need to use an external cache (e.g. Redis) or cookies or some combination to allow proper scaling.

The next thing we're doing is making use of middleware. Negroni embraces the middleware concept, allowing us to inject pre- and post-handlers and to wrap handlers with code like an authentication check. In Listing 10.1, we're wrapping the userHandler function with the isAuthenticated middleware. This will force an authentication before our userHandler is invoked.

In other frameworks for languages like Java and .NET, you may have seen functionality like this supported with attributes or annotations.

Listing 10.2 shows the code for our middleware function, isAuthenticated.

### Listing 10.2  server/middleware.go

```
package server

import (
        "net/http"

        "github.com/astaxie/beego/session"
        "github.com/codegangsta/negroni"
)

func isAuthenticated(sessionManager *session.Manager) negroni.HandlerFunc {
  return func(w http.ResponseWriter, r *http.Request, next http.HandlerFunc) {
        session, _ := sessionManager.SessionStart(w, r)
        defer session.SessionRelease(w)
        if session.Get("profile") == nil {
                http.Redirect(w, r, "/", http.StatusMovedPermanently)
        } else {
                next(w, r)
        }
  }
}
```

This code is extremely simple. In every handler wrapped with this middleware, we attempt to pull the authenticated user's profile from the session. If such a profile doesn't exist, then we redirect away to the home page.

On the home page handler, shown in Listing 10.3, we expose some JavaScript via server-side templating that creates a login button. This login button takes our users over to Auth0 to be prompted either to login or register. When the user redirects back from Auth0, they'll have an authentication token.

Listing 10.3   **server/home_handler.go**

```go
package server
import (
  "net/http"
  "text/template"
)
var bodyTemplate = '
  <script src="https://cdn.auth0.com/js/lock-8.2.min.js"></script>
  <script type="text/javascript">
  var lock = new Auth0Lock('{{.ClientID}}', '{{.Domain}}');
  function signin() {
    lock.show({
    callbackURL: '{{.CallbackURL}}'
    , responseType: 'code'
    , authParams: {
    scope: 'openid profile'
  }
  });
  }
  </script>
  <button onclick="window.signin();">Login</button>
  '

func homeHandler(config *authConfig) http.HandlerFunc {
  return func(w http.ResponseWriter, r *http.Request) {
    t := template.Must(template.New("htmlz").Parse(bodyTemplate))
    t.Execute(w, config)
  }
}
```

The authentication token that comes back from Auth0 is parsed by our `callbackHandler`. This function cracks open the token, validates it, and then stores the user information in a profile object that gets stuffed into session state. As mentioned, this is all boilerplate we got from Auth0.

Listing 10.4  **server/user_handler.go**

```go
package server

import (
        "fmt"
        "net/http"

        "github.com/astaxie/beego/session"
)

func userHandler(sessionManager *session.Manager) http.HandlerFunc {
  return func(w http.ResponseWriter, r *http.Request) {
        session, _ := sessionManager.SessionStart(w, r)
        defer session.SessionRelease(w)

        // Getting the profile from the session
        profile := session.Get("profile")
        fmt.Fprintf(w, "USER DATA: %+v", profile)
  }
}
```

In Listing 10.4, we're taking advantage of the existence of a user profile in the session. In this extremely simple sample, we're just dumping the user profile data. However, in a full-fledged web application, we would make the user profile data available as an object exposed to the server-side template processor.

What we've demonstrated in very few lines of code is that we can secure a web application written in Go with OAuth as easily as we could do it for any other language or framework. If your friends tell you that you can't have easy-to-configure, robust security in your Go web applications, you should get rid of those friends. You don't need people like that in your life.

## Running the SecureWeb Application

The easiest way to run the application is to clone it from GitHub (https://github.com/ cloudnativego/secureweb). Type the following in your terminal window:

```
./runlocal
```

This is a script we wrote to allow you to run the application inside a Wercker docker image, using a little templating magic to allow you to inject some values for your Auth0 account.

When run without any parameters, it displays some usage information, instructing you on how to build an environment file to prep the application for running. To do this, create a file called env in the local_config directory. It should look like this:

```
X_AUTHZERO_ID=(your auth0 ID)
X_AUTHZERO_SECRET=(your auth0 secret)
X_AUTHZERO_DOMAIN=(your auth0 domain, e.g. foo.auth0.com)
X_AUTHZERO_CALLBACK=http://192.168.99.100/callback
```

Because our Docker machine default runs on the IP address 192.168.99.100, that's how we've set up the callback (remember that the Wercker build runs inside a Docker image).

Before any of this will work, you have to set up your Auth0 account. The simplest way to set it up is to allow it to use social networking authentication so you don't have to configure your own database. However, if you want private credentials, then you can create your own database, but you have to make sure that you *link* the database you created to the application you created in Auth0 (all of this is documented on their site).

Finally, you will need to add the value you supplied for X_AUTHZERO_CALLBACK to the list of authorized callback URLs for your application.

Now run your application with your configuration:

```
$ ./runlocal local_config/env
```

You'll see a bunch of Wercker and Docker spam and then your application will come up on port 80. Open a browser to http://192.168.99.100 (or whatever the IP address is of your Docker machine). You should see a simple login button. Click it, and you'll get a screen that looks like the one shown in Figure 10.2.

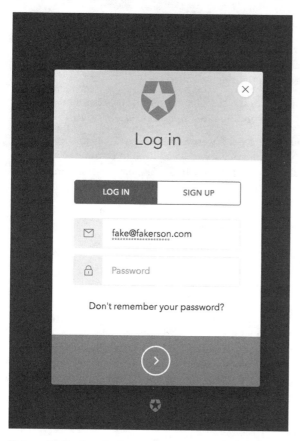

Figure 10.2   Logging Into Our Application via Auth0

Source: Auth0

After either signing up or logging in as an existing user, you'll be redirected back to our application via the callback URL. When our callback handler has finished processing the OAuth token and populating session state, it then redirects to the /user URL.

The user handler then dumps the user profile stored in session state so we can see the kinds of information available to our application. Of particular interest are the `alias`, `email`, and `picture` fields, which are invaluable for helping personalize a user's experience on a secure website.

# Securing Microservices

In this section of the chapter, we're going to cover how to secure a microservice. Earlier we walked through how easy it is to take a web application and wrap it in OAuth security, but that relies on being able to redirect between your web application and an identity provider.

In this next section, we'll talk about how to secure microservices that don't have any UI and cannot participate in any authentication scheme that requires redirects.

## Overview of the Client Credentials Pattern

There are as many authentication patterns for services as there are architects in the world. Many developers often go and implement their own proprietary token dispensary and validation system that only works on services within their organization.

Others use client certificates, or encryption, or some combination of tokens, certs, and encryption. The pattern we're going to discuss here is among the simplest: *client credentials*.

When we signed up as a user for the Auth0 service, we were granted an **API key** and an **API secret**. We use those to tell the Auth0 service that our service is allowed to communicate with it. When we use the Google Maps API, the Facebook API, Twitter's API, or countless others, we run into a very simple pattern where our code must use a key and secret pair to authenticate.

What this boils down to is that there needs to be a discrete difference between authenticating the human consumer of our services, and the *client* code consuming an individual service. There are two questions we're asking, each with different ramifications:

- What is the identity of the human that originally initiated the request?
- Is the service making the request authorized to do so?

In some cases, our service doesn't care about human identity. For example, a service that returns warehouse availability for individual SKUs doesn't care whether this request is being performed at the behest of a human or by other parts of the system. In fact, as a best practice, this service *should never care* whether it is doing work on behalf of a human or another service. Of course, as with all rules, there are exceptions. In this case, you might make an exception if the service was wrapped in RBAC (Role-Based Access Control) and thus needed to know the identity of the request initiator in order to determine whether to execute the request or reject it with *401 Unauthorized* or *403 Forbidden*.

> ### Tip—403 vs 401
>
> We often see secured RESTful services that return 401 when your credentials aren't good enough. This is technically not the way the 401 code should be used. Code *401 Unauthorized* should be used when an attempt has been made to access a secure resource and *no credentials were provided*. *403 Forbidden* should be used when an attempt to access a secure resource was made, credentials *were* supplied, but the calling client was determined to have insufficient privilege to perform the request. There is a subtle, but important distinction here. Keeping this in mind when securing a web service may save you some trouble in the future, especially if you're building a public API.

Many enterprise service ecosystems feel the need to carry the originator's identity throughout an entire chain of service calls. For compliance and auditing purposes, sometimes this is required, but you should try and avoid tightly coupling your services to the assumption that they are being consumed by people unless that really is the only way your services work.

In the *client credentials* pattern, a client service passes a pair of values to a service with each request it makes. This value pair is most often referred to as a *key* and *secret* but can also be labeled as a *username* and *password*. The latter is usually avoided for the same reasons we've already discussed—you should never assume anything about why and by whom your service was invoked. Just authenticate and respond to requests and nothing more.

## Securing a Microservice with Client Credentials

We've already seen how to implement middleware that opens up a JSON Web Token (JWT) issued by an OAuth identity provider to authenticate requests to a web application.

We can use the same middleware pattern to secure routes to our microservice. The only difference will be in the implementation of the middleware. First, let's take a look at the simple server code that sets up a secure root (/api/*) that will be authenticated using client credentials.

Listing 10.5   **server/server.go**

```
package server

import (
        "github.com/codegangsta/negroni"
        "github.com/gorilla/mux"
        "github.com/unrolled/render"
)

//NewServer configures and returns a Server.
func NewServer() *negroni.Negroni {
  formatter := render.New(render.Options{
        IndentJSON: true,
```

```
    })

    n := negroni.Classic()

    // Public Routes
    router := mux.NewRouter()
    router.HandleFunc("/", homeHandler)

    // Protected API Routes
    apiRouter := mux.NewRouter()
    apiRouter.HandleFunc("/api/get", apiGetHandler(formatter)).Methods("GET")
    apiRouter.HandleFunc("/api/post", apiPostHandler(formatter)).Methods("POST")

    router.PathPrefix("/api").Handler(negroni.New(
            negroni.HandlerFunc(isAuthorized(formatter)),
            negroni.Wrap(apiRouter),
    ))

    n.UseHandler(router)
    return n
}
```

In the code in Listing 10.5, we've set up our security such that all of the routes bundled with apiRouter will be secured by the middleware function isAuthorized. This pattern should look familiar and you'll see it used everywhere in idiomatic Go.

Next, Listing 10.6 shows the implementation of the isAuthorized function.

Listing 10.6   server/middleware.go

```
package server

import (
        "net/http"
        "os"

        "github.com/codegangsta/negroni"
        "github.com/unrolled/render"
)

func isAuthorized(formatter *render.Render) negroni.HandlerFunc {
  apikey := os.Getenv(APIKey)
  return func(w http.ResponseWriter, r *http.Request, next http.HandlerFunc) {
        providedKey := r.Header.Get(APIKey)
        if providedKey == "" {
          formatter.JSON(w, http.StatusUnauthorized,
            struct{ Error string }{"Unauthorized."})
        } else if providedKey != apikey {
```

```
      formatter.JSON(w, http.StatusForbidden,
          struct{ Error string }{"Insufficient credentials."})
    } else {
      next(w, r)
    }
  }
}
```

This function uses an environment variable to determine the expected value of the API key required for authenticated consumption. In a real-world application, we would compare both a *key* and a *secret* against some backing store of authorized clients.

## A Note on SSL

The keen observer may have noticed that we haven't written a line of code that appears to do anything related to SSL. There is an extremely good reason for this: *we hate writing SSL code.* More importantly, *you should too.*

There are a myriad different infrastructure tools that deal with SSL certificate validation and SSL termination. There are so many, and they are so ubiquitous, that it has essentially become an anti-pattern to tightly couple the code in your microservice to any particular SSL implementation or rule enforcement.

Whether you are manually deploying your code behind a reverse proxy that terminates SSL on your behalf, or you're deploying your code to Cloud Foundry that does SSL termination for you, your app shouldn't have to deal with the low-level SSL details unless you're explicitly whitelisting client certificates, and even that can be done outside your microservice in a gateway.

# A Word on Privacy and Data Security

Security is an overloaded term. There are countless different types of security. We have already talked about two of the main types of application and service security: securing access to your web application to only authenticated users and securing access to your services using client credentials.

Another type of security that has been in the news a lot lately is **data security**. Any discussion of building massive-scale applications in the cloud and security would be incomplete without at least mentioning this topic.

There was a time when enterprises dealt with security by making sure that their data centers were in remote, undisclosed locations, and guarded day and night by trained staff. They would put firewalls around every component of their network, and lock down their databases and their printers and everything in between. This is how Hollywood would have you believe secrets are guarded in the mythical world of Jason Bourne and James Bond.

This "hide behind the walls" mentality has merit, but does it really apply in the era of the cloud? What if you don't have physical access to your own servers? Can you put a uniformed security guard outside the door when half of your infrastructure can float from New York to Nebraska to California seamlessly, or when the number of running copies of a database can scale up or down at a moment's notice?

## Hackers Can't Get What You Don't Have

One universal rule of hacking is that given enough time and resources, *any* infrastructure can and *will* be compromised. If you spend all of your worst-case scenario planning trying to prevent an intrusion and spend no time thinking about what happens *when* the intrusion occurs, your company's name will be plastered across both paper and social media alike and the customers whose information you lost will find somewhere else to take their business.

So what happens if someone does penetrate your service and somehow gain unauthorized access? What do you do then? If you've been following the *way of the cloud* and your applications adhere to the 12 factors of cloud native applications, then you will have built a *stateless* service that uses *externalized* configuration. In other words, there will be nothing compromising in the memory space of your service, and an intruder will not be able to see the URLs and credentials used to communicate with your backing services.

Let's assume someone got into one of your databases, and had full access to roam around and query whatever they like. What would they find? Would it be useful or profitable to them?

The key to deterring data theft isn't in making it impossible, it is in making it impractical and *unprofitable*. If it takes the hacker too much time to find what they're looking for, they'll move on to juicier targets. If, when they do get into your database, and all of the useful information is encrypted (and the *keys are stored somewhere else!*) or that useful information is stored in *yet another* database, then the hacker is also likely to move on to less prepared targets.

Here are some *very general* rules of thumb when designing secure systems for the cloud. This list is not exhaustive, and if you are really interested in the topic of information security, that is a deep subject that we can't even scratch the surface of in this book.

- Never store compromising information *adjacent to* the information of the person who could be compromised. For example, if you must store credit card numbers, don't store them in the same database as the people who own them, and for the love of unicorns and kittens *do not use the social security number as the correlating key*. Better yet, when a customer supplies a credit card, use a third party to exchange the card number for a token that has no meaning or value outside the context of your application.

- If a hacker can make money or do damage with the contents of a field, *encrypt it at rest* and *encrypt it in motion*. There are a number of shrink-wrapped offerings that can keep data encrypted all the way until it reaches the customer who owns it.

- Never, ever, EVER (ever!) store the decryption key anywhere near the encrypted data to which it applies. This is like leaving your house key in the flowerpot and then putting up a sign saying, "Don't look in the flowerpot, it's a secret."

- Never emit PII (personally identifiable information) to STDOUT or STDERR. You would be shocked at how many attacks are possible by sniffing a relatively insecure log stream rather than compromising the actual system. Developers *love* to emit diagnostic details like "About to store record in repository..." and they use a shortcut like the `%+v` marker in Go ... and the entire contents of the record, including field names, are dumped into the log stream.

- In the interest of both statelessness *and* security, never store any confidential information in memory longer than it takes to process a request.

Finally, there is the guideline of the three R's. While not a *rule*, it is a philosophy many of us try and embrace in every environment in which we work:

- **Rotate, Repave, Repair**—In an article by Justin Smith, he discusses the notion of rotating data center credentials every few minutes, repaving servers frequently, and repairing operating systems right after patches are available.

I once had a conversation about this topic with a brilliant security professional. He indicated that to get any meaningful data from his system, a hacker would have to compromise three databases in three different zones, plus a fourth location to get the encryption keys. If someone was able to compromise this much of his system, information security would be the least of his problems.

# Reader Exercise

In this chapter we built a web application that was secured by OAuth using a third party identity provider, Auth0. We also built a secure web service that validated clients by querying for an API key.

As a reader exercise, we would like you to make this example a little more real-world as well as bring some more integration to it. We'd like you to integrate the secure web application with the secure web service to simulate an extremely common, real-world scenario.

1. Add a resource to the secure service that requires a piece of information about the user consuming the resource. For example, you could create a resource collection like `/customer/email address/orders`, which would dump order information for a customer indicated by that e-mail address. Make sure to include the email address in the JSON response from the service so you know it works for different customers.

2. Add a web page to the secure web application that displays information obtained from the secure web service. For example, you could create a "my orders" page that renders the list of orders retrieved from the secure service.

   a. To make this happen, you'll need to extract the user's e-mail address from the session state (there's already an example of accessing this data in the existing sample), and use it to build the REST request to the secure service.

    b.  You'll also want to create a user-provided service so that the URL of the backing service is not hardcoded in the web app. There are patterns throughout the book of getting the URL of dependent services, both in and out of Cloud Foundry.

Once you've completed this, you should have an extremely good feel for what it's like to build a web application that relies upon backing services. You'll also have a good indication as to the level of work required and complexity involved in securing both the web application and its services.

## Summary

Security can never be an afterthought. Even if you explicitly decide that your application can be used with no authentication, that decision must be explicit. Nothing about the security of your application or its data can be an accident.

This chapter walked you through an overview of some of the main concepts around how applications can be secured in the cloud and discussed some of the more common and popular strategies like bearer tokens.

While we didn't cover every possible topic related to security, after reading this chapter you should hopefully have a foundation upon which you can begin asking more informed questions about securing applications and services in the cloud.

# 11

# Working with WebSockets

*"Simplicity is prerequisite for reliability."*

Edsger W. Dijkstra

Some of us are old enough to remember the days of the web when it was expected that you had to hit the *refresh* button on your browser to see new data. It wasn't until fairly recently that websites truly started embracing the interactive style, where users could expect the page to update itself as necessary.

Despite this being a recent innovation, it is now ubiquitous. Just about everyone using web applications *demands* such reactive behavior. If your web application isn't dynamically updating information and notifying the user of important changes to their data, your customers are going to flee in droves. If someone impacts our data in our browser and our browser is unaware of it, we're going to find another web application to use, right after we take to Twitter for an epic rant to end all rants.

WebSockets and Server-Sent Events (SSE) are two technologies that help deal with the problem of providing a more intuitive and interactive browser experience. In this chapter, we'll talk about these technologies and, more importantly, what kind of impact they have on cloud native development.

In this chapter, we will:

- Examine WebSockets and their applicability to the cloud.

- Use a third-party messaging provider to build a WebSocket-style application.

# Demystifying WebSockets

For many developers who spend most of their time working on servers and backends, the idea of WebSockets may feel like magical UI stuff that we can safely ignore. Unfortunately, this isn't the case. Today's web applications, even some of the simplest you can find, make use of WebSockets everywhere.

When you're sitting on your Facebook feed, catching up on how everyone's life is so much better than your own, and you see a notification indicating that someone liked that amazing video of cats you posted yesterday, you're seeing WebSockets (or SSEs) in action.

When you order a pizza from Domino's and you watch the themed progress bar change as your pizza goes from the concept phase to completion to delivery without refreshing your browser tab, you're seeing WebSockets (and possibly the downfall of society as we know it) in action.

## How WebSockets Work

As the web demanded the ability to have bi-directional communication between the server and the browser, they also required that it still somehow work on top of existing HTTP standards without breaking the traditional, "request only" web model.

WebSockets work by *upgrading* your HTTP connection. This is *always* initiated by the client by hitting an endpoint on the server and including the `Connection: Upgrade` header, as shown below:

```
GET /game HTTP/1.1
Host: server.mygame.com
Upgrade: websocket
Connection: Upgrade
Sec-WebSocket-Key: x3JJHMbDL1EzLkh9GBhXDw==
Sec-WebSocket-Protocol: awesomegame
Sec-WebSocket-Version: 13
Origin: http://mygame.com
```

There are also some WebSocket-specific headers, such as a key, protocol, and version. The key and version are used by the high-level WebSocket protocol itself. The `Sec-WebSocket-Protocol` header allows your client to establish a custom handshake with the server to agree upon a standard or definition of the *content* of the newly upgraded WebSocket channel. In this case, we've requested that we use the `awesomegame` protocol. If the server is aware of this, then it will reply accordingly. This doesn't prevent mismatch errors between server and client, but it does give us a chance to try and level-set prior to doing any real work.

We should then get a response from the server indicating that the connection has been upgraded from a regular HTTP connection to a WebSocket connection:

```
HTTP/1.1 101 Switching Protocols
Upgrade: websocket
```

```
Connection: Upgrade
Sec-WebSocket-Accept: HSmrc0sMlYUkAGmm5OPpG2HaGWk=
Sec-WebSocket-Protocol: awesomegame
```

At this point we have now left open an HTTP connection and we are using it to ferry back and forth WebSocket traffic rather than traditional HTML content. Of course, we don't write JavaScript that manually issues the connection upgrade. Instead, we just write code using the standard JavaScript WebSocket libraries (or whatever wrapper our favorite JS framework has exposed):

```
var socket = new WebSocket('ws://server.mygame.com');
```

Once we have the socket variable, we can define the function that will be invoked every time data is *pushed* from the server to the JavaScript running in our browser, and we can use the send method to send data up to the server.

## WebSockets vs. Server-Sent Events

Server-sent events are a slight variation on WebSockets. They are lighter-weight, but they are also uni-directional. As their name implies, they can only be used to *push* data from the server to the browser. Because of this, many large scale web applications often favor this approach rather than using full WebSockets.

Some of the key differences between WebSockets and SSEs are:

- WebSockets are full-duplex; SSEs are, as the name implies, server-send-only.

- WebSockets can sometimes have issues with older routers and proxies due to the connection upgrade, where WebSocket traffic is not contained within a traditional HTTP connection.

- The more complex an app, the more HTTP connections you need for SSEs, while many apps, despite their complexity, can manage with just a single WebSocket connection for each user.

In this chapter, we're going to be discussing WebSockets, though the vast majority of the discussions and design patterns can be applied to SSEs as well.

## Designing a WebSocket Server

You've decided that you love WebSockets and you now want to expose WebSocket functionality to the JavaScript in your application's front-end. If you're using any modern server-side web development framework, then you probably have an "easy button" that just lets you write a little bit of code in your handler function (or controller method, if you're doing MVC). Even with such an easy button, there are a number of things that need to be done:

- Support connection upgrades.

- Support and handle full-duplex WebSocket network connections.

- Maintain some sort of map of all connected WebSockets.

  - Looping through this map to send the same data will *broadcast* a message to everyone on your site.

  - Finding a specific socket (likely keyed by user) will allow the delivery of a message to a single target, e.g. notifying you when your cat video gets another like.

  - Clean up this map when WebSocket connections are closed.

## On WebSockets and Cloud Nativity

Knowing what we know about WebSockets and the tasks that we have to perform on the server in order to support them, what does this say about how well WebSockets play in the cloud?

First, let's take a look at *statelessness*. All truly cloud native applications are stateless. The fact that we have to maintain references to all of the open WebSockets in order to simply function as a proper WebSocket server should raise alarms. When we start adding maps on top of the sockets that identify the individual owners of those sockets, it gets even more worrisome.

If our application goes down, we lose all the WebSockets. Many of you have likely seen this happen and might not have known the underlying cause. You're sitting on your social media feed and it suddenly stops updating. Nothing new is happening! The cats have stopped playing their pianos!! Finally, as a last resort before full-on panic, you hit the *refresh* button and, thankfully, the page behavior returns to normal. This is a classic example of a WebSocket connectivity loss.

The stateful nature of WebSockets has even more insidious consequences when we scale horizontally. Being able to dynamically grow the number of instances of our application to deal with increasing load is an *essential* part of deploying applications to the cloud. Unfortunately, this also causes problems with WebSockets.

Let's imagine that you're playing a multiplayer in-browser game with a friend and, naturally, you're winning. The experience is fantastic and communication between you and your friend is seamless, including the ability to send insulting private messages to him as you play.

Now what happens if the game becomes super popular and we're now running eight instances of the app in the cloud? The game is a single-page app that does most of its communication via WebSockets as well as some REST calls to augment data in response to WebSocket messages.

You log on to resume your game on **instance one** of the app. Your friend logs in on **instance four**. When he sends a private message to you, the instance is going to look up the socket that should belong to you by checking the *in-memory map*. Since your socket is actually sitting on **instance one**, your socket won't be found. An error like this might get suppressed, or surface in weird ways on your friend's game. The net result is that, despite both being connected to the game, and both of your clients thinking they have functioning connections to the server, you and your friend cannot communicate.

This architecture is illustrated in Figure 11.1 below:

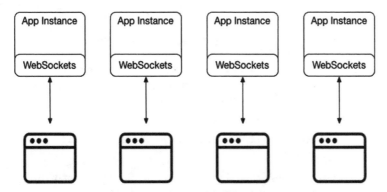

Figure 11.1    WebSockets and Bad Horizontal Scaling

Whether we're using SSE or WebSockets, or whether we're rolling our own WebSocket server implementation or we're using one that came with our framework, we still have a big problem with creating impenetrable silos around each of our app instances. Data and notifications cannot be sent from one instance to the other.

If we want any browser connected to our server to be able to participate in message exchanges with any other browser, *regardless of the number and location of our application instances*, then we're going to have to extract our WebSockets component away from our instances and hide it behind a facade. We can either implement our own facade or we can take advantage of any number of existing messaging services already set up for cloud enablement.

Such an architecture is illustrated in Figure 11.2.

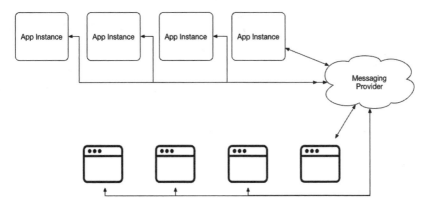

Figure 11.2    Scalable, Cloud-Friendly WebSockets Architecture

In the next section, we'll take a look at some sample code that implements the architecture illustrated in Figure 11.2.

## Building a WebSocket App with a Messaging Provider

In order to build a WebSocket application with a messaging provider, we're going to need a messaging provider. As with all decisions to use third parties that we've made in this book, we wanted something that was easy to use, reliable, well-supported, and, most importantly, would not require a credit card up front to start experimenting.

It is our opinion that any service that requires you to pay before you try their service lacks confidence that you'll feel you got your money's worth.

One messaging provider that provides publish-subscribe messaging (among a plethora of other features) is **PubNub**. PubNub is available as a marketplace service in Pivotal Web Services and they are available to use directly simply by going to their website (http://www.pubnub.com) and signing up for a free account.

If you find you like their publish-subscribe messaging (the simplest of their offerings), then you might really like some of their other features such as presence and data streams.

One major advantage of using a publish-subscribe system is the ability to segment your messaging traffic by intent or by audience. For example, if you're building a multiplayer game and your servers don't need to see the contents of chat messages, then that entire facility could be handled by your messaging middleware, leaving your microservices blissfully unaware of chat traffic and allowing them to focus on the important game messages.

If we want to enable our web pages to communicate with the messaging system, we can use code like what is shown in Listing 11.1 to subscribe to a channel as well as publish to it.

Listing 11.1    **assets/templates/index.html** (JavaScript snippet)

```
<script src="http://cdn.pubnub.com/pubnub-3.14.4.min.js"></script>
<script>
  var source = "{{ .Email }}";

  pubnub = PUBNUB({
      publish_key   : '{{ .PubKey }}',
      subscribe_key : '{{ .SubKey }}'
  })

  console.log("Subscribing..");

  pubnub.subscribe({
      channel : "hello_world",
      message : function (message, envelope, channelOrGroup, time, channel) {
        console.log(
        "Message Received." + "\n" +
        "Channel or Group: " + JSON.stringify(channelOrGroup) + "\n" +
```

```
          "Channel: " + JSON.stringify(channel) + "\n" +
          "Message: " + JSON.stringify(message) + "\n" +
          "Time: " + time + "\n" +
          "Raw Envelope: " + JSON.stringify(envelope)
        );
        var newDiv = document.createElement('div')
        newDiv.innerHTML = message
        var oldDiv = document.getElementById('chatLog')
        oldDiv.appendChild(newDiv)
      },
        connect: pub
    })

  function pub(txt) {
      console.log("About to publish: " + txt);
      pubnub.publish({
          channel : "hello_world",
          message : "[" + source + "]: " + txt,
          callback: function(m){ console.log(m);}
      })
  }

function publish() {
  console.log("Going to publish on demand")
  txt = document.getElementById("theText").value;
  pub(txt)
};
```

The {{ }} bracket syntax should look familiar to you if you remember the chapter on web applications where we explored server-side templating. This allows us to inject information the server obtained, such as configuration as well as OAuth identity information (discussed in Chapter 10).

We make this information available in the template so that the rendered JavaScript has variables that match the server-side data. The vast majority of this code is sample taken from the PubNub website. Essentially, it subscribes to the hello_world channel and, upon connection, immediately publishes a message to the channel. Then, we have a publish function that can be invoked from a button that sends the contents of an HTML text input control prepended by the current user's e-mail address.

The users of our application could all have a complete, real-time conversation in their browsers without ever invoking any RESTful handlers in our Go code. What your server needs to route through messaging middleware and what it doesn't is an architectural decision that is up to you and should be a choice you make without regard to what vendor or technology you're using for messaging.

If we want our server to also be able to send messages on this channel, which will then be displayed in the browsers of connected users, then we can write a handler that looks like the one in Listing 11.2. Again, most of this is taken from PubNub's sample code.

Listing 11.2  **server/broadcast_handler.go**

```go
package server

import (
        "fmt"
        "net/http"

        "github.com/pubnub/go/messaging"
        "github.com/unrolled/render"
)

func broadcastHandler(messagingConfig *pubsubConfig) http.HandlerFunc {
    formatter := render.New(render.Options{
        IndentJSON: true,
    })

    pubnub := messaging.NewPubnub(messagingConfig.PublishKey,
        messagingConfig.SubscribeKey, "", "", false, "")
    channel := "hello_world"

    return func(w http.ResponseWriter, r *http.Request) {
        successChannel := make(chan []byte)
        errorChannel := make(chan []byte)
        go pubnub.Publish(channel, "[SYSTEM] Broadcast from the server!",
          successChannel, errorChannel)

        select {
        case response := <-successChannel:
                fmt.Printf("pubnub publish response: %s\n", string(response))
        case err := <-errorChannel:
                fmt.Printf("pubnub publish error: %s\n", string(err))
        case <-messaging.Timeout():
                fmt.Println("pubnub publish() timeout")
        }
        formatter.JSON(w, http.StatusOK, nil)
    }
}
```

Here we're doing a little work with Go's channels and goroutines. We use the `go` statement to *asynchronously* push a message onto the `hello_world` channel. We then use the `select` statement to *block* and wait for a message to arrive on the success, failure, or timeout channels. Whichever channel gets a message *first* will unblock the select statement and execute the corresponding case.

We strongly urge you to check out the code in the GitHub repository (https://github.com/cloudnativego/websockets) and play around with it. It was built with the security sample as a starter, so it will use OAuth to identify you before you navigate your browser to the /chat page.

## A Note on JavaScript Frameworks

You may have noticed that the code we wrote in our HTML page to communicate with the messaging provider and manipulate the page DOM was primitive and somewhat ugly. This is actually by design.

We wanted to show you the bare bones of what it looks like to interact with a messaging provider *without* bogging you down in the details of any particular UI framework or bulky and cumbersome toolchain. This is absolutely one of those situations where we show you the ugly way so that you'll appreciate the more elegant way (Chapters 12 and 13) all the more.

Also please check out PubNub's website for more samples and documentation for the rest of their features. Cloud-based messaging middleware enables a degree of real-time programmability for websites that would have seemed impossible just a few years ago. We would be foolish to ignore services like this when designing and building our own reactive applications.

## Running the WebSockets Sample

To run the sample that we've included in github, you will need to pull the latest version of it from the repository. Next, run `glide install` to make sure you have the dependencies defined by the Glide lock file in your vendor directory (these dependencies are not checked into GitHub).

Next, make sure you've got an environment file in the `local_config` directory just like you did for the `secureweb` sample from the previous chapter. In addition to supplying your Auth0 credentials, you'll also need to supply the publish and subscribe keys from your PubNub account.

If you don't yet have a pubnub account, you should head over to https://www.pubnub.com/ and create one now.

At this point you should be able to run `./runlocal local_config/env`. This will start the web server inside the Wercker build's Docker image.

You can now open your browser to the IP address of your Docker machine (e.g. 192.168.99.100) and go through the OAuth login routine that you went through in the previous chapter. Once you get redirected to the user info screen, just change the URL to /chat and you should be able to participate in a conversation that looks like the one in Figure 11.3.

Also note that you can POST to the /broadcast resource to trigger the Go code to send a broadcast message to all chat clients:

```
$ curl -X POST http://192.168.99.100/broadcast
```

**Welcome, fake@fakerson.com**

the server is talking to m   [ SEND ]
[fake@fakerson.com]: hello_world
[fake@fakerson.com]: hello?
[fake@fakerson.com]: CHAT ALL THE THINGS!!
[SYSTEM] Broadcast from the server!
[fake@fakerson.com]: the server is talking to me! This is amazeballs!

Figure 11.3   Sample Chat Session

The first image is the book's logo (a cloud native gopher!). The second image was created for us by Auth0 since our user (*fake@fakerson.com*) doesn't have a stored image or a registered Gravatar.

In the sample transcript, you can see the browser getting push notifications of a user submitting chat text, as well as the Go code running in the server process also sending messages on the PubNub channel as system broadcasts.

As an exercise, you should deploy this to a server where more than one person can access it (preferably a cloud, like PWS), and take note of how it behaves with multiple users and browsers open, as well as how it behaves with the same person logged into multiple tabs in a browser.

## Summary

Given what we now know about the CQRS and Event Sourcing patterns, being able to build a web application that can receive push notifications from a server and react to them becomes fairly important.

In this chapter, we learned a little bit about the difference between traditional WebSockets and why we need a third-party messaging provider to do *cloud native* web sockets. We saw how to integrate a third-party messaging provider into both our Go services as well as JavaScript running in a browser.

# 12

# Building Web Views with React

*"Java is to JavaScript what Car is to Carpet."*

Chris Heilmann, Web Evangelist

We can build microservices until we're blue in the face, and create the most powerful and scalable back-ends imaginable, but most of us don't have the luxury of stopping there. At some point, a human being will likely need to interact with our application.

As we will discuss in this chapter, if someone is going to use a browser to interact with our application (or a mobile device), they will probably do so using JavaScript. JavaScript is an inescapable force permeating every corner of the web.

In this chapter we'll provide a little bit of perspective and context around JavaScript and what that landscape looks like today and where we think it's heading. True to our opinionated stance throughout this book, we'll be picking a JavaScript framework, React, and using it to build a simple single-page web application, and we will carry this knowledge and experience forward to use with the rest of the samples and content in the book.

Our aim is not to make you React experts, or even to teach you React. Instead, we want to show you how you can integrate React applications with the Go skills we have been developing up to this point so that you'll be ready for the final chapter.

In this chapter we will:

- Take a look at the fundamentals of React and why we chose it.

- Examine the anatomy of a React application.

- Build a basic React application.

- Illustrate how to test React apps.

- Suggest strategies for learning more about React.

## JavaScript State of the Union

We can only hide behind the elegant, pristine walls of our Go ecosystem for so long. Once we step into the morass of the JavaScript ecosystem (perhaps *mosh pit* would be more appropriate), we must get down off our high horse and set aside most of our hardline stances on consumption of third-party libraries, code cleanliness and elegance, dependency management, and simplicity.

In short, JavaScript is a hot mess.

If you sit down and ask the omniscient Google, "How do I solve problem X in JavaScript?", you will surely be inundated with millions of possible responses. The problem is there isn't a clear distinction between the right answer and the wrong answer. The truth is that for nearly every front-end, web-based UI problem you have, there are a staggering number of frameworks and libraries that purport to ease your woes.

If you're looking to build single-page apps and love the model-view-controller (MVC) pattern, then you might look into AngularJS. Of course, you've also got Backbone, Cappuccino, Ember, Meteor, Knockout, SproutCore, React, and countless others. Likely by the time this book has been published, another dozen frameworks will have appeared and the list we just included will seem horribly out of date.

If you're just looking for pure GUI and want a good library of widgets, then look no further than AngularJS. Or maybe Bootstrap. Or CycleJS or ExtJS, or jQuery UI, or... you get the idea.

JavaScript is an endless sea of frameworks, all floating to the surface like so much flotsam. The single hardest task you will have in building web applications isn't in writing the code, it is in deciding which frameworks you're going to adopt, and how strong your stance will be on that adoption. Among all the floating bits of debris, how do you find the treasure?

There is no single answer to that question. However, in the next section we'll talk about the decision we made, and how we came to that conclusion.

## Why React?

To build the user interfaces that we know are inevitable, we decided to go with React (https://facebook.github.io/react/). React is a JavaScript library for building user interfaces. It is not an MVC system, nor is it an all-encompassing library that attempts to "abstract all the things".

Throughout the book we have been open and transparent about our opinions, the decisions we've made, and why we made them. The same is true with React. However, as we go through the reasons why we chose React, keep in mind that as a human being you have the right to question and challenge windbag authors. Critical thinking is the only reason we aren't all using QuickBASIC right now.

We strongly encourage you to do some googling of alternatives to React and see if you end up in the same place we did when considering not just the framework overall, but how the framework enables massive-scale GUIs designed to thrive in the cloud.

Also check out SurviveJS (http://survivejs.com/). Here you will find an invaluable set of objective comparisons between React and other frameworks as well as detailed tutorials to learn an opinionated set of basics.

## The Virtual DOM

Whether you're using jQuery or AngularJS or any number of other libraries, whatever high-level abstraction you use to manipulate the contents of the browser ultimately resorts to making direct changes to the browser's DOM.

If you haven't experienced the special kind of pain this can cause, then you should consider yourself lucky. When building modern, reactive applications that can receive stimulus from users and servers alike asynchronously, you frequently end up spending inordinate amounts of time building guard clauses to protect the DOM from being stomped on by competing interests.

Direct manipulation of the DOM is also really inefficient, *especially* when you're dealing with frequent changes. If you're getting assaulted with an incoming stream of tiny changes to your UI, you're now going to have to write your own code to batch those changes, aggregate them, and then make changes on some regular interval. In essence, we end up building frame rate emulators in our apps just to avoid twitchy, jittery interfaces and poor performance from high-frequency DOM updates.

A **virtual DOM** solves these problems and gives us additional benefits. Since your React code manipulates a virtual DOM, React can then manage funneling changes down to the real DOM in a way that avoids write contention and optimizes performance.

Finally, one of our favorite benefits of the virtual DOM is that the virtual DOM concept is portable. You can use tools like React Native (https://facebook.github.io/react-native/) to allow your React code to work on mobile devices like Android and iOS. React Native takes your virtual DOM and makes changes to the mobile device GUI instead of a browser DOM, all while keeping your code at a level higher than the device.

### Caution

One of the most frustrating newbsauce problems we encountered when originally evaluating React was that it's really easy to *think* that you're creating real DOM elements when they are actually virtual DOM elements. It's very easy to forget that layer of abstraction and wonder why you can't simply pass-through HTML attributes directly.

## Component Composition

More than any other library we experimented with, React allows for the smallest impedance mismatch between whiteboard architecture and actual implementation. It does this through **component composition**.

When you're standing at a white board, and you're roughing out the high-level pieces of your GUI, you draw boxes, not actual controls with UIs. These boxes have smaller boxes inside them, and those might have even smaller boxes within them.

Let's say you're building a web page that monitors zombie virus outbreak activity. You might say out loud, "We're going to have a list of outbreak reports. The reports each have a source station, links to more details, and a severity indicator."

When you go to implement your components in React, you might end up with the following:

- A component called `OutbreakReports`. This renders a list of `OutbreakReport` components.

- A `SourceStation` component that displays the origin of the outbreak report.

- A `SeverityIndicator` that graphically displays (this is where it could get fun) the severity of the outbreak.

Once you get past the learning curve for React, the way you define and compose components feels extremely natural. We're not going to lie, there *is* a learning curve. However, despite it feeling intimidating at first, especially to people who spend most of their time on the server side, React is definitely one of the easier frameworks to learn. This is both a bonus for React and a sad statement about the JavaScript UI framework community as a whole.

## Reactive Data Flow

React uses what they call **one-way reactive data flow**. This means is that everything you build is designed to *react* to incoming changes in state. One of the reasons we like React so much is that it embraces the spirit behind Event Sourcing and CQRS at the UI level. If you remember back in Chapter 8, we spent a tremendous amount of time discussing the scalability, flexibility, and performance benefits you get when you shift mindset from "everything is mutable" to "all change is done as a reaction to immutable messages."

When we talk about *Flux* in the next chapter, you'll see this concept exploited to allow the kind of scale and performance you get from the Facebook web site, which deals with tens of millions of requests per second and each of those millions of users is getting an extremely responsive, interactive experience.

## Narrow Focus

React does not attempt to abstract or encapsulate everything. It doesn't want to extend its tentacles into your network communications with the server or your persistence mechanisms or anything else you do when no one is looking.

Instead, React has a singular focus—the UI. It aims to provide you with a framework for building composable components that interact with a virtual DOM. This narrow focus makes us happy, and satisfies our goal for simplicity and makes it easier for us to take a dependency on a framework like this.

## Ease* of Use

We've sat and watched as service developers have set up their first React application. We've also cackled with a level of glee usually reserved for mad scientists and super-villains as they exclaim, "What do you mean my bundle file has 35,000 lines?!"

React is actually *relatively* easy to use. It's simple, it's straightforward, and it doesn't try to do more than one thing. That said, it is a *JavaScript* library. This means you're going to have to deal with tools like npm, and webpack, and accept some level of chaos that you might not ordinarily be used to dealing with.

If the crisp, clean, elegant world of Go is a tidy workspace, the world of JavaScript is a clutter-strewn desk replete with spilled coffee cups, unidentifiable stains, and a potpourri of stale odors that may never come out of your clothes.

This experience is jarring to the average Go developer, but we feel that React is one of the best performing, elegant, and simple frameworks out there, and it is an ideal choice for the UI layer of any cloud native application. Once you get over the initial shock and the frustration of the learning curve wears off, React (especially Flux) can feel refreshing and almost enjoyable to use.

Believe it or not, the chaos is far, far worse with some of the other libraries with which we experimented. Some of those frameworks will be supplying nightmare fuel for years to come.

# Anatomy of a React Application

Every React application has a number of puzzle pieces that all must fit together nicely in order for everything to run properly. Like any good JavaScript framework, if one of these pieces is incorrect, everything could explode in spectacular fashion.

This next section provides a brief overview of the aspects of a React application that you will see every time you work with them.

## The package.json File

The package.json file is a project file. It contains the metadata that describes the package, which is especially important if you intend to publish this package to make it available to others via npm. This file also contains a definition of scripts, which are commands invoked via npm such as build, start (we prefer the command name of watch instead of start), or test.

Listing 12.1 shows what our `package.json` file looks like for the sample we're going to build:

**Listing 12.1   package.json**

```json
{
  "name": "react-zombieoutbreak",
  "version": "1.0.0",
  "description": "A Zombie Outbreak monitor app written in React.",
  "repository": {
    "type": "git",
    "url": "https://github.com/cloudnativego/react-zombieoutbreak.git"
  },
  "main": "index.js",
  "scripts": {
    "test": "echo \"Error: no tests\" && exit 1",
    "build": "webpack",
    "watch": "webpack-dev-server"
  },
  "keywords": [],
  "author": "",
  "license": "ISC",
  "devDependencies": {
    "babel-core": "^6.7.2",
    "babel-loader": "^6.2.4",
    "babel-plugin-array-includes": "^2.0.3",
    "babel-plugin-transform-class-properties": "^6.6.0",
    "babel-plugin-transform-object-assign": "^6.5.0",
    "babel-plugin-transform-object-rest-spread": "^6.6.5",
    "babel-preset-es2015": "^6.6.0",
    "babel-preset-react": "^6.5.0",
    "babel-preset-react-hmre": "^1.1.1",
    "css-loader": "^0.23.1",
    "style-loader": "^0.13.0",
    "webpack": "^1.12.14",
    "webpack-dev-server": "^1.14.1",
    "webpack-merge": "^0.8.3"
  },
  "dependencies": {
    "react": "^0.14.7",
    "react-dom": "^0.14.7"
  }
}
```

## Webpack.config.js

Webpack (and in turn *Babel*) is responsible for running through all of our JavaScript on the server-side and producing a single *bundle* that can be used in the browser. Webpack has a ton of configuration and listing it here would likely confuse more than elucidate.

For more information on the contents of this file, take a look at SurviveJS (mentioned a few times throughout this chapter) or any of the other online React references.

## The .babelrc File

Babel is the tool that converts your browser-agnostic JavaScript into something the browser can understand. There are a lot of different options for this, allowing you to take advantage of newer versions of JavaScript on the server than you can in the browser.

You configure the different plugins and translators you want to use in your `.babelrc` file. Here's a sample one for the project we're building in this chapter:

```
{
  "presets": [
    "es2015",
    "react"
  ],
  "plugins": [
    "transform-object-rest-spread",
    "transform-class-properties",
    "transform-object-assign",
    "array-includes"
  ],
  "env": {
    "watch": {
      "presets": [
        "react-hmre"
      ]
    }
  }
}
```

From this file, you can see that all of our pre-processed JavaScript will conform to the ES2015 standard as well as utilize React. We're also using a few fairly standard plugins.

## Understanding JSX and Webpack

The single goal of our entire collection of JavaScript files in our application directory is to produce a bundle. This bundle is an optimized JavaScript file that works well in browsers. As you'll see in this chapter, the code we're going to write in JavaScript is not straight-up browser-compatible JavaScript (and that's a good thing).

In essence, we're isolated from the browser dependencies of the JavaScript engine by compiling our JSX files (JavaScript files that can contain embedded virtual DOM markup) and additional JavaScript files into a single unit called a **bundle**.

## React Components

The real magic of React happens in the components. These are JSX files that are processed by webpack, trans-compiled by babel, and eventually generate functioning JavaScript that will end up in our bundle.

React components let us divide our page's UI into logical pieces that, as we mentioned earlier, often has a nearly identical correlation to how we might whiteboard out our page's architecture.

By convention, we typically start with an outermost component called App. This component renders itself into a root <div/> element. Component composition and the generated React code bundle is then responsible for rendering our views and handling user interaction with them.

For example, we might have a root App component that contains within it a GameBoard component. Within the GameBoard component we might have a Background component and a bunch of GamePiece components.

This composition makes it incredibly easy to build up powerful user interfaces as well as maintain and troubleshoot them.

# Building a Simple React Application

The zombie apocalypse is upon us. Outbreaks are everywhere, and death awaits us around every corner and within every shadow. What are we going to do? Why, *write an app*, of course!

As much as we would like to escape boilerplate entirely, we can't—especially when dealing with JavaScript applications. Rather than setting up the skeleton of each project yourself, we suggest you copy the full sample React application from GitHub (https://github.com/cloudnativego/react-zombieoutbreak) or one of the other templates we have in the repository.

The project anatomy that we discussed in the previous section largely represents the boilerplate or skeleton, leaving us to define the component model. In our application, we're going to have a root App component. Within that, we'll have an Outbreaks component that renders a list of OutbreakReport components.

We're going to look at the code from a bottom-up point of view, examining first the lowest-level component and moving up the hierarchy from there to the root application.

The OutbreakReport component, shown in Listing 12.2 has two rendering modes—one while in the editing state and one while in the default state. While editing is enabled, you can edit the description of the outbreak report. Note that to keep the code simple and easy to read, we deliberately didn't enable editing all of the other fields on an outbreak report.

Listing 12.2  **OutbreakReport.jsx**

```jsx
import React from 'react';

export default class OutbreakReport extends React.Component {
  constructor(props) {
    super(props);

    this.state = {
      editing: false
    };
  }

  render() {
    if (this.state.editing) {
      return this.renderEdit();
    }

    return this.renderOutbreakReport();
  }

  renderEdit = () => {
    return (
        <div>
          <div className="date">{this.props.outbreak.date}</div>
          <div className="origin">{this.props.outbreak.origin}</div>
          <div><br/></div>
          <div className="severity">{this.props.outbreak.severity}</div>
          <div className="description">
            <input type="text"
                ref={
                    (e) => e ? e.selectionStart =
                      this.props.outbreak.description.length : null
                }
                autoFocus={true}
                defaultValue={this.props.outbreak.description}
                onBlur={this.finishEdit}
                onKeyPress={this.checkEnter} />
          </div>
        </div>
      );
  }

  edit = () => {
    this.setState({
      editing: true
    });
  };
```

```
  checkEnter = (e) => {
    if(e.key === 'Enter') {
      this.finishEdit(e);
    }
  };

  finishEdit = (e) => {
    const value = e.target.value;
    if(this.props.onEdit) {
      this.props.onEdit(value);

      this.setState({
        editing: false
      });
    }
  }

  renderOutbreakReport = () => {
    const onDelete = this.props.onDelete;

    return (
      <div>
        <div className="date">{this.props.outbreak.date}</div>
        <div className="origin">{this.props.outbreak.origin}</div>
        <div><br/></div>
        <div className="severity">{this.props.outbreak.severity}</div>
        <div className="description"
          onClick={this.edit}>{this.props.outbreak.description}</div>
        {onDelete ? this.renderDelete() : null }
      </div>
    );
  }

  renderDelete = () => {
    return <button
      className="delete-outbreak" onClick={this.props.onDelete}>X</button>;
  }
}
```

The renderEdit method renders the component while in the editing state, which contains
a standard HTML input tag with a few attributes that hook up various events to the methods in
this component. The renderOutbreakReport method renders the non-editing version of the
component.

If you click on the description of an outbreak report, the component will switch into editing mode and present you with the input. Once you hit enter, tab out, or otherwise exit the input control, the component returns back to read-only state.

Listing 12.3 shows the code for the `Outbreaks` component, which is responsible for rendering a list of outbreak reports. Compared to the individual report component, this code is tight and compact.

Listing 12.3  **Outbreaks.jsx**

```
import React from 'react';
import OutbreakReport from './OutbreakReport.jsx';

export default ({outbreaks, onEdit, onDelete}) => {
  return (
    <ul className="outbreaks">{outbreaks.map(outbreak =>
      <li key={outbreak.id} className="outbreak">
       <OutbreakReport outbreak={outbreak}
           onEdit={onEdit.bind(null, outbreak.id)}
           onDelete={onDelete.bind(null, outbreak.id)}
       />
      </li>)}
    </ul>
  );
}
```

If the `onEdit.bind` and `onDelete.bind` syntax bothers or confuses you here, don't worry. This is one of those things that looks fairly natural to JavaScript developers but looks very foreign to back-end and service developers.

We're passing a reference to a method down into this list from the `App` component, which is in turn passed down to the individual outbreak report component. This keeps the event handler type functions in the `App` component. As we'll see in the next chapter when we discuss Flux, this is pretty ugly and we won't use this in production applications.

Finally, let's take a look at the source for the `App` component in Listing 12.4.

Listing 12.4  **App.jsx**

```
import React from 'react';
import uuid from 'node-uuid';
import Outbreaks from "./Outbreaks"

export default class App extends React.Component {

  constructor(props) {
    super(props);
```

```
      this.state = {
        outbreaks: [
          {
            id: uuid.v4(),
            origin: "Station Gamma",
            severity: "Yellow",
            description: "This was bad",
            date: "03-04-2016 12:00"
          }
        ]
      }
    }

    render() {
      const outbreaks = this.state.outbreaks;

      return (
        <div>
          <button onClick={this.addOutbreak}>New Report</button>
          <Outbreaks outbreaks={outbreaks} onEdit={this.editOutbreak}
              onDelete={this.deleteOutbreak}/>
        </div>
      );
    }

    deleteOutbreak = (id, e) => {
      e.stopPropagation();
      this.setState({
        outbreaks: this.state.outbreaks.filter(outbreak => outbreak.id !== id)
      });
    };

    editOutbreak = (id, description) => {
      if(!description.trim()) {
        return;
      }
      const outbreaks = this.state.outbreaks.map(outbreak => {
        if(outbreak.id === id && outbreak) {
          outbreak.description = description;
        }
        return outbreak;
      });
      this.setState({outbreaks});
    };

    addOutbreak = () => {
      var d = new Date();
```

```
    var datestring = ("0" + d.getDate()).slice(-2) + "-" +
        ("0"+(d.getMonth()+1)).slice(-2) + "-" +
        d.getFullYear() + " " + ("0" + d.getHours()).slice(-2) +
        ":" + ("0" + d.getMinutes()).slice(-2);

  this.setState({
    outbreaks: this.state.outbreaks.concat([{
      id: uuid.v4(),
      origin: 'Alpha Fortress',
      severity: 'Green',
      date: datestring,
      description: 'New Report'
    }])
  });
 };
}
```

Here, `editOutbreak`, `addOutbreak`, and `deleteOutbreak` provide the handlers for the CRUD functionality you would normally expect with a single-page JavaScript application. What may feel awkward to you is that all of this code is just sitting in the root component, and isn't stuffed into a controller.

This is absolutely one of those times where the teachers (in this case, windbag authors) are being jerks and showing you the hard way before they give you the more elegant solution. Understanding how this React application works this way, and playing with it before moving on, will put you in a far better position to understand the *what*, *why*, and *how* of Flux in the next chapter.

With everything ready (you grabbed the sample from GitHub, right?) we can ensure that all of our dependencies are installed properly in the `node_modules` sub-directory:

```
npm install -i
```

This goes through all of our project files and puts all the dependencies we need into the right place. With these ready to go, we can run our application in a live-updating web server that makes it particularly easy to tinker with the React sample:

```
npm run watch
```

At this point we should now see output that looks like this:

```
$ npm run watch


> react-zombieoutbreak@1.0.0 watch /Users/khoffman/Code/Go/src/github.com/
cloudnativego/react-zombieoutbreak
> webpack-dev-server
```

```
http://localhost:8080/
webpack result is served from /
content is served from /Users/khoffman/Code/Go/src/github.com/cloudnativego/react-
zombieoutbreak/assets
404s will fallback to /index.html
```

```
webpack: bundle is now VALID.
```

We can now open a web browser to the address provided and we can run our application. Take note of the sample outbreak report the application starts with, then experiment with adding and deleting reports as well as clicking the report descriptions to change those.

Once we're done tinkering with the live-updating version of the app, let's build a more permanent version of it that we can eventually use to deploy to the cloud. To do this, we need to generate our bundle.js file with the following command:

```
$ npm run build
```

```
> react-zombieoutbreak@1.0.0 build /Users/khoffman/Code/Go/src/github.com/
cloudnativego/react-zombieoutbreak
> webpack
```

```
Hash: f0b5b5e1d84529a3067a
Version: webpack 1.12.14
Time: 1636ms
    Asset     Size  Chunks           Chunk Names
bundle.js   813 kB       0  [emitted]  app
   + 189 hidden modules
```

We now have a bundle.js file sitting in the assets directory. With this in place, we can build our Go application (included in the sample and the templates) and run it:

```
$ go build
$  ./react-zombieoutbreak
[negroni] listening on :8100
```

Notice that the default port number for the Go application is 8100 while the default for the dynamic, live-updating version of the application (non-Go) was 8080.

It's totally up to you as to which one of these you use for development, but we *strongly* recommend that you do all of your React development with the live-updating Webpack server. Otherwise, you will find yourself getting carpal tunnel from stopping your Go server, re-generating your bundle, and re-starting the server.

Figure 12.1 shows an example of our fantastic UI. Try and contain your shock as we explain that we are not graphic designers.

Figure 12.1    React Application UI

There are some nice little bits of CSS that we borrowed heavily from other sources in order to get a nice shadow and border effect around the report over which the mouse is hovering, but other than that the UI is as basic as it gets.

Our goal is to show you how to hook up React UIs to cloud services you're building in Go, not to teach how to build rich user interfaces. There are countless books already available on that subject.

Once you have this running, you should absolutely experiment with changing various aspects of the code and see which pieces of the UI update automatically versus which ones require you to refresh your browser. You should almost never have to stop and start the Webpack watcher.

## What We Didn't Like

The sample we built in this chapter is contrived, overly simplistic, and doesn't make any network calls. However, it's easy to figure out where some of the problem points might be once we start adding complexity.

The biggest problem is what we do when we have a far more complex page hierarchy, and we have multiple components all on the same page that need to be alerted when things change. React's virtual DOM makes re-rendering in response to state change nice, but force-feeding event handlers down to nested controls is not going to scale. We're going to want a new abstraction for state management while still maintaining the elegance of the component model.

We'll start experimenting with *Flux* in the next chapter, which should address some of the concerns we have about the React application we built in this chapter.

## Testing React Applications

Testing React applications could be a subject for another book, or at least a large chunk of a separate book on React. Throughout this book we've been very strict about testing all of our Go code. However, we felt that spending a full chapter on writing unit tests for React applications would dilute our main goal of building cloud native services and applications in Go.

The basic idea behind testing React applications is you add another command to the `package.json` file to run your tests. If you've looked at the one in our template, you'll see we just display a message indicating there are no tests.

If you're using a JavaScript testing suite like Karma (which requires a whole separate pile of boilerplate and dependencies in your project), then you would just add a command to `package.json` that invoked `karma start`.

As with any other unit tests, your goal would be to invoke methods on your components and assert that their state has been modified accordingly. You'll have to check out in-depth React references to get into the details of how to assert the state or contents of the virtual DOM.

## Further Reading

As we've said numerous times throughout this chapter, our goal here is not to teach you everything you need to know about React. Our aim with this chapter was to give you enough information about React so that you could get to the next few chapters where we delve into Flux and then put together all of the techniques we've used throughout the book to create a fully functioning application.

### React Websites

As we were exploring React and its many alternatives, the single best reference we found was SurviveJS by Juho Vepsäläinen. This book provides an amazing guide to material that has a serious learning curve, taking you on a progression from the simplest concepts to the most powerful and complex. Vepsäläinen also expresses opinions and chooses among multiple frameworks and explains why, favoring simplicity and explicitness. These opinions align nicely with the way we feel about Go code. To explore or buy this book, go to http://survivejs.com/.

## React Books

Other React-specific books that you might find useful are:

- *Learning React Native: Building Native Mobile Apps with JavaScript* by Bonnie Eisenman
- *Pro React* by Cassio de Sousa Antonio
- *React: Up and Running: Building Web Applications* by Stoyan Stefanov

## Other Materials

Udemy (http://www.udemy.com) has a course called *Build Web Apps with ReactJS and Flux* that may provide an easier-to-consume course on the topics we're covering in this chapter and the next.

# Summary

This chapter was the first of two that cover UI technology. While the focus of this book is on *cloud native Go*, we felt it necessary to provide at least some coverage of how to to build *highly scalable* user interfaces that consumed services exposed by Go.

While not every microservice is going to be consumed by a front-end, knowing how to practically apply all of the knowledge learned so far in the book is extremely useful.

# 13

# Creating UIs that Scale with Flux

*"The risk of a wrong decision is preferable to the terror of indecision."*

Moshe ben Maimon (1135–1204 CE)

In the previous chapter, we took a look at React, a JavaScript framework that focuses solely on the views within your browser. It takes a strong, opinionated stance on one-way data flow, and its controls are all rendered in response to notifications of state change and the reverse should never happen.

This felt like a diversion from our steady progression of building up our Go microservice development skills. This chapter is also going to focus more on the UI, though we will be creating a microservice that supports our highly scalable front-end.

In this chapter, we'll discuss:

- The Flux pattern and choose an implementation of it.
- Building an application that uses Flux designed to support high-volume usage.

## Introducing Flux

As with the rest of JavaScript, Flux is confusing. However, we feel that it offers enough benefits to make the learning curve worth it if you're building massive scale web UIs. If you are going to do anything more complicated than the sample in this book, you're going to want to spend some time reading documentation and consulting other books.

The first thing that you need to know is that Flux is *not* an implementation. Flux is not a library or a set of code. It is an architectural pattern. You can think of Flux as an alternative to MVC. Both MVC and Flux are patterns, each with many different implementations.

Flux builds on the one-way data flow concept introduced in React and adds additional concepts such as the **store**, the **source**, and **actions**. The main goal behind Flux is to give us working concepts that we can use to separate data and application state from our views.

If you remember from the previous chapter, our OutbreakReport component was littered with state query and state manipulation code. Further, we had a ton of state management code stuck in the top-level application component and had to do all sorts of ugly binding and forwarding in order to manage our views.

Flux fixes this problem with the introduction of stores and actions. Figure 13.1 shows an overview of how data flows between components in a Flux architecture.

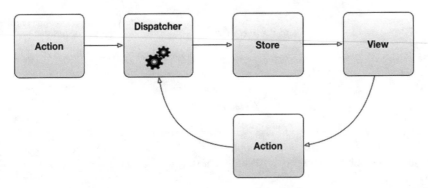

Figure 13.1    Data Flow in Flux

In the next section we'll talk about each of these components in a little more detail.

## Dispatcher

The dispatcher is responsible for broadcasting payloads to registered callbacks. As its name implies, the dispatcher is responsible for all of the central coordination of data flowing through the system.

Looking at the arrows in the diagram above, you can see that even though Flux has added a few more concepts to the basic React architecture, data is still flowing *in one direction*. It flows from the dispatcher to stores, and from stores to views.

## Store

The store is an abstraction around some arbitrary piece of data. If your component or application needs to maintain data or state, that will be in a store. This also implies that the components will *not* maintain their own state as is the case with React. Events coming from the dispatcher notify the store of changes to state. Changes in the store then trigger the view to render.

Again, it's important to point out that unlike some other two-way binding architectures (like AngularJS), views do not directly manipulate state nor can they communicate directly with the store.

## View

The view is your React component. This is the component that boils down to a single `render` function (even if you're using a wrapper or abstraction around that function). This function is called whenever a page loads, and called every time a store the view is interested in changes.

## Action

Actions are generated either by users or by any other stimulus. They can indicate that a user clicked a button, or they can indicate that something else happened that requires a change to state, such as receiving a message from a web socket or messaging provider.

The key thing to remember about actions is that, in an event-sourcing world, these map to *commands*. A command could be something like "reload the table" or "sort by last name" or "add a new record" or "delete record". Actions are handled by the dispatcher, which then broadcasts the appropriate information so that stores can react accordingly.

## Source

A component of the sample we're going to build that isn't in the architectural diagram in Figure 13.1 is the *source*. Stores rarely ever exist in a complete vacuum, isolated to within the confines of the page in which they were loaded.

For example, we could have a store that maintains a to-do list, which is then rendered by the `Todos` component, which in turn renders individual `Todo` components. While it might be illustrative for a sample to contain this data privately within the page, ideally we want the source of the data in the store to come from a backing service. In our case, we want these to be backing services written in Go.

As we'll show in the sample application, we'll be responding to the right events so that when our store needs to dispatch data or respond to requests to change data, it can communicate with the source to get that done.

## Complexity in Flux

At this point you're probably wondering why there are so many abstractions. We've spent the majority of this book harping on the fact that we must favor simplicity, so now we're looking at something that seems to go against this rule.

We also have another rule, and that is to favor explicit over implicit. While this may seem controversial to many developers, as developers of Go microservices in the cloud, it has served us quite well.

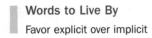

**Words to Live By**

Favor explicit over implicit

Building a JavaScript-based user interface that can respond to stimulus from the user, communicate with a RESTful service, and possibly respond to inbound stimulus from WebSockets is extremely complicated. Doing this on your own usually results in a huge pile of spaghetti that is impossible to maintain.

On the flipside, doing this with frameworks that do everything for you (in other words, "magic"), result in a smaller amount of code but when you go to troubleshoot you have absolutely no idea what's going on or how to diagnose and repair problems. You end up with a fantastic, magical unicorn that no longer works and you can't fix it.

What we like about this model with Flux is that while you have a large number of components, they are all *extremely small* components that all have a single responsibility. Also, you don't typically need to write your own dispatcher. As we'll see in the sample we're going to build, depending on the implementation of Flux you use, some of the boilerplate can be hidden.

What we get with Flux is a unidirectional data flow through extremely small, microservice-like components within our page. This means that we might have some initial sticker shock when we see the number of files we're creating for an app, but when something goes wrong, or we need to add a feature, we know exactly where to look.

The *explicit* nature of this architecture is far more valuable than the *magical* nature of some of the other frameworks when it comes to maintenance, support, and adding features rapidly.

## Building a Flux Application

In this section we're going to take the React sample we built in the preceding chapter (the zombie apocalypse tracker) and simplify the state management and component design through the addition of three new concepts: **actions**, **sources**, and **stores**.

Recalling the App.jsx component from the previous sample, it was an extremely cumbersome top-down design. We injected our event handlers into the top-level component, which was then forwarded all the way down the component hierarchy. We used awkward binding syntax and everything felt very forced and bloated.

If you want to see the finished conversion, check out our GitHub repository https://github.com/cloudnativego/flux-zombieoutbreak. In our Flux example, we have extracted all of our state management code into a **source** and a **store**. We've extracted all notifications of important events into a set of **actions** which are then subscribed to by interested parties.

Take a look at our new, simplified `App` component in Listing 13.1:

Listing 13.1    **App.jsx**

```jsx
import React from 'react';
import Outbreaks from "./Outbreaks"
import OutbreakStore from '../stores/OutbreakStore'
import OutbreakActions from '../actions/OutbreakActions'

export default class App extends React.Component {

  constructor(props) {
    super(props);

    this.state = OutbreakStore.getState();
  }

  componentDidMount() {
    OutbreakStore.listen(this.storeChanged);
    OutbreakStore.fetchOutbreak();
  }
  componentWillUnmount() {
    OutbreakStore.unlisten(this.storeChanged);
  }

  storeChanged = (state) => {
    this.setState(state);
  };

  addOutbreak = (event) => {
    OutbreakActions.addOutbreak();
  }

  render() {
    const outbreaks = this.state.outbreaks;

    return (
        <div>
          <button onClick={this.addOutbreak}>New Report</button>
          <Outbreaks outbreaks={outbreaks}/>
        </div>
    );
  }
}
```

In this component, once it has mounted (initialized), we're indicating that we're going to listen for changes to the `OutbreakStore` via the `storeChanged` handler, and then we're going to invoke an initial fetch. In our case this initial fetch retrieves mock data, but we could easily modify our source to retrieve data from a RESTful service.

Take a few minutes to compare this code to the code in the last chapter (https://github.com/cloudnativego/react-zombieoutbreak). While we have a few more files now, responsibilities have been separated and things are arguably much easier to read and maintain.

It might not seem like it for such a small application, but once we get into the realm of larger and more complicated apps (like the one we build in the next chapter), this type of segregation will be invaluable.

In Listing 13.2, we see *actions*. We invoke these methods when we want to send a change back through the dispatcher. The values we return from the actions will eventually end up as parameters to the *store*, which can then be used to affect state change.

You can think of this as a page-local publish-subscribe system where the components are publishers and the stores are subscribers, and the dispatcher is, well, responsible for dispatching.

Listing 13.2  **OutbreakActions.js**

```
import alt from '../lib/alt';
import uuid from 'node-uuid';

class OutbreakActions {
  updateOutbreak(outbreak) {
    return outbreak;
  }

  fetchOutbreak() {
    return [];
  }

  deleteOutbreak(outbreak) {
    return outbreak;
  }

  changeOutbreak(outbreak) {
    return outbreak;
  }

  outbreakFailed(errorMessage) {
    return errorMessage;
  }
```

```
    addOutbreak() {
      var d = new Date();
      var datestring = ("0" + d.getDate()).slice(-2) + "-" +
          ("0"+(d.getMonth()+1)).slice(-2) + "-" +
         d.getFullYear() + " " + ("0" + d.getHours()).slice(-2) + ":" +
          ("0" + d.getMinutes()).slice(-2);

      var newOutbreak =
        {
          id: uuid.v4(),
          origin: "Station Gamma",
          severity: "Yellow",
          description: "This was bad",
          date: datestring
        };
        return newOutbreak
      }
}

export default alt.createActions(OutbreakActions);
```

Rather than our components making changes to state directly like they did in the previous sample, we now follow a much more *event-sourcing* like model. When something happens, we indicate it via an action. The stores listen for actions and respond by changing their internal state. Change in state within a store then causes *only the affected components* to re-render themselves.

In these methods, we *return* the data we are affecting, we don't directly manipulate state. None of this would be possible without React's virtual DOM, a concept we had high praises for in the previous chapter.

A source, like the one in Listing 13.3, is just a JavaScript module that connects actual data with a store. In this sample we're using mock data, but we could very easily connect it with a RESTful service.

The main takeaway from sources is that we want to decouple the *raw* source of our data from the store used to feed our components. Remember again that all data flows in a single direction in React and Flux.

### Listing 13.3  **OutbreakSource.js**

```
import uuid from 'node-uuid';
import OutbreakActions from '../actions/OutbreakActions'

var mockData = [
    {
      id: uuid.v4(),
      origin: "Station Gamma",
```

```
      severity: "Yellow",
      description: "This was bad",
      date: "03-04-2016 12:00"
    }
  ];

const OutbreakSource = {
  fetchOutbreak() {
    return {
      remote() {
        return new Promise(function (resolve, reject) {
                resolve(mockData);
            })
      },

      local() {
        return null;
      },

      success: OutbreakActions.updateOutbreak,
      error: OutbreakActions.outbreakFailed,
      loading: OutbreakActions.fetchOutbreak
    }
  }
};

export default OutbreakSource;
```

Now that we have a source for our data, and we have actions that represent stimulus to our components, we need a store, an abstraction around in-page persistence of data. Changes in the state within the store automatically trigger re-rendering of the DOM that corresponds to the React virtual DOM.

In other words, we get binding for free, and it's one-way binding. Unlike Angular, where the pattern is to allow edit forms to manipulate the same data used to feed read-only views, here everything is downstream from the dispatcher. The code for this store is shown in Listing 13.4

Listing 13.4  **OutbreakStore.js**

```
import alt from '../lib/alt';
import OutbreakSource from '../sources/OutbreakSource'
import OutbreakActions from '../actions/OutbreakActions';

class OutbreakStore {
  constructor() {
    this.outbreaks = [];
    this.errorMessage = null;
```

```
  this.bindListeners({
    handleUpdateOutbreaks: OutbreakActions.UPDATE_OUTBREAK,
    handleFetchOutbreak: OutbreakActions.FETCH_OUTBREAK,
    handleOutbreakFailed: OutbreakActions.OUTBREAK_FAILED,
    handleChangeOutbreak: OutbreakActions.CHANGE_OUTBREAK,
    handleDeleteOutbreak: OutbreakActions.DELETE_OUTBREAK,
    handleAddOutbreak: OutbreakActions.ADD_OUTBREAK
  });

  this.exportAsync(OutbreakSource)
}

handleDeleteOutbreak(outbreak) {
  this.outbreaks = this.outbreaks.filter(target => target.id !== outbreak.id)
}

handleAddOutbreak(outbreak) {
  this.outbreaks = this.outbreaks.concat([outbreak]);
}

handleChangeOutbreak(outbreak) {
  // make last-minute changes if we need to
}

handleUpdateOutbreaks(outbreaks) {
  this.outbreaks = outbreaks;
  this.errorMessage = null;
}

handleFetchOutbreak() {
  this.outbreaks = [];
}

handleOutbreakFailed(errorMessage) {
  this.errorMessage = errorMessage;
}
}

export default alt.createStore(OutbreakStore, 'OutbreakStore');
```

The call to exportAsync tethers our source to the list of actions. The constants exposed by the
actions module (e.g. CHANGE_OUTBREAK) are generated when we call createActions in the
actions module.

Figuring out how everything stitches together to weave a fully functioning Flux application is admittedly very confusing the first time you go through it. We've found that the best way to learn this stuff is to get in there, roll your sleeves up, and change something to *watch it break*.

Open up the Chrome JavaScript developer console, change something around and watch it fail. Walking backwards from the failures you see in the generated `bundle.js` to the code you manipulated in the pre-Webpack JavaScript is probably the single most enlightening thing you can do to really get a firm grasp of React, Alt, and Flux.

Most of the code for `OutbreakReport.jsx` remains unchanged. However, instead of manipulating control state in response to edits and deletes, we defer those by invoking actions. These actions then churn through the dispatcher and end up triggering function calls bound as listeners in our store. Once our store makes changes, the control can then re-render itself. We cannot overstate the importance of one-way data flow in supporting complex UIs. Listing 13.5 shows the new `OutbreakReport` component.

Listing 13.5  **OutbreakReport.jsx**

```
import React from 'react';
import OutbreakActions from '../actions/OutbreakActions';


export default class OutbreakReport extends React.Component {
  constructor(props) {
    super(props);

    this.state = {
      editing: false
    };
  }

  // Master function for rendering, chooses render mode(s).
  render() {
    if (this.state.editing) {
      return this.renderEdit();
    }

    return this.renderOutbreakReport();
  }

  // Renders the control in edit mode.
  renderEdit = () => {
    return (
        <div>
          <div className="date">{this.props.outbreak.date}</div>
          <div className="origin">{this.props.outbreak.origin}</div>
          <div><br/></div>
```

```jsx
          <div className="severity">{this.props.outbreak.severity}</div>
          <div className="description">
            <input type="text"
                ref={
                    (e) => e ? e.selectionStart =
                  this.props.outbreak.description.length : null
                    }
                    autoFocus={true}
                    defaultValue={this.props.outbreak.description}
                    onBlur={this.finishEdit}
                    onKeyPress={this.checkEnter} />
          </div>
        </div>
      );
}

// Switch the control into edit mode. Does NOT invoke a store-changing action.
edit = () => {
  console.log('Switching to edit mode.');
  this.setState({
    editing: true
  });
};

checkEnter = (e) => {
  if(e.key === 'Enter') {
    this.finishEdit(e);
  }
};

// Blurred out of edit control. Commit changes to store via Action.
finishEdit = (e) => {
  console.log('Exited edit')
  const value = e.target.value;
  //this.props.onEdit(value);
  this.setState({
    editing: false
  });
  if(!value.trim()) {
   return;
 }
 this.props.outbreak.description = value;
 OutbreakActions.changeOutbreak(this.props.outbreak);
}

// Invoke delete action to modify store.
onDelete = (e) => {
```

```
      console.log('Clicked delete');
      OutbreakActions.deleteOutbreak(this.props.outbreak);
    }

    // Renders read-only version of report.
    renderOutbreakReport = () => {
      const onDelete = this.props.onDelete;

      return (
        <div>
          <div className="date">{this.props.outbreak.date}</div>
          <div className="origin">{this.props.outbreak.origin}</div>
          <div><br/></div>
          <div className="severity">{this.props.outbreak.severity}</div>
          <div className="description"
              onClick={this.edit}>{this.props.outbreak.description}</div>
          {this.renderDelete()}
        </div>
      );
    }

  renderDelete = () => {
    return <button
      className="delete-outbreak" onClick={this.onDelete}>X</button>;
  }
}
```

We've highlighted a couple of the important changes to this component. As mentioned, user interaction with this component has now been refactored to trigger actions. The actions go through the dispatcher and are then monitored by the appropriate store. The store changes, which then causes affected components to re-render. We've repeated it a few times, so hopefully the repetition of this data flow has made it easier to remember.

OutbreakReport still maintains its own internal state to manage whether or not it is in edit mode. Ideally we would also have factored this part out to utilize the concepts of stores and actions. We left it this way so you could see a little bit of both worlds in the same sample. As an exercise, you might want to try adding the isEditing flag as state to individual records in OutbreakStore and see if you like that model better.

Alt.js is the cog in the machinery here that supplies some of the binding wrappers that allow us to avoid working directly with the React dispatcher. We've seen some of the sample code people have written to work directly with the dispatcher at the lowest levels of React and Flux, and it's an ugly mess. Alt hides just enough of the boilerplate without becoming a source of frustration on its own.

If you're looking at the GitHub repo, you'll see that there's a lib/alt.js module that creates an instance of Alt. Little of what we're going in this chapter would be possible without it.

To see all of this in action, get the latest from GitHub (`git pull`), and issue the following commands:

```
$ npm install
$ npm run watch
```

You should now be able to open the application on ***localhost:8080*** just like in the last chapter. The UI should appear absolutely identical to the last chapter, but the code is now separated and refactored and ready to support substantially more complex UIs. In short, we're now ready to write UIs that scale to match the scalability of the microservices we have deployed in our cloud.

As always, you can also host this application in the provided Go server. You can see this by issuing the following commands:

```
$ go build
$ npm run build
$ ./flux-zombieoutbreak
```

This will generate the `bundle.js` file using `webpack` and then use the Go server to host the static assets to start the application.

If you want to run this without having to build anything, you can just execute it straight from Docker Hub:

```
docker run -p 8100:8100 -e
  WEBROOT=/pipeline/source cloudnativego/flux-zombieoutbreak
```

# Summary

We are not JavaScript programmers. We are not React or Flux or Alt experts. In fact, we will be the first to admit that we are just muddling through in this arena. Our expertise lies squarely in the microservices realm and building microservices with our favorite language, Go.

If you are a React or Flux expert, you may have noticed some things in the previous two chapters that are not idiomatic JavaScript or adhering to commonly accepted React and Flux best practices. Given the amount of newbsauce covering our Flux and React skills, this would not surprise us in the least.

All of our work for these chapters is open source, so if you see something you don't like, feel free to submit a pull request to improve the work.

Our goal with these chapters has not been to teach you JavaScript, React, Flux, or Alt. Our goal has been to show you the intricacies of how to stand up interactive front-ends that work with microservices that support them. There are tons of resources and books available on all of these front-end technologies that provide more detail than we could possibly hope to cover in a book on cloud native programming in Go.

In the next chapter we're going to put all of the skills to use that we've covered so far in this book and hopefully your suffering through two chapters of JavaScript and UI will have been worth it.

# 14

# Creating a Full Application— *World of FluxCraft*

*"It's dangerous to go alone! Take this!"*

Old Man NPC, *Legend of Zelda*. February 21, 1986

When we build microservices, we know that we're really building an ecosystem of services. Nothing we build that will add real business value, satisfy stockholders, or make our customers happy will ever be just a tiny service that exists in a vacuum.

A microservice ecosystem is, at its core, a distributed system. Distributed systems are hard. Microservices are hard. Building an application made up of many individually deployable and separately scalable components is *hard*.

When we read programming books, we want to apply the knowledge learned from building a dozen or so isolated samples to creating a cohesive, production-ready application. The problem is we miss something *vitally important* when we just dish out a dozen chapters of isolated content. All we've done at that point is teach you how to create isolated samples, and not shown you how to apply the knowledge in a practical manner to creating a *real-world* application.

In this chapter, we're going to take a look at everything we've learned so far, and we're going to apply it to building an application designed for massive scale. This application is a collection of microservices that are all separately deployable, and scalable on their own. In short, we're going to build a large, cloud native application that applies all of the skills we've learned from Chapters 1 through 13.

While we're going to build a game called *World of FluxCraft*, nearly every technique and architectural pattern discussed in this chapter can be applied to a myriad problem domains.

Throughout this chapter, we will:

- Introduce the game concept behind *World of FluxCraft*.
- Walk through the high-level architecture of this distributed game system.
- Discuss the Flux GUI.
- Provide an overview of the command processors.
- Provide an overview of the event handlers.
- Discuss the concept of the **reality server**.
- Discuss map management.
- Provide an overview of automating acceptance tests for a distributed system.
- Point you to the code for a fully functioning example.

## Introducing *World of FluxCraft*

One of the hardest aspects of writing a programming book is choosing the code samples. We are often tasked with illustrating how to solve enormously complex problems, and we need to do so in a way that doesn't bore the reader to death, but doesn't gloss over important details. We also can't bind a book big enough to hold the thousands of lines of source code from a production-ready application.

We also need to juggle scope. Scope creep is a problem for real-world production applications just as it is for the applications and services we build for the books we write. Hopefully, in *World of FluxCraft*, we have achieved a balance of scope, complexity, and readability that will combine all of the techniques in this book into a simple sample without being overly complex or too hard to read.

*World of FluxCraft* is a browser-based multi-player game. Rather than presenting one perpetually evolving world as many MMORPGs (massively multiplayer online role-playing games) do, we're limiting our scope by allowing small groups of players to create a very small game.

The rules of the game are simple—*reach the winning spot on the map*. We believe in building software in an agile fashion, by targeting the smallest possible functioning application (MVP, or minimum viable product) first. Once we've built that, we can add features and enhancements incrementally, all the while still using our core product.

The first player to start the game gets to choose the map. From there, this player can then invite other players into the game. Players get an avatar image that represents them on the map as they move around. You can chat with other players, and you can even attack them, but that's about it. The attack is the simplest possible implementation (MVP) of multi-player combat in that it just does a random amount of damage to you.

Whether you use *World of FluxCraft* as a starting point to build your own browser-based MMO, or whether you take the patterns and code and use it to build a real-time, interactive line of business application is up to you. Throughout this chapter, we'll be discussing architectural concepts, high-level designs, and the sequence of data flow through a microservices ecosystem. We're not going to include any code in this chapter.

To get the code, as well as instructions for building *World of FluxCraft* and deploying it in the cloud, check out the repositories that begin with `wof-` in our GitHub repo (*http://github.com/ cloudnativego/wof-\**).

Figure 14.1 below shows a screenshot of an early prototype of a *World of FluxCraft* game map rendering (we purchased some nice tile sets and avatar images from talented folks online, because between the two of us we can barely manage to draw a straight line).

Figure 14.1    An Early Prototype of *World of FluxCraft's* UI

## Architectural Overview

When we play a game, or check our bank balance, or check into our favorite restaurant using social media, we are only interacting with the tip of the iceberg. Beneath every point of contact with the customer is usually an enormous amount of code and infrastructure.

In the case of our sample game, *World of FluxCraft*, as players we interact with the game's main website. This has the usual functionality we would expect, as well as a way to navigate to a page running Flux-based UI.

Once we're in a game, as we move around the game board and interact with the game and other players, we are sending our moves to a command processor. This command processor works like the one we illustrated in Chapter 8 ("Event Sourcing and CQRS"). Commands are converted into events and sent to a message queueing system.

From there, one or more event processors do what their job implies—process events. In the course of event processing, each event is persisted so we have it for a historical archive. Some events might require that we emit messages to the real-time messaging (e.g. Websockets) infrastructure. This lets us send **push** messages directly to running games. Finally, the calculated state of the game is sent to the reality server for caching.

Each game can take place on a different map, and as such we need a way to store and retrieve the metadata (e.g. tiles, graphics, barriers) for these maps. This is what we use the **map service** for, as shown in the next diagram.

Figure 14.2 shows the microservice ecosystem that supports *World of FluxCraft*. There are a couple of other microservices in the final implementation (like the *user profile* service) that aren't shown in this diagram, just for the sake of keeping things simple.

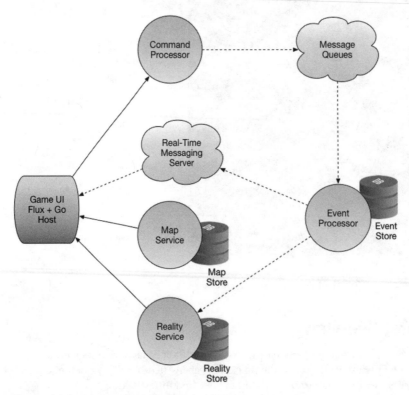

Figure 14.2   High-Level Application Architecture

In the next few sections of the chapter, we'll talk about the design, architecture, and decisions that went into each of these components in depth.

## Independent Scaling, Versioning, and Deployment

Taking a look at Figure 14.2, each of the green circles is a microservice. As you'll see throughout the chapter, the design of these microservices ensures that we can deploy, version, and scale them independently.

Deployment can be done while the system is still running. If we need to release a new microservice, then we can do a blue/green deployment. This essentially lets us deploy the new version alongside the old, test the new version, and when we're satisfied that everything is in order we can drain the traffic from the old service to the new. There are a number of ways we can screw this up, such as releasing a new version of a service that has a breaking API change.

This leads us to our next notion: **versioning**. It's physically possible to deploy new versions without impact to the system, but we need to adhere to some basic guidelines, such as avoiding breaking public API changes whenever possible. We can do this with techniques like semantic versioning, and including version information either in our REST payloads or in the resource URI (or both).

Each of the microservices in the diagram is stateless. While you might see a persistence medium stuck to it, the service itself is stateless. The services are designed to start up quickly and to allow a quick death. This means that we can scale up or down the number of instances of each of these microservices based on demand and usage patterns *live, in real-time*, and *without stopping the system*. More importantly, we don't have to change or redeploy configuration in order to adopt a new number of instances.

Further, this architecture also allows us to *automatically* scale. We can spin up more instances of services based on CPU utilization, queue depth, or other high-level business metrics within the system. For a game like *World of FluxCraft*, we might scale based on the number of concurrent users or active games.

## Databases are not the Integration Tier

We cannot stress enough that *databases should never be used as an integration layer*. In the preceding diagram, you'll see that each microservice has its own *private* data store. This is a fairly well understood and widely adopted pattern of microservices that you can read more about in Sam Newman's book.

## One-Way Immutable Data Flow

Look again at Figure 14.2 and count the number of two-way arrows or bi-directional communications. There are *none*. Every interaction with the system follows a single, consistent, and predictable flow. Data flows from a source to a destination, and never in the opposite direction.

This very much mirrors the architectural principles that govern the design of React and Flux as well as the guiding principles behind Event Sourcing and the Command Query Responsibility Segregation (CQRS) patterns that we discussed in Chapter 8. This is not a coincidence.

*Mutability is the scale-killer.* The more we adopt these reactive, uni-directional flow patterns the more scalable our systems are. We also often get huge performance benefits from these and we can often extend these systems in amazing and powerful ways once they're running because of the flexibility of the architecture.

# The Flux GUI

The user interface for *World of FluxCraft* is obviously not up to the standards by which most gamers judge online role-playing games these days. We are both old enough to remember when you could play Donkey Kong at a stand-up arcade machine for 25 cents per play. We also remember the first 8-bit video game console.

As an homage to the childhood of millions of today's developers, we decided to make WoF a classic top-down, 8-bit map crawler game. You can find the full code for the WoF Flux GUI at https://github.com/cloudnativego/wof-ui.

The main interface for a game consists of a top-down map view, on which player avatars move around. The players can only move in legal directions and can only interact with the map in ways in which the Flux GUI and the backing services allow.

The bulk of the heavy lifting of the Flux GUI is all done in the `MapSource` and `MapStore` components. We need to get the map metadata from our map service. Once we've got players moving around the map, we need to modify the store to reflect this. Once the store is updated, all of the relevant components like `MapTile` are then re-rendered to reflect the new position of the player.

One trick that we found particularly helpful in rendering the Flux UI without the aid of a full-fledged 2D game engine was the use of **sprites**. In the traditional sense, a sprite is just a 2D image that can be moved around a screen or some section of it.

What turned to to be of huge benefit to us was an often overlooked feature of CSS that allows you to set the backgrounds of HTML components to only a sub-rectangle of a larger image. This allowed us to go get some classic-looking 8-bit *tile sets* (collections of tile-friendly images) that manifest as a single PNG image. Then, we set up a stylesheet that declares class names for each of the tiles that sit at various coordinates within the graphic.

So, let's say we have a tile that contains a sewer grate on stone, and it is at offset 768 by 384 within the image. We can declare a CSS style that will use this image as the background for a div easily:

```
.tile-sewer-grate-on-stone {
  background: url('/tiles/dungeon_tileset_128.png') -768px -384px;
}
```

Now, anytime we declare a div that has this class name, it will have a background of that sewer grate. If we want to put a player avatar, or some other icon like a lever, a switch, or an impassable obstacle, we can just stick an image tag in that div and center it. This gives us the impression of having one sprite walking on a map, without us having to do any of the hard work of building a real 2D engine.

This lets us have an extremely simple div to represent a map tile in our MapTile component:

```
<div className={className} onClick={tileClicked}>
   <img id={tile.sprite} src="/sprites/img_trans.gif" onClick={spriteClicked}/>
</div>
```

The simple string in the `tile.sprite` state variable corresponds to the CSS style for a sprite image, which can be mapped to a sub-rectangle within a sprite layer image just like we do for the background tiles. Setting the class name on the div changes the background tile.

With some very simple, clever CSS tricks we can dynamically lay out an entire game map that supports sprites on top of map tiles. Since we're just using simple images, we need to resort to a little more cleverness to indicate that more than one player is currently occupying the same map tile.

Remember that our goal with this game isn't to make something to compete with multi-million dollar budget MMORPGs, our goal is to show you how to put all of the skills we've built up throughout this book together to make a running application. As such, we decided to make the simplest UI that would work for our game and then stop there, preferring to spend our time enhancing gameplay and the Go-based backing services than fuss with things like fancy animations, sound, parallax scrolling, etc.

## The Go UI Host Service

Various actions taken by the player, such as moving, chatting, or joining or quitting a game, all result in commands being sent to the command service. We don't want the Flux JavaScript to communicate directly with the command service because doing so brings up a number of security and infrastructure problems like cross-site scripting execution security measures.

When these actions occur, instead of posting to the command service, we post to the local service. The local service then simply takes the payload and sends it on to the command service.

If we were building something more complicated, or we intended to support mobile device gameplay as well as web-based, we might want to utilize a third-party API gateway service like that provided by Apigee. With all traffic going through an API gateway, you get all sorts of powerful features like conditional transformations, security, attack prevention, intrusion detection, and even geographically optimized service edge deployment.

For our purposes in demonstrating this game and its associated services, having the Go application that hosts our Flux UI act as a simple proxy for the command service should suffice.

## Sample Player Move Sequence

The sequence diagram in Figure 14.3 shows the flow of information through the entire system in response to a player indicating that they would like to move to a new map location.

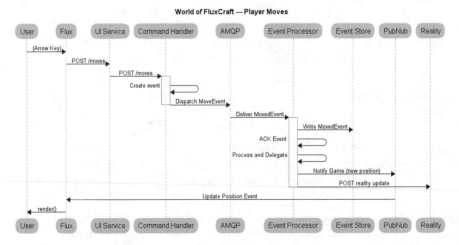

Figure 14.3    Sequence Diagram for Player Movement

Source: websequencediagrams.com

The sequence goes like this:

1. User presses an arrow key for a legitimate move.

2. Flux UI reacts to the key and modifies the local map store and components render accordingly.

3. JavaScript sends the JSON payload for a move command to the local `/api/moves` URL.

4. The UI host service forwards that payload to the command processor service.

5. The command processor produces an event from the inbound command and dispatches it to a queue.

6. The event processor picks the event up off the queue and performs any necessary processing.

   a. The event is written to the event store.

   b. Notifications are sent (if applicable) to the real-time messaging system.

   c. New game state is calculated and submitted as an update to the reality server.

These steps will all be covered in more detail as we discuss each of the microservices we've built.

# Processing Commands

As we saw in Chapter 8, the job of the command processor is just as its name implies: *process commands*. A command is a *declaration of intent*. This is a client issuing a command to the system, without knowledge of how that command will be fulfilled or what will happen to it.

More importantly, the issuance of a command is understood to be inherently asynchronous. When we submit a command to a command processor, we get back a result code that indicates whether the payload was understood and whether the command was successfully dispatched, but the processing and fulfillment of that command could take seconds, minutes, or hours depending on the type of application we're building.

Most commands in *FluxCraft* should be handled in near-real time, or as fast as the system can handle it. There are some pros and cons to this approach. The benefits are that if we want things to be processed faster, we spin up more processors or we spin up more consumers on the other side of the event dispatch.

The downside to having near real-time fulfillment is that when the system gets bogged down, players will immediately see problems. Other player movements will lag behind reality, chat messages might slow down, and so on.

The *World of FluxCraft* command processor has the following responsibilities:

1. Expose RESTful API that accepts new commands via POST.
2. Convert the command into an event, augmenting the event with environmental metadata, e.g. timestamp.
3. Dispatch the event *without knowledge of potential consumers*. In our case, we're dispatching the newly generated events to RabbitMQ queues.

When the command processor converts a command into an event, it is essentially converting a *desire for something* into a *record of something happening*. Put another way, commands are in the present tense and events occur in the past.

This is actually a fairly small set of responsibilities (as close to *single responsibility* as we can practically get), and that's intentional. This is the *micro* in *microservices*. The smaller the responsibility, the less impact there is when we change it, and the less reason we have to modify it to add features to the overall application.

The following is a list of some of the types of commands that a game like *FluxCraft* would support:

- Create Game
- Join Game
- Send Text Message

- Attack
- Move
- Leave Game

These commands are all player-initiated.

# Processing Events

The event processor is the closest thing we're going to get to pure functional programming in a book like this. Its job is to receive and process events, where the processing of an event is really the calculation of new state by applying an event to old state.

As we've mentioned a number of times before, event processing in an event-sourced system *must be idempotent*. We must be able to reliably, and *always*, get the exact same result when we apply an event to a known state. This makes for an incredibly easy-to-test module, but it is also the keystone of a truly scalable and reliable system.

Our *FluxCraft* event processor handles events it receives from queues, including events such as:

- Player Joined
- Player Left
- Player Sent Text
- Player Moved
- Player Attacked
- Game Started

Again note that these events are deliberately described so that they reflect the fact that they occurred *in the past*.

When the event processor receives an event, it performs the appropriate function by applying it to the old state. The newly computed state is sent off to the **reality** service (discussed shortly) and the event itself is persisted in the event store.

If applicable, a notification will be broadcast back out to the system to interested parties to inform them of the new state (or some subset of it) as a result of event processing. You might be thinking, *emitting a notification is a side-effect, so that's not purely functional*. You're right.

Emitting a notification as a result of processing a function is not purely functional. If we were building this sample in a 100% purist fashion, the event processor would produce a secondary stream of events, which could then be processed. In this secondary stream, you would have the notifications which then get broadcast to interested parties.

In the interest of avoiding scope creep, we decided against this approach because the notifications we're emitting *are not mutating data*, they are simply a *convenience* broadcast of changes to data. This same information would be available through queries, and we're just opting to *push* some of this new information (like player hit points and locations) via our messaging subsystem (*FluxCraft* uses PubNub).

As a convenience, as well as to make sure our event processor plays nice in the cloud, we expose a REST endpoint that allows us to query some counters that indicate the number of events processed. In a more complex system with a larger problem domain, we imagine that the REST endpoint on the event processor might expose methods to query the event store.

## Maintaining Reality

In Chapter 8, we stated that *reality is event-sourced*. Our reality is the end result of our brain performing insanely complex calculations on multiple never-ending streams of events (stimuli).

In much the same way, the "reality" of *World of FluxCraft* is the end result of performing calculations on a stream of game-related events. The state (reality) of any given game can be determined by playing the stream of game events in sequential order through the event processor function.

When a browser opens a game page for the first time, it needs to know the state of the game in progress. Because the browser doesn't have the event history, and does not have the event processor logic, it needs to ask the reality service for the state of the game.

When an event processor applies a new event to existing state, it will update the reality service with this new state so that this same state can be made available for the case we just mentioned (loading the game player web page).

The reality server has a very simple job, but it is vitally important. In our implementation, to avoid scope creep and realizing that we're writing book samples, we backed our reality server with a simple MongoDB database. In a real-world scenario where you could have tens of thousands of concurrent games (realities) active at once, you could upgrade the reality service so that there is a caching tier between it and the persistence service.

As with all the other services, we can deploy new versions of this service at any time without impact to the rest of the system. In keeping with Conway's Law, this also means it would be very easy for us to have different teams working on different services and still be able to rapidly build and deploy new features.

## Map Management

When you start a new *World of FluxCraft* game, you get to pick the map. All multiplayer games worth their salt have epic maps: *Nuketown*, *Blood Gulch*, *Rainbow Road*, *Gold Rush*, and the *Goldeneye Archives* all come to mind.

FluxCraft is no different than these, except that our maps are far less epic, less interactive, less fun, less graphically intense, developed with a $0 operating budget, and only run in a browser. If it weren't for these and a few hundred other reasons, our maps would be right up there with the all-time multi-player greats.

Some multi-player maps are huge graphs of interconnected geometry—polygons and meshes and light sources and countless other complexities. Our maps are inspired by the top-down maps of the prime of the 8-bit gaming era. As such, *World of FluxCraft* maps are 2D grids of map tiles.

Each tile within the map has an image property (the image is supplied by the browser via CSS), as well as metadata indicating whether players can traverse that map tile or, if the players can occupy that space, which directions they can and cannot use to exit the tile.

Every tile on the map has a unique ID, and every map available to a *World of FluxCraft* installation also has a unique ID. When you look at the code in GitHub, you'll see how the unique IDs of the maps and map tiles are used by the event processors and by the UI.

One of the extremely cool side-effects of having the maps managed by a separate microservice is that we can borrow technology from the map renderer in the game's main UI and create our own **level editor** or **map designer**. This saves us from the arduous task of manually constructing the JSON for our maps.

When a player starts a game, the UI host service queries the map service in order to get map metadata, and if we made a level editor, it would submit new maps or changes to existing maps to the map service.

It's worth mentioning that reality (game state) operates on a copy of the map. This insulates the game from changes to the map, and allows us to satisfy the *no external data* requirement of an event-sourced system. If we have to reach out to the map service constantly throughout event processing, our event processing is neither predictable nor idempotent.

## Automating Acceptance Tests

Even in our remarkably dumbed-down example of a multiplayer game, there are a lot of moving parts. We have a command processor, an event processor, a reality server, a real-time messaging component, and we have queue-based messaging and the game's main user interface. There's also a map server, a user profile service, and if we continue to add features it isn't unreasonable to expect the number of microservices to grow as well.

If we've been adhering to *the way of the cloud*, then we've built everything test-first and we've tested everything in isolation. However, isolated testing is rarely ever enough. We want a reliable predictor that once all of these isolated services go into production, they'll all work as intended.

To do this, we're going to need acceptance tests. With a multi-player game like this, a fairly straightforward way to test is the use of **game scripts**. A game script is essentially a sequence of player actions taken within a game. An acceptance test for a single game might consist of the following:

1. Deploy all of the microservices into a clean environment. They should pick up the clean/ acceptance test environment configuration.

2. Issue a *start game* command to the command server.

3. Issue a few *add player* commands.

4. Run through a known sequence of commands taken by the players within a game. This would include every possible type of command, preferably multiple times, exercising some scenario with an expected outcome.

5. Wait for things to settle a bit to allow the game's plumbing to work.

6. Query the reality server to ensure that the state of the game is as you expect it to be.

This not only re-tests all of the individual components, but it tests that they all work together as expected. You don't need the Flux/React UI as part of your acceptance test, because this is really just a thin veneer on top of a websocket receiver and a sender of POST commands to the command service.

Once you've got individual acceptance tests that run through the various key permutations of gameplay scenarios, you might want to bump up the complexity of your acceptance tests.

This is a multi-player game, after all. In addition to multiple players participating in a single game, *World of FluxCraft* is designed to support a massive number of concurrent games.

To really be sure that *FluxCraft* is behaving as it should, we should start multiple games at the same time, and we should issue commands for those games simultaneously. We could accomplish this pretty easily with the use of **goroutines**—each goroutine could just load up a game script (which could be just a file containing a sequence of JSON payloads to send to the command service) and start sending.

Now when we check the status of each game in the reality service at the end of the test, we're also ensuring that the state from one game hasn't bled into or interfered with the others. This acceptance test could also be adapted to push configurable load on our *FluxCraft* environment. If we scale up the number of acceptance test clients and the number of concurrent game scenarios each test runs, we can stress the servers and still assert that all of our games have played out properly.

Finally, we'll also want to include a number of game scripts that have invalid moves in them. We want to ensure that if someone reverse engineers the protocol for communicating with the command service, they would still be unable to move to prohibited spots, attack players they cannot reach, or otherwise cheat or abuse the system.

As we've done throughout the book, every commit would trigger a CI (e.g. Wercker) build that runs all of our unit tests and all of our integration tests for the single microservice that was changed. Then, we can continue the CD pipeline by spinning up an acceptance test that exercises the newly modified microservice along with all the others, ensuring that the change we made doesn't break the overall gameplay.

*Without* such an automated acceptance test in a microservice ecosystem, we have absolutely no confidence about the ability of our ecosystem to support proper gameplay. The only evidence we would have that the game works would be the lack of complaints from our players. That kind of model is a terrible way to run a stable, scalable, production-grade system.

We've been on teams in the distant and recent past that have rigged the status of a time-delayed or nightly acceptance test suite to a large monitor so that everyone on the team is *immediately* aware of the fact that a recently committed change has broken the game. In fact, in some places we've worked, teams have rigged lava lamps or angry Darth Vader heads to the status of the acceptance tests.

For obvious reasons, when the acceptance tests fail, fixing them becomes a stop-everything-else priority because a team that is pushing to production daily or weekly can't maintain that pace if the acceptance tests are broken.

Of course, all of this implies that you've built your tests in such a way that they do properly exercise all critical gameplay scenarios. If you skimp on this, the green acceptance test light will just be a false sense of security, and then the first people to discover problems in your software will be your customers.

## Summary

*World of FluxCraft*, despite the incredibly original name, is not a commercial-grade game that we would expect to charge a lot of money for. Instead, it is a sample designed to illustrate *just one* of the many ways in which the techniques, patterns, disciplines, philosophies, and code laid out in this book can all be applied to a single problem.

The WoF repositories in our GitHub organization should show you a React+Flux UI that sits on top of a backing service that acts as a broker to other microservices in the ecosystem. The Event Sourcing and CQRS patterns are implemented to show how the stream of game *moves* produces an event stream that can be processed, which in turn emits an output stream of events to be delivered to active games via a real-time messaging system.

We wrote WoF for a number of reasons. First and foremost, it was a lot of fun. Secondly, we wanted to give you a sample template that you can use as a reference; not as a source of copy-and-paste code that solves your business problem out of the box, but as a source of inspiration and a means of reminding us all that software development in Go is not just productive and powerful, but it is *truly enjoyable*, whether we're solving complex business domain problems or building a real-time, web-based RPG.

# 15

# Conclusion

*"If bridge building were like programming, halfway through we'd find out that the far bank was now 50 meters farther out, that it was actually mud rather than granite, and that rather than building a footbridge we were instead building a road bridge."*

Sam Newman, Building Microservices

Congratulations! You have suffered through the work of two windbag authors, read our drivel, compiled our code, and run our samples. Hopefully, at the end of all that, you have learned a few things that you will take with you after using this book as kindling in your fireplace or lining the bottom of a bird cage.

In this final chapter, we'll:

- Recap what we've covered throughout the book.
- Suggest next steps for learning and growth in cloud native Go development.

## What we Learned

Hopefully there has been some payoff as a reward for making your way through this entire book unscathed. While there's no badge, level-up, or experience points, perhaps there is some knowledge or information that may be useful to you after this book is discarded in a heap.

### Go Isn't Just a Niche Language

There is a vicious stereotype floating around the Internet that, while handy, the only real place for Go code is in building command-line tools and tiny little one-off utilities. We hope that we have disproved this slander and that you now know the real power of Go, which is solving complex problems with simple and elegant code.

## How Micro Should a Microservice Be?

As we have built samples of varying complexity, we have mentioned patterns and techniques for determining where you should split the boundary lines of your microservices.

While there is no silver bullet answer, there are a couple of guiding principles that should remain in the back of your mind during design and architecture:

- A microservice should do *one thing*. It is a self-contained, RESTful embodiment of the Single Responsibility Principle (SRP). It should be easy to change and upgrade, and the changing of it should make ripples not waves.

- The golden rule from Sam Newman's book: *can you make a change to a service and deploy it by itself without changing anything else?*

## Continuous Delivery and Deployment

All the tools and technology in the world won't help you if you don't have *confidence* in your application. If you don't know how its going to behave in production *before* you deploy it, then the cloud will be your enemy rather than your greatest ally.

You should be running builds as soon after every commit as possible, on *all branches*. Your build pipelines should execute unit tests immediately, and they should execute integration tests as soon as possible.

Assuming everything tests out clear, your build pipelines should be automatically deploying your applications to various environments. At the very least, you should be automatically deploying to a testing environment and then using one-button deployment for higher environments like staging and production.

## Test Everything

Confidence only comes from testing. Only by *strictly* adhering to the principles of Test-Driven Development (TDD) can you have any confidence in the reliability of your code or its ability to perform as designed. Integration tests should certify your code *at the seams*, and acceptance tests should certify all the moving parts of your application within a single environment.

Many people think the choice of programming language is the silver bullet to solve all of their problems. If there is any one thing that solves the majority of all problems, *it is testing*. It's hard to do, it requires effort, and it may *feel* like it takes more time in the beginning, but it is absolutely essential to success and your ability to maintain existing applications and rapidly build and deploy new features.

## Release Early, Release Often

*Fear of releasing* is a real thing among many enterprises and even many organizations that would label themselves as agile or a lean startup. These organizations often put off releases until the last minute, or they schedule them for every quarter or even every 6 months.

The solution to the *fear of releasing* is not to release less often, it is to release *more often*. As features are tested and certified, they should be released and made available. You can use techniques like *blue/green deployment* to gradually introduce these features to customers consuming your application. This model is how many of the giants perform releases, including Google and Facebook.

Automated releases are essential, and frequent releases are directly correlated to your ability to maintain and enhance applications. As we mentioned early in the book, the phase of your application's life where it is not "in production" is extremely short. You need to plan for the long game; for how your process is going to deliver what you need rapidly and reliably while your app is being used by millions of people.

## Event Sourcing, CQRS, and More Acronyms

We also learned that language and technology is not a substitute for scalable architecture and design. You can implement terrible patterns in so-called cloud native languages and completely ruin your application's ability to scale.

In this book we talked about patterns and practices that enable massive-scale operations, including Event Sourcing, the Command Query Responsibility Segregation (CQRS) pattern, and the concept of eventual consistency. Knowing how these work, when to use them, and when their complexity is warranted will serve you well as you build truly cloud-scale applications.

# Next Steps

Now that you're an expert on building microservices in the cloud with Go, what are you going to do next? Where do you go from here?

*Build.* It doesn't matter what, but if you don't use the skills and techniques outlined in this book, then you'll quickly forget them and the authors will become sad and depressed. Come up with crazy ideas and implement them. The building of an application should be as enjoyable as the consumption of it.

*Contribute.* Give back to the community. Write libraries for other Go developers building microservices. Create samples; add to the samples repositories for this book. The more code we contribute to the community, the bigger the community gets and the quicker we can reach a point where folks stop underestimating the power, flexibility, and elegance of the Go language.

*Share.* Tell your skeptical friends about this book. Buy them a copy, show them the code samples. Spread the word and get more people addicted to writing cloud native code in Go.

# Troubleshooting Cloud Applications

*"If I had an hour to solve a problem I'd spend 55 minutes thinking about the problem and 5 minutes thinking about solutions."*

Albert Einstein

If you've survived this book from start to finish, then there's a very good chance that you've got several sample applications deployed and running in the cloud. You're probably also contemplating what your next project is going to be—are you going to migrate some legacy code to be cloud native, do some green field work, or take over the world one microservice at a time?

Regardless of the project, at some point you will find yourself looking at your monitor, observing your applications that have been deployed and are running in a production cloud. Now what?

In this appendix we'll discuss some concepts and techniques around troubleshooting problems that might occur with applications *after* you've written them. All too often we assume that our work is done when the application compiles and this is never the case. We own our applications until we retire them in favor of their replacements, so we should know how to monitor, assess, and diagnose them in the cloud.

## Working with Log Streams

A truly cloud native application does not write its logs to disk. Rather, it emits a log stream to either STDOUT or STDERR. Applications running in the cloud should *know nothing* about the ultimate destination and consumers of their logs. The only thing they should be concerned about is emitting the right information into a log stream to aid in monitoring and diagnosis (without exposing sensitive information, of course).

If you're using Pivotal Web Services or you've got Pivotal Cloud Foundry installed in your enterprise, then you can use the `cf logs` command to examine the logs for your application. This might be useful for real-time monitoring but the logs you see with this command do not last forever. The sheer volume of data being transmitted for logs in the cloud is staggering and, as a result, most clouds are only going to give you real-time monitoring and a *very* short history.

The log stream is likely going to be the first place you look when trying to figure out what's wrong with your application. Whether you're looking at it in real-time or whether you're poring over historical data stored in Splunk, the ELK stack, Sumologic, or another tool, *logs are your friend*.

The log stream emitted by your application should be treated like a stream of telemetry coming from a satellite in orbit. You can't reach out and touch your application, you can't pull out a wrench or a hammer to repair it. It's in the cloud. It could move from one coast to another, or switch continents, or change from one instance to one hundred. The only thing that stays constant in any of those scenarios is the stream of emitted log events.

Implicit in all of this is the assumption that your application is actually emitting *useful* information. While the platform may augment the logs with counters, metrics, and detailed messages coming from the router, your app is still ultimately the one responsible for choosing what information to log.

## Monitoring Health and Performance

As we mentioned earlier in the book, once deployed, your application should be treated more like a probe launched into space than something tethered to you with a cable. Visibility is everything in supporting an application in production, especially one deployed in the cloud as a microservice ecosystem with independently scaling components.

You need to be able to see, at a glance, the overall health of your entire system. If you need more detail, you need to be able to see the health and performance of each individual component. Without this, you can't support your application or promise the kind of "5 9s" uptime that consumers have come to demand.

### Application Performance Monitoring (APM) Tools

There are countless tools available today that allow you to monitor your application. You need to know the average throughput of each of your services. You need to know when a component is getting bogged down, or when you might need to change the scaling profile to accommodate new requirements or peak events.

One such tool is **New Relic** (https://newrelic.com). This tool, and others like it, works by having the application emit performance metrics to some form of central aggregator. This aggregator is then responsible for storing and processing the information received from the applications to provide administrators, developers, and operations people with dashboards and drilldowns.

Many APM solutions like New Relic work through the use of **agents**. These are either libraries loaded with your application or processes that are loaded "sidecar" style that facilitate the emission of APM metrics. While New Relic's page doesn't link to a Go agent, you can find an OSS one here: https://github.com/yvasiyarov/gorelic.

Regardless of the type or complexity of your application, if you deploy it to production without a combination of robust log aggregation and APM, you're essentially flying blind and you'll be relying on hope and blind speculation when something bad happens to your live environment. We're not explicitly saying New Relic is the only way to go, but we are saying that you should have *some kind* of APM solution in place for production applications of any reasonable size.

### Monitoring Your App via the Platform

APM tools give you the ability to track timing metrics for method calls, latency and throughput of your REST API, and many other things. Your platform, however, should also give you access to vital metrics about your applications and how they are performing at the platform level.

For example, any decent cloud provider should give you access to raw data or dashboard GUI (preferably both) that shows summary and detail level for platform statistics.

Some of the metrics that your platform should expose to application developers and operations are:

- CPU usage, per app instance.
- Memory consumption, per app instance.
- Response time, per request per app instance.

If your platform doesn't provide you access to at the very least these basic bits of information, then perhaps you need to consider a different provider. Without this information available to you *at all times* when supporting a production app, you're essentially operating with handcuffs.

# Debugging Applications in the Cloud

Many times throughout this book we have encouraged you to think of your applications as deployed scientific instruments, satellites circling the earth in orbit. These applications are not within reach, and they certainly do not have a tether through which you can perform low-level communication.

This presents a problem for those who feel as though troubleshooting cannot be accomplished without the use of a debugger.

If you're working on your local workstation, running a local copy of your application, then you can certainly make use of the Go debugger (https://golang.org/doc/gdb). However, when your application is in production, with multiple instances deployed across multiple availability zones in production, your debugger is not going to do you any good.

Even if it were physically possible to remotely attach your debugger, you still have to figure out which instance you want to debug. In many cases, the problem might be spread across multiple instances of the application. For example, a request could be handled by instance 1 and then a subsequent request from the same user could be handled by instance 2. Assuming that both applications are truly cloud native, they are stateless and these instances might not even be running in the same physical data center.

In a stateless application, what information would be available on a call stack or in a locals watch that would help you diagnose a problem? With microservices in the cloud, you are usually far better served by an analysis of transactional flow, logs, and event stream monitoring than you would by poking around in the bowels of a service's process space.

Not relying on an interactive debugger is like letting go of a safety blanket for many people. However, the sooner you embrace the other tools available for diagnosing problems in the cloud, the better off you will be.

Envision your application as a satellite in orbit and you, the developer, are on the ground. What information do you need your application to emit via telemetry (logs and diagnostic endpoints) so that you can diagnose problems in testing and in running production applications?

# Index

# X

# Y

# REGISTER YOUR PRODUCT at informit.com/register

## Access Additional Benefits and SAVE 35% on Your Next Purchase

- Download available product updates.

- Access bonus material when applicable.

- Receive exclusive offers on new editions and related products.
  (Just check the box to hear from us when setting up your account.)

- Get a coupon for 35% for your next purchase, valid for 30 days. Your code will
  be available in your InformIT cart. (You will also find it in the Manage Codes
  section of your account page.)

Registration benefits vary by product. Benefits will be listed on your account page
under Registered Products.

---

**InformIT.com–The Trusted Technology Learning Source**

InformIT is the online home of information technology brands at Pearson, the world's foremost
education company. At InformIT.com you can

- Shop our books, eBooks, software, and video training.
- Take advantage of our special offers and promotions (informit.com/promotions).
- Sign up for special offers and content newsletters (informit.com/newsletters).
- Read free articles and blogs by information technology experts.
- Access thousands of free chapters and video lessons.

**Connect with InformIT–Visit informit.com/community**

Learn about InformIT community events and programs.

the trusted technology learning source

Addison-Wesley • Cisco Press • IBM Press • Microsoft Press • Pearson IT Certification • Prentice Hall • Que • Sams • VMware Press